Lifestyles
of the
Rich in Spirit

By Alan Cohen

Books:

Are You As Happy As Your Dog?
Companions of the Heart
Dare to Be Yourself
*A Deep Breath of Life
The Dragon Doesn't Live Here Anymore
Have You Hugged Your Monster Today?
I Had It All the Time
*Joy Is My Compass
*Lifestyles of the Rich in Spirit
The Peace That You Seek
*Rising in Love
Setting the Seen

Audiocassettes:

Deep Relaxation
Eden Morning
I Believe in You
Journey to the Center of the Heart
    (also available as a CD)
Peace

Videocassette:

Dare to Be Yourself

(All of the above are available through Alan Cohen Publications: 800-462-3013. Items marked with an asterisk may also be ordered by calling Hay House at 800-654-5126.)

Lifestyles
of the
Rich in Spirit

LIVING IN A WIN-WIN WORLD

Alan Cohen

Hay House, Inc.
Carlsbad, CA

Published and distributed in the United States by:
Hay House, Inc., P.O. Box 5100, Carlsbad, CA 92018-5100 (800) 654-5126

This book was originally published by Alan Cohen Publications under the title *The Healing of the Planet Earth: Personal Power and Planetary Transformation.*

You are free and encouraged to reproduce this book, in whole or part, by any means, without written consent of the author or publisher. This book is given to be shared; as is everything that comes of love.

The author wishes to acknowledge his gratefulness to the following authors and composers for the kindness of their permission to print their words and lyrics in this book: Dr. Patch Adams, Gesundheit Institute, for permission to use his photographs; Awakening Heart Productions, for permission to use their photographs; Bhaktan, Integral Yoga of Seattle, for permission to use his photograph; DeVorss & Company, for permission to quote from *The Life and Teachings of the Masters of the Far East,* by Baird Spaulding, © 1972 by DeVorss & Co.; Steven Longfellow Fiske, for permission to quote from "Bridges of Love," © 1983 by Fiske Music; Foundation for Inner Peace, for permission to quote from *A Course in Miracles,* © 1975 by Foundation for Inner Peace; Barry Neil Kaufman and Suzy Lite Kaufman, Option Institute, for permission to use their photograph; John Randolph Price, for permission to quote from *The Planetary Commission,* © 1984 by Quartus Foundation for Spiritual Research; Sovereignty, Inc., for permission to quote from *Ramtha,* Steven Lee Weinberg, Ed., © 1985 by Sovereignty, Inc.

A Course in Miracles can be obtained from: The Foundation for Inner Peace, P.O. Box 635, Tiburon, CA.

I also wish to express my deep appreciation to Joan Fericy, Anne Wiley, Elise Harvey, Judy Marlow, and the many others who assisted me with loving service in preparing the manuscript for publication.

Library of Congress Cataloging-in-Publication Data

Cohen, Alan, 1950-
      Lifestyles of the rich in spirit : living in a win-win world /
  Alan Cohen.
          p.   cm.
      Rev. ed. of: The healing of the planet earth.
      ISBN 1-56170-339-7 (trade paper)
        1. Spiritual   2. Cohen, Alan, 1950-   ,   I.   Cohen, Alan,
  1950- Healing of the planet earth. II. Title.
  BL624.C594 1996
  291,4--dc20   96-30689
                                              CIP

ISBN 1-56170-339-7

00 99 98 97 96   5 4 3 2 1
First Printing, Hay House Edition, October 1996

Printed in the United States of America

To the vision of Father Pierot
and all of us who share it

Contents

PART II—THE HEALING

WALKING IN LIGHT

Introduction

When John Robbins received an invitation to be interviewed on the popular television series *The Lifestyles of the Rich and Famous,* he was astounded. "Why would you want me to be on the show?" he asked the producer. "I am certainly not in the same ballpark as the rest of your fabulously wealthy subjects."

"You come from a wealthy empire," the executive told him, "and we are interested in what you are doing."

The producer was right about the lineage. John Robbins was the heir apparent to the Baskin-Robbins ice cream kingdom. From childhood, his father groomed him to take over the business and pro-liferate the wealth. When John became a young man, however, he adopted values quite different than his father's. John recalls, "My parents' idea of 'roughing it' was when room service was late."

John went off to meditate, study yoga, and embrace a vegan diet, which excludes all animal products, including dairy. Quite a turnabout from a dairy-made fortune! John went on to renounce the Baskin-Robbins throne, and he wrote the landmark book, *Diet for a New America,* documenting how a meat- and dairy-based diet has undermined our health and environment. The book went on to be nominated for a Pulitzer Prize.

"When the production team came to my humble rented house in the hills near Santa Cruz," John recounts, "I could tell they felt disoriented—this scenario was a far cry from the mansions they were used to filming. But then something amazing happened. My wife and family welcomed the crew and invited them to eat and relax with us. We opened our hearts and laughed and played with them. Before long, the crew lightened up, and I could tell they were having a good time. By the end of the shoot, we were all like a fam-ily; many of them didn't want to leave. One camera operator came to us with tears in her eyes and told us, "This is the most wonderful shoot we have ever done. Thank you for opening your home and hearts to us. So many of the places we go are incredibly opulent and beautiful, but devoid of spirit. It seems that our hosts' lives are just about collecting more stuff. Here, however, I felt real love, and I will never forget this.'

"After that, John added, "I thought it might be a good idea to start a television series honoring people who are fabulously wealthy in love. We could call it *Lifestyles of the Rich in Spirit.*"

This book celebrates life lived from the heart. These pages contain many true anecdotes about people who have made love the first priority in their lives and have become happy as a result. My intention is not to put these people on a pedestal, but to offer them as shining models to show that anyone, including you and me, can become a love millionaire the moment we choose peace rather than fear.

We were not born to live in pain and limits, nor are we intended to endlessly chase after values that continually frustrate and disappoint us. We are heirs to the kingdom of love, and nothing less will ever satisfy us. As divine beings, we deserve material abundance, prosperity, and security. Indeed, we are offered all the wealth of the planet as our playground. In the long, run, however, we recognize that our real security and prosperity rests in Spirit. As we remember our identity as spiritual beings, our life is transformed, and we become the wealthiest people in the world.

This book is given to inspire you to live the lifestyle of one who is rich in spirit. It is to remind you that you deserve so much more than you have been settling for. You are invited to reclaim your soul as your most cherished possession, and then live in the style to which love would have you become accustomed.

Part I

THE VISION

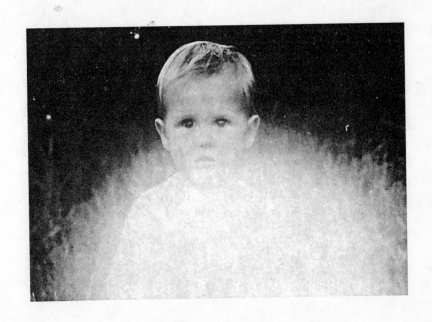

VISIONS, DREAMS,
and WONDERS

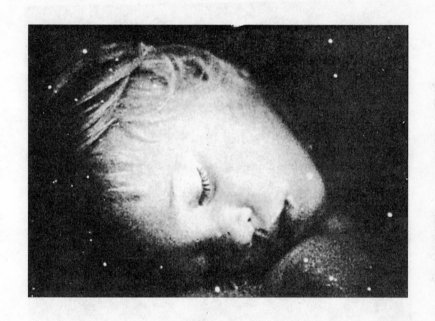

The Glimpse of the Eternal

The early spring sun cast its golden beams across the dusty room, bringing to life a pathway of long-awaited light. The winter had been long and arduous, and the warmth that entered with the sun was as healing as it was welcome. The rays found their way to the contoured glass of the television screen, partly obscuring the movie in progress, yet twinkling gracefully like angels dancing on the surface of a mountain lake. My first impulse was to draw the shade, but somehow the play of light upon the images on the screen seemed mystically appropriate, and I decided to let it be.

The movie was *Lost Horizon* and it seemed as if I had stumbled upon it by the same quirk of Grace which led the five lost travellers in the film to the hidden realm of *Shangri-La*, the land of eternal contentment. As the tale unfolded I was amazed at the profound lessons the story was offering — an unexpected gift of awakening on the threshold of a healing season. Spellbound, I watched the handsome Robert Conway, statesman, author, and visionary, enter the etherically candlelit chambers of Father Pierot, the ancient High Lama of *Shangri-La*. It was there that the holy man revealed to Conway that he had been benignly guided to *Shangri-La* for the purpose of handing over to him the responsibility for the future of the community of light.

When Conway questioned the possibility of actually establishing a peaceful community of good will, Father Pierot gazed into the younger man's eyes, and with the gentlest of fatherly smiles asked, "Are you not the same Robert Conway who in one of his books wrote, 'There are moments in every man's life when he glimpses the eternal'? And are you now so surprised to see your own dream come true before your eyes?"

These profound words rang through my heart like the huge cathedral bells that signal the entrance to *Shangri-La*. I realized that Father Pierot was not speaking only to a fictitious personage, but to me. I understood that I am Conway. And if you share the vision of a world in harmony, so are you.

Then I understood that Father Pierot is real. Within each of us there is a great and wise soul, born of undying purity, inspired by the sacred vision of a

5

planet at peace, living to deliver a golden destiny to a world that has nearly given up hope for real abiding love. This ancient one sits serenely within the chamber of the heart, patiently awaiting the joyous day when we will share the vision and dare to live it. Quietly, silently, he whispers warm words of loving encouragement, nobly reminding us who we are, powerfully urging us to accept our charge as teachers and healers of the Planet Earth.

Many times have I returned to those ancient, secret, most holy chambers within my heart, and met with the Father Pierot within me. Each time, I receive deep consolation and guidance that affirms my dedication to that noble ideal that Father Pierot declared. It may seem strange that I have been so deeply touched by a man who may never, perhaps, have lived in a body, and yet I am reminded of how powerfully One of Nazareth has guided so many into the light, inspiring and teaching through the temple of living spirit that dwells within every heart.

Thus it is to the vision of Father Pierot that this offering is dedicated, with the high intention that these words will awaken the Robert Conway in all of us, and quicken the lifting of our hearts and hands to accept the torch of Truth that our Father is so joyous to pass to us. In a broader sense it is to all the Conways of the new world that these words are directed, for as Father Pierot told Conway before that illuminated altar that my soul so loves to embrace, "I am placing the entire future and destiny of *Shangri-La* in your hands." By the Grace of the Living God I am willing to accept it. Now I invite you to share with me a new vision of humanity's destiny, a vision that will most certainly flower in the healing of the Planet Earth.

The Song of the Ancients Returned

In a dream, I saw myself as a great butterfly
With wings that spanned all of creation;
Now I am not sure if I was Chuang-Tsu
Dreaming I was a butterfly,
Or if I am a butterfly dreaming I am Chuang-Tsu.
                        - The Chinese Patriarch Chuang-Tsu

Some dreams are more real than our waking life. When such a gift is received, the power it bestows is so compelling that we can never really go to sleep again. One night I was shown a vision in the form of a dream which outshines any wonder I have seen in my waking days.

In this vision I was babysitting for a child, a young boy, at his suburban home overlooking the New York City skyline. Standing with him on the lawn of the house, I looked up into the night sky where I saw a group of shimmering blue lights appear on the horizon, just over the silhouette of the skyscrapers. These lights were not arriving from another physical location, but coming into sight from another dimension, materializing in a form that I could see.

One of the lights — a breathtaking shade of royal blue — came very close to us. Before our eyes it took the form of a spacecraft. I began to feel afraid and I tried to grab the boy and rush inside for shelter. But he wanted to run to the spacecraft, from which was emerging a group of extraterrestrials — small, happy beings like playful children. I had the sense, however, that these were not really children, but fully matured and very advanced beings. As I continued toward the house for protection, these little giggling aliens unleashed a laser-like ray that struck the house and instantly burned it to a crisp, leaving but a few flimsy rafters.

Piqued, I began to admonish the spacelings, "Hey, now wait a minute! You can't do that! I'm responsible for this house! What will the owners say when they come back?!?'' (The mouse that roared.)

The aliens had little interest in my pettiness. In a wave of laughter they telepathically communicated, "Come with us...We'll show you something that will take your mind off real estate."

With that I was lifted up, not in a spaceship, but in consciousness, and taken on a guided tour over the skyline of New York City. It was as if I had no body, floating, mentally hovering like a leaf on an easy wind.

Then a feeling flowed through me that is nearly impossible to describe in words. It was a feeling of completion so deep that every cell in me was burning in ecstacy. The closest way I can hint at this feeling is "bliss." I felt as if every part of me was vibrating with the entire universe, flooded with brilliant aliveness, as if I was being nurtured in a soft amniotic bath. I felt completely protected, fluently whole, and eternally loved. It was a taste of Heaven.

In this state I was shown a vision of a New Age. Emerging from the streets of the city below I saw glorious lights, astral fireworks exploding in happy patterns, a playful mosaic of brilliant white, rich burgundy, and vibrant blue. These colors burst forth in an amazing show of pure light. As I looked down at the people gathered together in the streets below, I saw them joyously watching this splendid display. Gleefully they applauded the birth of each new emanation. The physical details here are fascinating, but the real essence of the scene was the feeling I received from the group of people gathered in the streets. There was a unity, a harmony, a togetherness of appreciation. It was a clean energy, a demonstration of the divine potential of human beings living together in the spirit of dedicated cooperation.

Then I was shown a little wooden cabin on the top of one of the skyscrapers. The building was not the tallest tower, but one of the lesser structures. In the cabin I saw a simple scene: there was a modest wooden desk and chair, a kerosene lamp, and a few books — nothing more. This, I was told, was the office of the leader of the world government of this new day. This leader was marked by humility and simplicity. The government had no need to aggrandize itself, for it was fully devoted to the well-being of the people it served.

Then I was shown the United Nations building. It was explained to me that the idea for the United Nations was not born of human consciousness, but was a seed idea planted on earth by loving guiding angels who held the future of the planet in great reverence. Their intention was to help the people of the earth enter a new era of unity. The United Nations is the symbol — in

8

potential — of the New World.

In the background of my visit to the New World I heard a softly sweet and hauntingly soothing chant. This music was far more subtle and delicate than a physical ear can hear. The tones were borne on a female voice, oriental in flavor. The chanting came in smooth, delicate ripples, as if it was flowing from a great and wondrous ocean. Though the sounds were at first foreign to me, I soon recognized in them an ancient familiar song, mysteriously comfortable, not describable in words, yet deeply ingrained within my soul's memory.

The experience was so overwhelmingly beautiful that I began to weep tears of joy. My body and mind were overflowing with a nectar-like love, rich in freedom and fulfillment. I wanted to stay forever and float endlessly in this ocean of bliss.

But my time was up. I had to return. I felt my guides beckoning me to start back to the physical world. I sensed that my vision was drawing to a close. Weeping profusely, I felt myself beginning to descend, moving through progressively denser layers of matter.

Soon a young and beautiful woman with long blonde hair came to my side, as a kind of loving companion to soften my journey back to the harshness of the earth plane. I did not want to return. This radiant woman was more of a comforter than a lover, more a guide than a peer.

As we descended together my head rested on her shoulder. In the sky I saw pairs of all living creatures, male and female, as if in showcase frames. I saw birds and lions and many other animals, drawn across the blue sky in couples. My guide was showing me how compassionately God provides for all creatures to be comforted in companionship in earth life.

The conclusion of the journey was equally fascinating. I clearly observed myself passing through different planes of awareness, coming back into my body. At one point I actually saw myself sleeping, about to awaken. When I awoke I felt my eyes brimming with tears of gratitude. I lay in my bed for a while, with my right hand on my heart, sobbing, quietly feeling the overflow of an experience that I cherish as a loving gift from a blessed source. Although I felt some sadness that I had to leave that peaceful New World, I felt no remorse. Deep within my soul I knew that what I had left was not lost in the past, but a promise of the future.

Visions of Future Passed

The trick, according to Chiang, was for Jonathan to stop seeing himself as trapped inside a limited body that had a forty-two-inch wingspan and a performance that could be plotted on a chart. The trick was to know that his true nature lived, as perfect as an unwritten number, everywhere at once across space and time.

- Richard Bach, *Jonathan Livingston Seagull**

We dream many dreams in a lifetime; some even say that all of life is but a dream. Yet each of us holds a handful of sparkling memories that seem to be gifts of vision from beyond a veil that fell over our eyes long ago. These are the insights that bolster us during the times when all else seems to have fallen away. They are the crystals of hope that give us the courage and a good reason to wake up tomorrow. They are the promises of happy endings that remind us that all of life is a gift, cherishable and worthy of appreciation and sharing.

I would like to share my most important visions with you.

I

At a New Year's gathering several friends and I were discussing the possibility that we have lived time after time through history. When I mentioned that I had never had any recollection of a past life, my friend Al invited me into another room to speak with him privately.

When we were alone he asked me to close my eyes. Then he led me into a soft meditation, very soothing in comparison to the activity in the rest of the house. When we reached a considerable depth in the meditation, he guided me back in time to see if I had any impressions.

To my surprise, I did.

I saw myself in the basement of a house of worship. The image seemed not so much like a vision, but a memory.

---

* Richard Bach, *Jonathan Livingston Seagull*, Avon Books, 1970

"Where are you?" I heard Al's voice pierce my thoughts.

"I'm sitting at a table in the basement of some kind of church or synagogue."

"That's right," he responded.

How did he know that was right? But I was too interested in what I was seeing to think about his response.

"Please describe the scene."

"The room is lit with candles on the walls and some on the tables."

"Yes," Al repeated enthusiastically. I wondered again, how did he know?

"What color are the walls?"

I looked more carefully. The walls were clearly a tone of orange, close to amber. I told him.

"Yes!" he almost shouted. His confirmation seemed much more than encouragement.

"Tell me more about the scene."

"I'm sitting at a table with a group of young men. Most of us are about nineteen years old, some older. We are wearing cloths over our heads, secured by dark sashes around our foreheads. All of us have *pais*, the long curls in front of the ears, prescribed in the Jewish tradition."

"That's right," Al interjected again. "What is happening?"

I scanned the vision on the inside of my forehead. It was clearer then a movie in a theatre.

"There is a sense of deep importance in the room. Our gathering is extremely auspicious. We are zealots. We have been trained in the ways of orthodox religion, and we have been brought together by the common realization that what we have been taught by our elders is not the complete truth. We are angry at having been misled, yet we are more hungry to discover what we can learn by seeking further. There is an air of great excitement in the assembly."

There was a long pause. What was Al thinking?

"Is there anything else you can tell me about this scene?"

"Yes. There is a feeling of secretiveness in our gathering; if we are discovered we will be scorned or punished. Yet our commitment to knowing the Truth is so strong that we are willing to risk it."

"Do you sense anything else about this memory?"

"Yes...Something very important will come from this meeting. We are like rays of sun on the dawn horizon, emerging slowly at first, but eventually bringing great change."

12

"Thank You."

It took a few minutes for Al to bring me back to the room we shared. He asked me to open my eyes. The room to which I had gone seemed as real as the room to which I returned.

I had to ask, "Al, why were you saying 'Yes,' and 'That's right' about my description?"

"Because," he answered, "I was seeing exactly what you were describing before you said it."

II

About a year later I had a dream that seemed equally real and intrinsically connected with that New Year's vision.

I saw myself as a rabbi in the temple during the time that Jesus lived and taught. It was just after he was condemned. As he was being ushered to his lashing, it dawned on me that he was who he said he was. What he taught was the truth. A veil of ignorance and fear lifted from my eyes and heart as I saw that he truly was the Son of God. I knew that he and his teachings were genuine, and that he sought only to bring light into a world of shadows.

I realized that I had made a great error in not coming to his support during his trial. I stepped forward to say something, but I knew that his lot had already been cast. It was too late to defend him.

My lesson, I felt, was simply to know that he and his message were true, and now I must live for this noble ideal for the rest of my life.

III

Hilda, my teacher of many years, has always worked diligently to create a harmony between the Jewish and Christian peoples. Much of her work has been to open up Jewish and Christian minds to the beauty and wisdom of both ways. In fact, Hilda once told us that this is one of the major purposes of her mission as a teacher of light.

One evening Hilda explained to us that she was aware of her previous life as "Colette, a nun in northern France." (She humbly neglected to mention that this was St. Colette, a dedicated reclusive nun who was a spiritual comerade of St. Joan of Arc.) We were startled to learn of this lifetime, yet not surprised to see that the mission of Colette's life is very similar to Hilda's purpose today.

During a prayer pilgrimage to Europe, Hilda and a group of students decided to take a day trip to Corbeille, the tiny village where Colette lived and where a church still stands in dedication to her memory and ideals.

The students returned with marvelous accounts of their adventures and some fascinating photographs. One picture showed a statue of Colette, with features remarkably similar to Hilda's. The one photograph that captured all of our attention, however, was that of a statue in Colette's church, a rendering that neither I nor any of the students have seen elsewhere: it was a statue of Moses and Jesus together, each with his arm around the other's shoulder. The sculpture was carved out of one stone, with no separation at all between the two brothers.

IV

At a group meditation I was asked to go back in consciousness to a time before birth, and then to inquire about the purpose of my life. Back, back, back I went, until eventually I found myself in a soft dreamy state, touched with gentle breezes and splashes of light from one shore of eternity to another.

"What is my purpose, Lord?" I asked when the moment was ripe.

"Demonstration," came the answer. It was not an answer from outside myself, but from *within.*

Then I heard, "Your mission is to demonstrate the truth of love while on earth; to prove to yourself and the world that love and forgiveness are the most powerful and practical healers of troubled hearts; and to be a living message that it is possible to live on earth as it is in Heaven.

I was also told that it has been given me to take difficult situations that would be handled one way by a fearful person, and to demonstrate how easily they can be resolved with the help of Spirit.

V

This, then, is my sense of my purpose in this life: to bear witness to the truth that Jesus lived and taught; to celebrate the unity of all the pathways to God; and to learn and demonstrate that God is a loving friend Who will remove all obstacles from our path as we allow peace to be our only guide.

The Possible Dream

Look, look, look to the rainbow
Follow it over the hill and the stream
Look, look, look to the rainbow
Follow the fellow who follows his dream
- Finnian's Rainbow

The blue lights bathed the stage in their kindly essence. A hush fell over the audience as the emcee completed his reverent introduction. The singer stepped forward, drawing her breath deeply inward. Even those in the farthest corners of this historic theatre could feel the poignancy of this moment.

"Do you think I should do it, Alan?" a voice asked as I felt a hand on my shoulder.

"Do what, Danny?"

Crouching in the stage wings, waiting for our musical group to be called for the next act, Danny looked me in the eye. I realized that he had something on his mind far more important to him than the number we had prepared.

"Do you know who that is on the stage?" he whispered.

"The program says her name is 'Odetta;' that's all I know."

"Odetta is one of the greatest gospel/blues singers that has ever lived," Danny explained. "For many years she has been one of my favorite stars. It's been a dream of my life to accompany her on '*Amazing Grace*'...and that's what she's going to sing now!"

I could feel the thrill in Danny's voice; his excitement felt like that of a boy on the threshold of becoming a man.

"Do you see that piano there?" Danny pointed. "...I could just walk out there and start playing with her...or I could sit here and watch. What do you think I should do?"

There was no question in my mind about what Danny should do. He was one of the most talented and inspired gospel pianists I have ever heard.

This moment of opportunity was no accident; it was a gift.

"Go for it, Danny - This is your moment!"

Danny stood up, walked like a master to the piano, and sat down. As Odetta breathed heartily into the second verse of *Amazing Grace*, Danny began to weave a mosaic melody around her inspired voice. I saw his trepidation dissolve into the courage that shines from those who dare to be who they are.

Then there was a moment of hesitation in my mind...What if she did not want accompaniment? What if she wanted to sing *a cappella*? Had I made a fool out of both of us by encouraging him to go out there?

My fears were allayed quickly. Odetta turned to Danny, smiled, and nodded gracefully. This affirmation inspired him even more, and together the two of them created one of the most powerful renderings of that inspiring tune that I have ever heard. The audience responded with thunderous applause. Before my eyes I witnessed a living example of *Amazing Grace*.

Who is Danny? Danny is not just an isolated musical romantic or hopeful fantasizer. He is the spirit of every awakening soul who has had a dream and given birth to the courage to make it come true. Danny is every aspiring musician, artist, dancer, and inventor; every master of any discipline who has sweated through years of practice, trials, and obstacles in the name of a cherished ideal. Danny represents all of us who know that our dream can become a reality if only we don't give up. Danny is every one of us who yearns to make a difference in our world, to bring our planet into a better condition than the one in which we found it. Danny is you and me; Danny is all of us.

Be Calm, Be Steadfast

Last winter I was riding aboard a United Airlines Boeing 727 en route from Seattle to Newark, eagerly anticipating a workshop I was to present that evening in Princeton, New Jersey. The workshop was especially important to me as it was being sponsored by a holistic health association I have long respected. For years I had wanted to work with this group, and here was my opportunity. I purposefully arranged to leave Seattle at 7 AM in order to arrive in ample time for the evening's event.

About 4 PM, one hour before we were to land, I was mentally preparing my presentation when the captain's voice came over the loudspeaker: "Ladies and gentlemen, you may have noticed that the airplane just made a wide left turn...I guess it's time to tell you the bad news: Every airport from Boston to Baltimore is fogged in, and there's no place on the east coast for us to land. We'll be in Detroit in about an hour.''

"*Detroit?!?!?!?!?!*"

Did he really say, "*Detroit*?!" If I didn't know what thought-forms were, I would have received my first lesson right there, as I saw about a hundred of them hit the ceiling at the same time. They were like the little water-propelled rockets we used to shoot from our lawns as kids, excitedly watching them *whooosh!* into the summer sky. Only this time it was not summer and there was no sky - just the pre-fab contoured plastic ceiling panels enfolding a hundred jet-lagged and conspicuously unenthusiastic travellers.

"Detroit?"

That moment gave me the auspicious opportunity to practice what Hilda had been teaching me for so many years, namely "a quick adjustment of the mind." I must report, in all honesty, that my adjustment was not so quick. For the next hour I practiced every metaphysical trick I had ever seen and read about, in a feverish attempt to get the plane to land in Newark. I visualized the plane touching down on a sunny airstrip (which would have been a real miracle, since the winter sun had already gone down). I called on all the saints, masters, and angels that I had ever heard of, ardently summoning their aid in my petition. To my chagrin, when I called on St. Francis I was told that he was out walking in the woods; redirecting airplanes, they said, was not really his department. Next, I subliminally vibed the pilot and cockpit crew, hoping to implant just-below-threshold suggestions in their subconscious via the airplane's musical entertainment channel.

Then, when all else had failed, I had no choice but to bring out the heavy artillery: THE VULCAN MIND MELD! Fervently aligning my mental faculties with Saint Spock, I beamed my thought-forms to everyone in charge of this awful dilemma, hoping that a Federation tractor-beam would draw us precisely to that New Jersey runway. Mentally I extended my fingers to the First Officer's brow, strategically placing them on the sensitive nerve centers indicated in the ancient Vulcan rite. "My mind is one mind with your mind," I concentrated all of my energies " - You will turn this aircraft right and land us in Newark by 5 PM."

But alas! The First Officer of this particular starship had no pointed ears and his eyebrows extended nowhere near his temples. Soon I felt the ship's landing gear touch down not upon the Federation coordinates I had prescribed, but instead on a cold and slightly snowy asphalt airstrip that led to none other than the Motor City.

Disappointed, disgruntled, and slightly disembodied from my hapless hijinks in metaphysical hijacking, I joined a hundred other displaced cling-ons in line for a bus pointed toward a hotel in the middle of the city that, as far as I knew, housed only automobiles and Tigers...

Several resisted hours later I flopped into a bed on the forty-fourth floor of a hotel overlooking an icy Lake Erie, a thousand miles from anyone I knew. "What am I doing here?" I asked God. "Didn't you want me to do that workshop? I mean, really, God, what gives?"

I picked up a book from my suitcase, *The Still Voice*, a collection of inspiring meditations by a gentle spiritual guide called White Eagle.

"O.K. God, could you please tell me the lesson?" I asked. "I'll open this book to any page, and whatever I read will be my lesson."

I inserted my thumbnail somewhere in the midst of the off-white leaves and let the book fall open. There before my astounded eyes, I read:

BE CALM, BE STEADFAST

When you try to do things, and they will not go the way you want, leave them alone. Do not try to force things the way you would like them to go. Just leave them alone. Do your best, obey the law of love, and you will be surprised at how circumstances will work out far better for you than if you had had your own way. Let God have His way, and you just be patient and wait. Be calm, steadfast and peaceful. Accept things as they come and do not be rushed into wrong decisions or overcome by the forces of ignorance. Be steadfast, with a quiet, inner, peaceful persistence, knowing that the Great Architect of the Universe holds the plan of your life in His hands.[1]

Well, that about summed it up. "Maybe I'm supposed to be here," I conceded. "...and if that's so, I might as well enjoy myself."

My attention was drawn to a triangular card on top of the television in the room, advertising the in-house movies available that night. Mentally I surveyed the offerings of "Body Heat," "Linda Lovelace Strikes Back," and a series of pictures that promised more x's than crosses. Before long I

---

[1] White Eagle, *The Still Voice*, The White Eagle Publishing Trust, Hampshire, United Kingdom, 1980

began to give up hope that I would find something I felt like seeing. Then I saw an advertisement for a movie called *Flashdance*. When I saw that word it occurred to me that within the last two weeks I had told several people that I had wanted to see *Flashdance* when it played in the movie theatres, but I had missed it. Could this be my opportunity?

I switched on the set to find a marvelously inspiring story of a young woman who has a lifetime dream to be a classical dancer. To pay her rent until her dream comes true, she dances in sleazy clubs at night and works as a welder during the days. She is not really doing what she wants to be doing, but her vision sustains her to carry on until her dream can become a reality.

This aspiring young woman meets a man who gets her an audition with a respected ballet school. But because she feels that she did not earn the audition on her own merit, she turns her back on the audition and the man.

I remember so clearly the scene in which she tells her boyfriend, "I give up...I'm going back to the club!" She turns to walk out the door.

But he is not willing to let her — and her dream — go so easily. He grabs her by the arm, swings her around, looks her straight in the eye and asks her, "Don't you realize what you're doing? You're throwing away your dream! And don't you know that *when you give up your dream, you're dead!*"

When you give up your dream, you're dead.

As far as I was concerned, that was the whole story. Perhaps that was why I was brought to Detroit, to hear that message. At first I thought I was in the middle of nowhere; at last I discovered I was in the center of everywhere. There I was given an important lesson, a practical lesson, a lesson that perhaps we all need to remember: *When you give up your dream, you're dead.* And when you hold fast to your dream — when you are calm and steadfast — you're alive. What more do we need to remember?

As the movie turned out, that young lady went on to that audition and really wowed them. She had the courage to believe in herself, to push past that lethally deceptive membrane of self-doubt. In so doing she proved the adage that the only time we fail is the last time we try. She succeeded not only for herself, but for me, for you, and for everyone who needs the strength to go all the way. And that determination made all the difference.

As my own movie turned out, when I arrived home the next day I was told that the same fog which kept my plane from landing at the airport prevented cars from driving on the highways. Very few people had been able to make it to the workshop, and the organizers decided to reschedule it for a later date. There was no real loss — but I did gain much in learning such a powerful and healing lesson.

Are you living your dream? Have you given up your most wonderful, cherished, and important aspirations and settled for a half-life? Do you have a reason to get up in the morning, a vision, an ideal, a quest? Or have you compromised your vision and let go of the bright-eyed child within you that gave you so much joy? Have you surrendered your personal destiny to conform to the pack?

You don't have to give up your dream; in fact, the hound of Heaven will keep lovingly urging you to do what you were born to do until you have bestowed upon the world the gift that only *you* can offer it. Spinoza, the great celebrant of love, proclaimed, "To be what we were born to be, and to become what we are capable of becoming, is the only end in life."

My friend Marsha is a good example of holding firmly to her vision. Marsha is a talented beauty consultant who has made a career of teaching women and models how to make the most of their appearance. Since she has been meditating, however, her work has taken on a new and exciting creativity.

"I realized that inner beauty is even more important than outer beauty," Marsha shared with me one day. "So I created a class called, *"Me — the Best I Can Be."* I gave the students oatmeal and honey facial packs and asked them to lie down on the floor for the half hour it took for the treatment to take effect. While they were lying there I put on a tape of meditative music and guided them through a progressive deep relaxation. When they got up they said they felt relaxed, healed, and beautiful — inside and out. They ended up getting everything they wanted, and more!"

This fresh originality is available to all of us. Another friend, Barbara, is a dedicated hairstylist. She explained it to me in this way: "When anyone comes to me in the shop, I know they are really coming for love and peace of mind. So I developed a method I call "the seven-minute vacation." I got permission from my boss to set up a booth in the rear of the salon, which I have dedicated as a place of peacefulness. Before each treatment I turn down the lights, put on some soft music, and give my client a gentle neck and shoulder massage. As I touch them I silently pray that I serve as a channel for the Christ light and that this client is healed through my haircut, my touch, and my presence. They love it! Now the manager can't figure out why so many people request me as their personal hairstylist. The secret is that I'm really styling their soul!"

Perhaps the most cogent demonstration that God works through *all* channels is an account given to me by Alberto Aguas, a gifted and dynamic

Brazilian healer. Alberto travels throughout the world working miracles through the laying on of hands and inspired prayer. Here is Alberto's story:

One week when I was working out of a motel in California, my secretary showed me that one woman had scheduled a five-hour appointment.

"Five hours?" I asked; "Why did you schedule her for so long? You know that my healing treatments usually take about half an hour."

"I know," the secretary responded, "...but this is a special case."

"What could be so special to require five hours?"

"Just trust me."

"Well, O.K. — I guess a faith healer should have some faith."

The next afternoon at 12:30 Alberto heard a knock at the motel door. He answered it to find, to his astonishment, a tall woman, early forty-ish, with orange hair, hot pants, gold go-go boots, and a cleavage that did not require much in the way of creative visualization. The woman's profession could not have been more obvious had she worn a billboard. After rubbing his eyes, Alberto looked again to see that she was accompanied by about a dozen younger ladies wearing the same uniform, obviously all players on the same team.

"Come in," Alberto cordially invited them, half-amazed, half-curious, half-laughing inside.

"What can I do for you?" was his introduction, almost ludicrous in light of its juxtaposition.

"Mr. Aguas, my name is Honey; I'm the manager of the Pink Pussycat Massage Parlor, and these girls are my staff."

(Alberto had to do all he could to keep from breaking up.)

"I know that this is a rather unusual request for you, Mr. Aguas, but we have been having some rather unusual experiences, and we thought perhaps you could help us understand them."

"I'll try." answered Alberto, holding his breath.

"About six months ago we moved to new headquarters, a lovely old building on La Quieta. We set aside a few days to clean the place up, and on the third day we went down into the basement. There we found some old boxes with many books in them. Curious, we opened some of the paperbacks with strange titles we'd never seen before: *Adventures in Reincarnation, Your Healing Power*, and many by some fellow named Edward Case or something like that, a quaint old man from Virginia Beach. The titles and subjects were so fascinating that we began to read excerpts out loud to one another as we rearranged the boxes.

"At first we thought these ideas were rather strange and sometimes we poked fun at them. But, Mr. Aguas, the most amazing thing happened — the more we read, the more interested we became. Eventually we stopped unpacking and we began discussing the material. It turned out that many of us had had experiences such as the ones described in the books, like picking up the phone to call someone and finding them on the other end of the line, or meeting someone and feeling like you've known them before. Susan, here, had seen angels as a child, but she stopped when her mother told her she must never tell anyone.

"We came to a chapter on healing, and we decided to try this stuff out to see if it really worked. So when we were with our clients we would see them in white light and, strange as it may sound, we would pray for them. It was easy to know what to pray for, for many men who come to ladies of the evening like to tell us their story; in an ironic way we have always been counselors of sorts. So when we were performing our services we would inconspicuously put our hand on the man's heart or his back or wherever he told us he had a problem. Then we would silently ask to have healing light flow through us to him.

"The results were amazing! When the men came back a week or a month later, we would casually ask them how their heart or back was. You wouldn't believe the reports they gave us! Like, 'Funny you should ask...This amazing thing happened: Right around the last time I saw you it started to get better; it's funny, but it used to be such a problem and now it hardly bothers me at all!'

"So, Mr. Aguas, quite frankly we believe in this stuff, and we'd like to learn more about it. Can you help us?"

"Yes, I think I can — and I would be delighted to!"

So Alberto spent the next five hours giving one of the most important healing classes of his life.

"I Dream for a Living"

One of my favorite dreamers, high on the list of visionaries I love is Steven Spielberg, the genius producer/director of such modern classics as *Close Encounters of the Third Kind, Raiders of the Lost Ark,* and *E.T.* It was no accident that I should see a picture of Steven on the cover of *Time Magazine* and subsequently open to his story entitled, "I Dream for a Living." With saucer eyes I dove headlong into the article, at times laughing out loud, at other times elbowing the fellow sitting next to me, cheering, "Yeah, yeah, that's it!"

I felt like I knew him. Making movies, the article explained, has been in Steven's blood since he was a child. Ever since he got his hands on his dad's 8mm home movie camera when he was twelve, Steven hasn't stopped. "Our living room was strewn with cables and floodlights," reports Leah Spielberg, his Yiddisha momma, now an extra in his films. "We never said no — we never had a chance to say no — Steven didn't understand that word."[2]

Steven, like all dreamers, has *chutzpah*. When he was seventeen he went on a tour of Universal Studios. At an opportune moment he slipped away from the tour and found a film editor, to whom he showed an early homemade film. The editor was impressed, but apologized for not being able to help him.

Did that stop young Steve? No, no self-respecting visionary would throw in the celluloid at such a minor setback. The next day Steven, like his fabled *Indiana Jones*, fudged his way past the guards at Universal, carrying his father's briefcase containing a sandwich and two candy bars. He started hanging out with producers, directors, and dubbers, found an empty office, and moved into it. He went out to a camera store, bought a plastic name title, and put his name on the building office directory. Thus began Steven's legend-in-his-own-time career with no authorization from anyone other then his higher self. And what an authorization it was! Twenty years later, at the age of thirty-seven, finds Steven Spielberg as the most successful producer/director in cinematographic history, with four films in the top ten attractions of all time, the highest-grossing film ever made, a four million dollar home built for him by Universal City on their own lot, and a major share in the ownership of the studios that not long ago didn't even offer him the closet of a self-authorized office through which he walked to greatness.

How does Steven explain his creative process? Simply. "Once a month the sky falls on my head, I come to, and I see another movie I want to make. I wake up so excited I can't eat breakfast. I've never run out of energy. I don't worry about a premium going on my energy. It's always been there."[3]

That was one of the moments my neighbor got elbowed; I got excited because it explained the way my books come. Right now I feel about half a dozen books in mental utero, brand new to the world, each inspiring me in its own special way. The best way I could describe this process is that these creations are like airplanes flying in a holding pattern, each waiting its turn to land, each carrying a full cargo of never-before gathered ideas as passen-

---

[2] *Time* Magazine, July 15, 1985
[3] Ibid.

gers. It is the most humbling experience and yet the most strengthening. This process of dreaming, thinking, and creating is a pure miracle to me. I see the birth of an idea into the world as the most powerful testimony that God is life. There is no greater opportunity in life than to be a dreamer drawing ideas into expression.

God is Your Agent

It may be said that there are two types of people in the world: those who are willing to live for their dream, and those who have forgotten how to believe in themselves. Those who live for their dream are the creators, the initiators, the artistically alive free souls, the women and men who stand out in a crowd and brighten the lives of those they touch in the simple interactions of daily living. They are the people around whom we feel energized, nourished, healed, important, and optimistic. They make us feel that we are capable, worthy, and lovable, for they feel that wonderful way about themselves. They radiate beauty because they find good in everyone they touch. They are the persons who move the world along, lifting normality out of inertia and into action. They are the shining ones who have heard and responded to the inner call, standing for all that destiny would have them glorify.

I had to stand up for my dream — We all do, and although the individual facts may appear to be different, the dynamics of integrity are always the same. When I finished writing *The Dragon Doesn't Live Here Anymore*, I trusted that the same God that gave me the book would get it published. I sent sample chapters to several spiritually-oriented publishers and received either no response or a "thank you for your material, but it does not fit in with our current publishing plans" form letter. One publisher, whom I telephoned directly, asked me what was the theme of the book. When I told him, "the healing power of true forgiveness," he scoffed, "Nah, nobody's interested in that; try writing something more dynamic." No room at the inn.

I did not want to wait until someone was willing to take the book on. I decided that if I had to publish it myself, though I did not have the money, I would do it.

The day I finished writing the book two friends approached me, and though I had not asked them, offered me the money to publish the book. One of them was my mother. When I told her I had written a book she asked me, "What's it about?" I told her, "truth, love, and God." "That's beyond me,'' was her immediate response. "How long is it?" was her next question. "About four hundred pages, Mom." "You're crazy!" was her second response.

The next day her third response came. She called me on the telephone and said, "If you want the money to publish your book, I'll give it to you." I guess it wasn't beyond her.

I found a reputable company in the mid-west to do the printing. Within a few weeks I found myself in New York City meeting with their agent to give him the completed copy, discuss the printing format, and hand him a check for five thousand dollars to print a book that a metaphysical magnate had scoffed at. As we concluded our arrangements he walked me to the door and as he shook my hand he told me, "You know, they say you don't make any money until you've published your third book!"

Momentarily taken aback by this narrow notion, I felt like an infant upon whom a wagonload of manure had been thrust unannounced. Yet I knew that I could not afford to give one moment's acknowledgement to this debilitating idea. Immediately into my mind arose the *Course in Miracles* lesson, "I am under no laws but God's."[4] I knew that I had to make a stand for the Truth. I thought for a moment, smiled at my skeptical friend and told him, "Yes, Keith, I understand that's what they may say, but one thing you may not realize is that my agent is God."

Keith just stood there scratching his head. I don't know if he got it, but I got it. I got that never again could I lean out on the values and expectations of the world to validate me. I realized that I would have to trust God and believe in myself even when those around me were lost in fear and limitation. I understood that the only source to whom I can turn in times of outer darkness is the Light within me, ever urging me to know myself to be magnificent, beautiful, and good. I found myself.

The first printing of *Dragon* sold out quickly, and before long my original investment was returned. Soon I began to make money on its sales — *before* my third book. *What the agent had told me was simply not true.* If I had believed him or allowed that limiting thought into my mind, I might have created that negative situation — not by virtue of its truth, but by the power of my thinking and believing that it was so. But because I refused to agree with that constricting idea, I experienced no limitation. *There is no limitation.* As we rise to our ability to create with God, miracles happen.

---

[4] W, p. 132

Stand by Your Dream

There is no dream in life that is beyond your ability to accomplish. God would not plant a seed in your mind if She did not plan to give you ways to help it grow into a flower. God is not a sadist. If anything, She is a philanthropist. Once we know that God is working *with* us and not against us, we can cherish our dreams as divinely-inspired visions of our new life. Then all we need to do is hold firmly to our dream, especially during the times when it seems as if the dream is being challenged. The key to transforming our life is to *keep your mind and heart on your dream.* As one great thinker said, "Obstacles are what you see when you take your eyes off the goal."

Your dream is a sprouting innovation that needs your loving help to grow to full maturity. Then it returns your caring by nourishing you as well as many others. Every great achievement in this world started out as a dream. A vision of success is a seminal idea that needs to be nurtured and strengthened by one who believes in it enough to stand by it through windy times.

Are you willing to stand by your dream in times of opposition? Are you willing to believe in yourself enough to say "Yes!" to yourself even when others do not stand with you? Are you willing to believe that God Itself planted that dream in your mind, and that selfsame Spirit will help you bring it to perfect fruition, even — and especially — when you seem to have exhausted all of your own resources? Are you willing to live for what you believe?

This is the dynamic law of living that empowers us to materialize our dreams. How can a dream come true unless we act to make it real? Too many great ideas have been thrown in the wastebasket before they were put on the drawing board. Within you now are the seeds of greatness. There is something that you have to offer the world, something special, something marvelous, something that can change someone's life for the better — perhaps many people's lives. Are you willing to plant these golden seeds? Are you willing to take a chance on having your life work now? Are you willing to be the magnificent radiant being that you really are, the shining light that God knows you to be, from the moment you were conceived?

God has never given up on you because God could never forget how precious you are. Are you ready to go out on the stage of life and play that piano like you've never played before, for the glory of love and the celebration of beauty? If so, then you are certain to succeed, for your dream is none other than God's dream for you.

I must believe there's a God Who believes in me.
                                                    - Joseph and Nathan

The HEALED MIND

Natural or Regular

Be true to yourself, be true to yourself
And you'll never be false to any man
Be true to yourself, be true to yourself
And stretch out your hand

- Chris Rudolf*

One afternoon my mother sent me to the supermarket to buy some applesauce on sale. As I made my way through the aisle I looked at the coupon and found a most interesting description of the product: "Foodtown Applesauce — 19 cents — *"Natural or Regular"*. "Natural or Regular" — What did that mean? I checked the labels. The regular applesauce contained sugar, artificial coloring, a list of preservatives requiring either a master's degree in organic chemistry or a working knowledge of Tralfamidorian to decipher, and a host of other ingredients that do not usually come with apples from a tree. The natural applesauce, on the other hand, contained just apples and water.

This distinction caused me to think more deeply about how we live our lives, about the values we hold to be true, about the goals we set for our livelihood. It is becoming clear to me that the way most of us have lived our lives has not been in harmony with the way the universe was intended to work for us to be happy. It seems that we have somehow lost touch with the loving flow of life, our rhythm of being, our sense of peacefulness about ourselves and satisfaction with what we are and what we are here to do.

We have sacrificed the natural for the regular, entrenching ourselves in patterns of living that have left us with a sense of being somehow incomplete, knowing that what we have is not it, yet not quite knowing how to get the "it" we feel we are missing. Many of us have found ourselves in jobs that give us little satisfaction, riddled by a sense of being trapped in relationships that do not seem to be working, living for goals that disappoint

---

* "Be True to Yourself," by Chris Rudolf, *Songs Along the Way*, Waking Up Productions, 1984

us almost as soon as they are reached. Yet we keep the same job because we are afraid to do what we would love to do, slowly dying under the macabre illusion that a job is real only if we are suffering in it. We stay in the same rut in our relationship because most of the relationships we have seen have failed, so why should ours be any better, and maybe interpersonal peace is just a myth anyway. And we continue to chase after the dreams that disintegrate in our hands like the powder of dead men's bones, the sad revenue of the elusive goals that have been attained by the apparently successful who seem to be happy, but whose terrible hurt returns to their drawn faces the moment the cameras turn away and the spotlights are dimmed. This is the story of the world, a house of distorted mirrors through which the original image has been turned upside down, a seductress masquerading as a saint, a demon with the face of an angel.

At some point in our soul's evolution each of us discovers that the world is not working according to the rules that we have been taught to serve. We learn that the way most people approach life is not a healthy guide for us. It becomes clear that the institutions to which we have been encouraged to pay homage are little more than empty shells of long ago withdrawn ideals, and the nations of the world are as lost, alone, and afraid as the individuals who make them up. To put it simply, the world is not succeeding according to the illusions after which it is pining. We see that if we are to find some kind of peace and solace we are going to have to hearken to the voice of an *inner* guide rather than the dictates of the masses.

The world we have made is the opposite of Heaven. We have used fear as a guide instead of peace, worshipping separation instead of unity. We have looked at ourselves as bundles of boundaries instead of the magnificent, unlimited beings we truly are. When we take just about all of the values we have honored and reverse them, we discover that what we have sought and learned is indeed the opposite of what we need to learn and be.

My friend Mike, a successful organizational development consultant with a sizeable income at A.T.&T., told me this story:

"My brother stood in danger of losing his home through a default on his mortgage payments. Feeling guided to help him, I went to the bank, withdrew seventeen thousand dollars from my savings account, put a cashier's check for it in an envelope, and mailed it to him. It wasn't a gift; it wasn't a loan; it wasn't anything I could name. All I knew was that he needed it and I had it, and it was more important to me to help him than to keep it. I want you to know that the moment I dropped that check in the mailbox I felt more peace than I ever have in my whole life."

More peace. It is said that God gives us feedback about how close we are to Heaven by the amount of peace that we feel when doing any act. Yet somehow we have learned to live as if we gain peace by separating ourselves from one another, when in fact we move along the road to healing by acknowledging our caring.

We have sadly come to the point where we feel we need to apologize for making contact. One night in a movie theatre a woman sitting next to me accidentally brushed her hand by my knee as she reached for her pocket-book.

"I'm sorry," she briskly apologized.

"Sorry?" I returned; "Please don't be sorry — I liked it!"

Perhaps if we admitted more often that "I like it!" when we really do like it, our world will reflect more of who we really are, how we truly want to live, and the way we would like to be with one another. Otherwise we are doomed to a horrible sense of confusion because the world in which we live is not in harmony with the truth of our being.

This truth is *totally within our power* to know, feel, and live *as we choose*. Often at the end of a weekend workshop I hear participants remark, "Wow! This was really great! I felt so comfortable with my feelings of real love for myself and those around me! Too bad we have to go back to the real world now."

Then I answer, "This *is* the real world. *This* is the world that everyone loves, for we understand this feeling as the reality of our heart. *This* is the world we all want to feel and live in all the time. There is no reason to stop now. We can create our life any way we choose. We *can* have caring people in our life, our relationships *can* work, we can *hug*, and we can say, "I love you" as much as we like. It's entirely up to us."

Then I tell them the story of Dan, my auto mechanic, who quit watching ticker tapes on Wall Street to consolidate carburetors in a local service station. Although he felt happier having made the move, Dan was still bothered by some physical symptoms of stress. Whenever I brought my car in to be repaired Dan and I would chat for a while. At first I felt a little distant from him, but as I got to know him I began to appreciate him. He was a deeply sincere and sensitive fellow, and although he would probably not term himself so, he was a spiritual man.

One day as Dan and I were standing in front of the garage he told me how much he wanted peace. He explained to me that his stomach was troubling him, some of his relationships could feel better, and other aspects of his life were not working as well as he would have liked. He told me that he was at the point where he was willing to do anything to be healed. This touched me deeply, for as I looked into his eyes I saw the eyes of the Christ.

At that moment something came over me; a feeling of deep closeness to Dan welled up within me, and I just wanted to reach out and hug him and tell him how much I appreciated his beautiful open heart.

So I did. Right there on Main Street. Right in front of the gas station. Right there where all the tough guys hang out swearing and smoking Marlboros. In the very heart of gasoline alley I gave him a big bear hug. It was one of those spontaneous acts that's more fun to do when you don't think about it first.

Then, a few moments into my embracing Dan another voice within my mind spoke to me. This voice was not as encouraging as the one that had prompted me to hug him. This voice, with sort of a John Wayne roll, informed me, "You're crazy!...Men don't hug other men in the gas station, and certainly not on Main Street. Why are you doing this? You hardly know this guy! When you let go he's going to punch you."

It was one of those moments known as an embarrassing predicament, when time just seems to linger in the air like a slow bomb taking its time dropping. "How did I get into this one?" I wondered — and more important, "How do I get out?"

Realizing that I had probably made a big mistake, I decided that my only hope was to delay the punch. So I kept on hugging him, thinking that he couldn't raise his fist if my arms were clenched around his.

But it couldn't go on forever. Eventually I had to release my embrace and see what he would do. I let go. There was a pregnant moment in which the two of us just stood there looking at each other. I wondered whether it would be a left jab or a right uppercut.

But the punch never came. Instead, Dan looked me right in the eye, took a big deep breath, and told me, "Thanks — I needed that!"

Dan and I became friends. I gave him one of my books and a meditation tape with my deepest blessings. Although we did not see each other often, he was very much in my heart.

About six months later, I was driving down Main Street and I stopped at a traffic light in front of the garage. Almost involuntarily my head turned in the direction of the garage bay, where I saw Dan's coveralled body, head submerged under the hood of a red Ferrari. Quickly and enthusiastically I tooted the horn.

Startled, Dan emerged like a dinosaur lifting its head from lunching on a patch of greens. When he saw me he smiled and yelled, "Where have you been? I need a hug!''

Being one who never turns down an offer for a good hug, I left the traffic signal, turned into the station, jumped out of my car, left the motor running, and gave Dan a big hug. Then I took off. My first pit stop for a hug.

About a year later I received a message that a Dan had telephoned me. ''Dan?'' I scratched my head, not recalling who the name belonged to. When I returned the call Dan's wife answered. When I told her my name she called out, ''Hey Dan! It's the gentle flowing waterfall!''

''What's the gentle flowing waterfall?'' I queried as he picked up the receiver.

''Oh, yeah,'' he laughed, ''My wife and I listen to your meditation tape every night before we go to sleep. You know—the one with the waterfall and the rainbows in it. I must tell you how much we both enjoy it—it really helps! My wife even took the tape into labor with her. I also want to tell you that my stomach is much improved, along with the relationships I told you about. Thank you so much for taking such an interest in me—I feel like a new person!''

Hugging on Main Street. It takes guts. I don't know if there is any fear so debilitating as the fear of popular opinion, and no freedom more rewarding than following the guidance of one's own heart. I know few people who are willing to hug on Main Street, to say, ''I love you'' when the popular script doesn't call for it. Some, not a lot. But there are more and more, more and more.

We can cite courageous persons like Shirley MacLaine, who while living in the public eye are willing to risk gossip and opinion for the sake of sharing the truth that has come to them. And yet it is not really a risk at all, for once one sees the truth there is not much choice about going back to illusion. Shirley's books, *Out on a Limb* and *Dancing in the Light*, are inspiring testimonies of a sincere person miraculously blossoming into the spiritual life. She has blessed millions simply by sharing her story.

Yet Shirley's story is no more powerful than yours or mine. The world is waiting for our stories to be told, despite what the norms may have been. The moment Shirley was willing to speak the truth she felt in her heart she began to be a channel, a vessel through which healing ideas, attitudes, and actions are being directed to those whose ears and hearts are open to hear and feel the truth of their own beauty.

The Path of Love

Each day we receive many opportunities to give healing simply by being our true self. It is up to each of us to accept the invitation to become who we truly are. Indeed every moment is a doorway to Heaven, every encounter a lesson in love.

One beautiful summer I had such an opportunity when I met Charley Thweatt of the joyously talented musical group, *Oman, Shanti, and Charley*. Instantly I knew he and I were kindred spirits. We had so much to say to one another, to share, to laugh about together. It seemed as if we were old and dear friends meeting after a long time away from one another. Opening our hearts and sharing stories, we discovered that we had travelled many of the same highways of life, and now we were being given the privilege to meet and catch up on all the places we had been and what we had done. It felt as if distant continents were being joined once again.

I shall always treasure that night we reunited in a restaurant on the windward side of the island of Oahu in Hawaii. We had just completed a successful presentation together, and a deep sense of joyful satisfaction was in our hearts. Charley walked over to the table where I was sitting with some other friends, and asked if we could have a word privately.

We stepped down to a terrace amid gently swaying palm trees. Torches illuminated the mystical contours of great wooden masks of ancient Hawaiian gods that smiled through the flowered aroma of the tradewinds that caress one's very soul on those magical islands.

Charley took my hand and told me, "I just want you to know how much I've enjoyed working with you. I hope we can share a program together again."

There was a moment of mutual gratefulness honored perfectly by the silence in which we felt it.

"And I, you."

There we were, just Charley and me, our inner glow poignant in contrast to the noise of the restaurant. We just sat there looking into one another's eyes like two sappy lovers in a linty old Bogart movie.

As we held each other's hands and spoke in gentle tones, a fearful little voice in the back of my brain began to slither: "This really looks weird. You better let go of his hand...People will think you're gay — You mustn't let anyone see this.''

But our being together had nothing to do with sexuality, romance, or bodies. It was a joining of spirit, and we could just as easily have been a man and a woman, a mother and child, or two lima beans. It was the essence of two brothers sharing a special moment. And it was far beyond time and into the eternity that brought the flowers on the breeze to our senses and then swept them on to the ocean and unto the dreamy Pacific skies.

It took courage to hold my brother's hand in that crowded restaurant, as it takes strength to be natural in a regular world. We have been hypnotized into believing that we are small, troubled creatures, while our souls are rooted in eternity itself. *All that we seek we already are.* We do not need to scrutinize our state of hypnosis or curse the stupor into which we have fallen. We need only to wake up. We need to remember who we are, make a stand for it, and live it. We must celebrate our spiritual identity. We must emerge from our cocoon of fear, open our hearts, and declare, ''I know that the ability to heal my life and our world lies within my hands.'' In thus committing ourselves, you and I create the most monumental transition our planet has ever been blessed to experience.

To change the world, we are required only to put fear aside and dedicate ourselves wholeheartedly to the Truth. At first we may hesitate to crawl out on those skinny new branches and declare who we are. But before long we discover that the only thing more painful than making a stand for the light is knowing the truth and living a life that does not reflect it.

In a sense we have all been double agents. Knowing reality and living in illusion is a torturous dilemma, and truly there is no split in life that creates more tension than this one. But tension is a gift that bestows its blessing when we are ready to seek relief from it. Being dissatisfied with the world as it is means that there is a part of our mind that knows there must be a better way. Let us thank God that we are not willing to settle for less than the complete peace we deserve.

One day each of us will arise and say, ''Dear friends, I am now ready to live for the light.'' On that momentous day, that holy day — not far away now — the natural will become the regular. That will be a day of great rejoicing, for with the acknowledgement of the truly natural comes all of the light that we know we deserve, but have temporarily forgotten how to see because we were covering our eyes with our own hand. On that day we shall fulfill Jesus' prophecy when he prayed, ''On earth as it is in Heaven,'' for this earth will not be complete until it reflects the Peace of Heaven in every way. It is you and I who must create this holy moment, which begins now and spans far into eternity. For this were we born, for this we live, and for this shall we continue to live until the aspiration of our soul becomes the reality of our life.

Who Told You
You Were Naked?

The holy instant does not require that you have
No thoughts that are not pure.
But it does require that you have none that you
Keep to yourself.

- A Course in Miracles[1]

As you may recall from Sunday or Hebrew School (in between perusing the Captain America comics hidden in your Bible or sketching hot rods on your desk), God created Adam and Eve in Paradise. Then God set them in a beautiful garden to be enjoyed eternally, with no service charge, finder's fee, or difference in price for cash or credit. Here the happy couple had dominion over all the elements of earth, free to play and be at peace literally forever.

"You may eat of all the fruits of the garden," the Heavenly Father told His Children, "even the Tree of Life. But there is one tree from which you must not eat — the Tree of Knowledge of Good and Evil."

God was telling Adam and Eve — you and me — that we cannot judge. This is not a commandment not to judge, but a statement that we could not judge even if we wanted to. Spirit, in its true essence, does not know good or evil. God is just pure love, pure energy, pure being. If we want to live in the high joy vibration, we must free ourself of the distinctions that the mortal mind has conjured to separate us from our Source.

So what did Adam and Eve do, for openers? The only thing they were told not to do, of course, and Eve took her famous bite. Now here's where the action really begins. Immediately Adam and Eve realize they are naked, and they take fig leaves to cover their loins, which beforehand were no less beautiful or holy than the rest of them. The moment they made a distinction between good and evil, that separation was projected onto their bodies,

[1] T, p. 289

39

making some parts of them good and other parts bad. This is the division in consciousness that has produced the world of separateness that we see.

Then, the Bible tells us, Adam and Eve hid from God (the first guilt trip), and God, like any self-respecting father, sought to find them. (*He* knew where they were, but *they* needed help to find them*selves*.) Then, the story goes, "They heard God walking in the Garden." It's interesting that now they perceived God as outside themselves; until that time, He was within their hearts.

And God asked, "Adam, where are you?"

Adam, realizing that he could hide no longer, answered, "Here I am."

"What are you doing in those bushes, Adam?...You were playing so nicely in the Garden! Come, *bubbala*, I have a grilled cheese sandwich and tomato soup for you. Have a little lunch."

"But I can't come out, Father — I'm naked!"

"Naked, what's 'naked'? What are you talking about, 'naked'?"

Enter Adam and Eve, stage left, adorned with the tackiest designer fig leaves you've ever seen, hastily tied around their waists, looking more like leftovers from a Soho costume party than Children of God. God almost fell on the Garden floor laughing — He made His Children in perfection and they decided perfection needed to be covered by a plant. Had it been a few thousand years later, it would have been polyester.

"What is this fig leaf business?" asks the Father. "What I gave you wasn't good enough?"

"No, it's not that," Adam begins to explain. "You see, the woman made me do it." (We won't even begin to comment on that one.)

Spotlight to woman. "Well, what's your story?"

"The serpent made me do it." Flip Wilson would have been proud.

Unfortunately for the serpent, he wasn't around to defend himself, else he might have blamed it on the tabasco sauce on last night's nachos. So the poor asp gets condemned to slither around on his belly and perform denigrating dances out of straw baskets in grade-b movies for several thousand years. Bad karma.

Now, if you would be willing to overlook the burlesque license I am taking, let's look at that one question asked of Adam by God, the inquiry around which the whole scene revolves: *Who told you you were naked?*

This is a question asked not only of Adam by God. It is one you and I must ask ourselves. Who told you you were naked?

There was a time early in our lives when we lived as innocent children, totally unashamed, free of fear of opinion, beyond the sordid realm of guilt and fear. This was the Garden of Eden within our heart. Here we were and *are* all Adam, all Eve.

Then something happened. Someone told us we were naked. Someone convinced us — beguiled us — to believe that we were not good enough as we were, that we had to be or do something more than we were to be approved. We believed that we had to work to change ourselves to be innocent, while our innocence stood inviolate just as we were.

Someone, like the first grade teacher of a child I know, told us that we could not color the clown's nose green. "All clowns' noses must be red," she commanded the child. That afternoon the little boy came home with a tear in his eye, a tear that was not there before.

It was the same child who stood at the door waiting for the schoolbus on the first day of school, stark naked, lunchbox in hand.

"Dov, you can't go to school like that!" mother laughingly told the little one.

"Why not?"

"Well...everyone wears clothes to school."

"Why?"

"Well...other people might feel embarrassed."

"Why?"

"Because people don't like to show their bodies."

"Why?"

"Frankly," the mother later told me, "I couldn't think of a good reason why."

I thought about it. I have thought about it a lot, and frankly, I can't think of a good reason either. I don't know why people wear clothes. I wear clothes because I would probably be embarrassed in public if I didn't. And yet somehow that reason doesn't satisfy me very well.

When I spent some time at Esalen at Big Sur a dozen years ago, I went naked with many people, and it was a wonderful experience. For the first day or two my eyes drifted below some navels, but soon I opened my mind and heart to the relaxed and peaceful atmosphere, and sexuality was not an issue. In fact, the experience was probably less sexually stimulating than in the world of clothes, where many garments are designed to highlight sexuality through accent and mystery. When nothing was left to the imagination, I felt a sense of ease, and sexuality was but a minor aspect of nudity. I remember returning to society after that experience, feeling very strange in clothing, wondering, like the little boy with his lunchbox, why people wore clothes anyway.

Now I am not pushing nudity, nor would I consider myself a nudist, although I think it would be marvelous if the leaders of the nations held a nude summit conference. (Can you imagine a naked U.N. General Assembly or a Security Council meeting in the tubs of the Esalen Hot Springs?) I see nudity more as a metaphor for a way of living, a refreshing attitude of being completely open with one another, with no hidden agendas. As Hugh Prather says, "We must be like plate glass buildings, with no areas shielded from sharing." Then, perhaps, we would see that there is nothing that we need to protect anyway.

Who told you you were naked? I remember one of my earliest feelings of embarrassment. I was sitting on a toilet at Mommy Babb's Nursery School, when another little friend came in the room with me. I remember feeling for the first time that I was not supposed to be with another person in the bathroom, that I must not be seen on the toilet. Perhaps I remember it because it was my moment of departure from the Garden, my turning point from peace to fear. Perhaps that was the moment I donned my first fig leaf and began to hide from my Father.

But it doesn't have to be that way now. Perhaps spiritual enlightenment is nothing more or less than awakening to the fact that we do not need to hide, and in fact we never did. Perhaps if we had the courage to hide nothing we would soon realize that all is forgivable. We keep our sins powerful by our unwillingness to hold them up to the light. Perhaps real healing is the undoing of all the coverings we have draped over what we thought should not be seen. Then we will see the radiance that we are.

There is a tale which quite eloquently tells our story: Once there was a western fort where a platoon of cavalrymen were feverishly fending off a band of Indians. After a long and grueling battle the ranks of the cavalry were diminished to two lonely infantrymen.

In the midst of pummelling shooting, one soldier came to the other, tapped him on the shoulder, and told him, "I have good news and I have bad news."

"Let's have the bad first."

"O.K.: Our defenses are failing miserably and there are no reinforcements."

"Well, if that's the bad news, I can't imagine what could be the good news. Let's hear it."

"There are no Indians."

That about sums it up. Our defenses are failing us, but perhaps that is the best thing that could happen; for it is only when our barriers fail us that we are forced to notice that we never needed them.

Can you remember some of the silly defenses you have erected to make you look good, which have backfired? I can remember working in a douche powder and laxative factory during the summer of my sixteenth year (definitely a lower consciousness job). Spending so much time in the warehouse, I had little opportunity to get to the beach and be in the sun. I felt embarrassed that I was rather a paleface, so I went out and bought some "Tanfastic," a lotion that I had seen on a television commercial. I was impressed when I saw a handsome actor attract a flock of beautiful bikini-clad girls simply by applying a dab of the chemical to his forehead.

"That's for me!" I thought, "I'll rub some on, and when I walk into work on Monday all the secretaries will swarm around me asking for dates!" And off to the drug store I dashed.

Come Monday morning, there I was in the locker room, punching in, datebook and pencil in hand. This was it; my moment had come. Smoothly I cruised through the office toward the shipping department, my ears perked for the first compliment.

It came: "Hey, Alan!" a man's voice gruffly called from the loading dock. "What's that orange stuff on your arm?"

There is a passage from the Talmudic *Ethics of the Fathers: "He who seeks to gain reputation shall lose it; he who does not seek reputation shall gain it."* (Could the ancient sages have known about *Tanfastic?*)

Who told you you were naked? Was it a television program, an aunt who slapped your hand when you touched your genitals, a friend of your mother's who was visibly embarrassed when mom brought her little boy into the ladies' room with her?

No, it was none of these. Let us not be tempted to blame anyone or anything outside ourselves, for *there is no outside world.* There is only awareness.

No, it was not the fault of a person, an event, or an experience. It was a thought, one tiny, almost imperceptibly subtle — like a serpent — thought that said, "You must hide." That's all it was. And that thought has snowballed through incredible convolutions, twisting and doubling back upon itself countless times, until it has formed the world we see. We have manufactured a senseless world in which an attractive young black woman is named Miss America for taking most of her clothes off, and then she is disqualified for taking them all off. It is an enigmatic world, a self-contradicting arena where illusions reign and the security of open sharing is overshadowed by heavy armor and the fear of gentleness.

Yet that senseless world has no power in the Light. Here in the light of truth, in the joyful openness of the dawning day, all is alive and fresh and as clear as the innocence in which we were born. We can be ourselves, we can love, we can know the truth about who we are. Still we walk in the Garden; the Tree of Life remains. Nothing has happened but love.

We need never hide from one another again. There is no sin that can stand before the healing power of forgiveness. No illusion can cover over the dignity in which we have learned to respect ourselves. Never again need we attempt to be someone or something that we are not. For now we know that who we are is wholly lovable and perfect in the eyes of the One in whose holy image we are created. As Alan Watts described the universe, "God is a flower that grew a nose to smell itself." We are the flower, the God, the nose, the aroma, and the self.

Who told you you were naked? It really doesn't matter now. All that matters is that we know who we are, from what great love we have sprung, and that we live in the Garden as we were intended. We remain as God created us. And for that we can be grateful.

> *And gladly will you walk the way of innocence together, singing as you behold the open door of Heaven and recognize the home that called to you. Give joyously to one another the freedom and the strength to lead you there.*[2]

---

[2] T. p. 399

Blue Highways

*Some of your greatest advances you have judged as failures, and
some of your deepest retreats you have evaluated as success.*

- A Course in Miracles[1]

Glancing to my right on Peoplexpress Flight 159 to Buffalo, I noticed
the woman sitting next to me reading a shiny-covered book called *Blue
Highways.*[2] Looking to my left, I saw my other neighbor reading a shiny-
covered book called *Blue Highways.* Being giftedly psychic and keen to the
subtleties of spiritual intuition, I deduced that I was supposed to find out
about *Blue Highways.*

I turned to the lady on my right, a pleasantly-professional looking
young woman who felt approachable. "What's that book about?" I asked.

"Oh, it's marvelous!" she returned. "It's by a Native American
named William Least Heat Moon who lost his marriage and his job as an
English teacher, both about the same time. Having next to nothing left, he
decided to follow his dream of travelling around the country as a pilgrim of
consciousness. He bought an old VW bus, packed up his gear and set out.

"Deciding where to go, William looked at a map. He saw that all of the
major routes, printed in red, were the regularly travelled superhighways and
toll roads that promised little more than tourist attractions and truck stops
every hundred miles. This prospect did not feel like it fit with William's
dream, so he looked at the map again. This time he saw that there were also
blue highways. These were the local lesser-known byways, routes that
promised more color and adventure than speed and comfort.

"William decided to follow the blue highways, and what marvelous
adventures he had! He visited the monastary where the Christian mystic,
Thomas Merton lived and wrote; he stayed at Native American Indian
villages where he learned more about his heritage; along the way he met
many fascinating people who gave him odd jobs and put him up for weeks. It

---

[1] T, p. 357

[2] William Least Heat Moon, *Blue Highways*, Little, Brown, 1983

45

was a true odyssey, a living voyage in personal awakening.

"As William went along he kept a journal," my lovely *raconteur* went on, her excitement waxing as she shared it with me. "After a year or two on the road he had recorded a sizeable collection of insights and experiences which he felt other persons who shared his dream might benefit from reading, so he sought to publish it. Little, Brown found it marketable, and it's been a huge success."

I looked at the book. On the cover I saw a round gold sticker boasting *"34 WEEKS ON THE NEW YORK TIMES BEST-SELLER LIST."* Between the covers I found a masterfully witty portrayal of one man's discovery of his country, his people, and — most important — himself. This author deserved to be read.

It was no accident that William Least Heat Moon lost his job and his wife. He had a different job to do, a larger family to serve. His destiny was to be a major writer with a gift to share. Had he remained with that career and family, he might have travelled only the red highways, learning of life mostly through newspaper headlines and coffee-break talk in the teachers' room. He might have published a poem in a literary quarterly every hundred miles or so. But being forced onto the blue highways, William Least Heat Moon stepped into his destiny — and shared its gift with millions.

We all have our blue highways, and blessedly so. Every minus in our lives is really half of a plus. A "negative" experience is simply the beginning of a positive awakening that is waiting for a stroke of vertical awareness to make it complete. We see the negative only when we are looking back or ahead, not up. The moment we look up and join our mind with the wisdom of God's infinite perspective, we can see that all of the minuses seemed to be bad only because we did not yet realize the blessing they brought into our lives. In his masterful book *Illusions*, Richard Bach writes,

> There is no such thing as a problem without a gift for you in its hands. You seek problems because you need their gifts.[3]

When we accept the gift, it ceases to be a problem. "Bad" is an interpretation, not a fact. Our hardships are not the whim of a wrathful God; they are the conclusions we draw from incomplete perception.

---

[3] Richard Bach, *Illusions: The Adventures of a Reluctant Messiah*, Delacorte Press, 1977

Tragedy to Triumph

One day after coming home from a weekend retreat I had conducted, I went to my mailbox to collect the day's mail. "Ah, another letter of thanks!" I smiled as I walked back to the house. Often after a retreat I receive letters of loving testimony from participants whose lives have been changed as a result of the workshop experience.

Opening the letter I expected a ray of gratefulness to shine out and bless me. Instead, to my chagrin, I felt engulfed by billows of dark, murky psychic smoke. Where I had anticipated finding, "How elated I am after your weekend!" I found instead, "What a disappointment your retreat was, and you owe me something!"

Thrown somewhat off balance, I read:

> *Dear Mr. Cohen, I want you to know what a terrible experience I had at your event. You misrepresented what the weekend was about...Your brochure stated that the facilities were comfortable, and I did not find them so; you called it a retreat, and it turned out to be a workshop; I did not like sharing the dorm facilities with others...*

The letter went on to offer a list of complaints, concluding with, "I would like my money back."

"Well," my ego responded, "Who does she think she is?...That was a really good retreat, and if she didn't like it, that's not my fault — Everyone *else* liked it! Besides, what does she want for $75, anyway?" (Do you know this train of thought?) I put the letter aside, too upset to think clearly about what to do about it.

A few minutes later I picked it up and read it again. This time I noticed that she had signed it, "In love and light, Elena."

"In love and light"? How could she sign an attack letter "In love and light?" Wasn't she trying to hurt me? If she loved and lighted me, how could she criticize my retreat so harshly?

I mulled over those thoughts for a while, wondering what to do about this difficult letter. My first inclination was to immediately write her back a

47

strongly-worded response explaining why she was wrong, and prove to her that I was right.

Then I remembered a Dale Carnegie quote that has saved me many times: "Do not do the impulsive thing — That is always wrong."[4] Along with the memory of that advice came the *Course in Miracles* motto: "The ego always speaks first, it always speaks loudest, and it is always wrong."

I listened again for Spirit's guidance. I heard, "Don't act hastily... Put the letter aside for a few days; consult the Voice of Peace inside yourself, and then act."

As I thought about the situation during the next few days I began to hear more and more clearly the teaching of the Course: "When you perceive an attack from one of your brothers, it is simply your faulty perception. Look at his action in another way, and you will see that it is actually a call for love. Give the love that is being sought, and a miracle will happen."

My ego did not want to acknowledge that Elena was calling for love, but the feeling to respond as if she was, was so compelling that I had to follow it. I realized that it really didn't matter who was right or wrong in this situation; the only way anyone ever wins is if everyone wins. When anyone ends up hurt, no one wins. I gradually saw more clearly that it was more important to feel peace and harmony with one of my fellows than to try to prove that I was right.

I remembered a verse from a song that we sing at my workshops: "All I ask of you is forever to remember me as loving you." I realized that if Elena and I never saw each other again, I would much rather have her remember me as someone who cared about her, than as someone who hurt her. I figured that saving a few dollars was nowhere near as important as giving love, and that if I really needed that money God would get it for me in another way.

I sat down and wrote this letter:

Dear Elena,

I am so sorry that you did not have a good experience at the retreat. It is very important to me that those who attend my workshop go home with a good feeling about it. If you feel that the workshop did not serve you, then I consider it my loss. Please find enclosed a refund check with my hopes that you will attend another of my workshops at another time, with my

---

[4] Dale Carnegie, *How to Win Friends and Influence People*, Simon & Schuster, 1936

48

deepest support for your good experience.
In love and light,
Alan

It felt right. I put the check in the envelope and dropped it in the mail with the prayer that only good would come of this interaction.

About a month later I received a beautiful Christmas card from Elena, with this note:

Dear Alan,
Thank you very much for your letter and the refund. I want you to know that I really appreciate it. If you would like to run another retreat, may I recommend the Harrison Farm, a beautiful center on a hundred well-kept acres, with cozy double rooms and very comfortable facilities. The telephone number is enclosed. I think you will enjoy it. Have a wonderful holiday season!

In love and light,
Elena

Was I glad I sent her the letter I did! I called the center and set up a visit. To my happy surprise it was one of the most beautiful conference centers I have ever seen! Lovely cottages, a large stone dining hall, a waterfall and lake, a delicately manicured flowered landscape, and a very amiable manager. Immediately I wrote a deposit check to reserve the site for my next retreat, blessing Elena as I did so.

The retreat turned out to be a marvelous, uplifting event, allowing a hundred and twenty persons to receive a deeply healing experience which touched many of their lives in a profound way. All this was a direct result of Elena's recommendation.

Elena's complaint was not an attack, but a blessing. Her dissatisfaction with the original camp was the steppingstone for our discovery of this new and much more enjoyable site. I originally perceived her letter as being against me, but in the grand scheme of things it was quite *for* me. It directly benefitted all the participants, hundreds more who have attended subsequent retreats, and the many thousands they ultimately touch, as well as everyone who reads this account. How powerfully Elena served the Holy Spirit by writing that letter! And how gracious was that same Spirit to counsel me to answer her the way I did. Elena's letter truly *was* written in love and light.

Bouncing Back

Hitting bottom sometimes helps us bounce to the top. In dance it is necessary to go into a deep *pliet*, crouching almost to the floor, to gain the leverage to jump high. If you consider the difficult times in your life, the periods when you entered a state of spiritual contraction, you will notice that these challenging times were often followed by a catapult into new spiritual awakening. You were squeezed through the birth canal of consciousness into a greater awareness, bringing with it many more possibilities than life in the womb could offer.

At a workshop in upstate New York a radiantly handsome man named Martin stood up to tell his story: "I began to drink when as a teacher, husband, and father, I felt that I could not cope with the pressures in my life. Gradually I found myself drinking more and more, until I had to move out of my home, away from my wife and daughter. I took a job in a city in the midwest, where I continued to drink even more heavily. I didn't want to admit it, but I was an alcoholic. "The turning point for me came one night when I found myself naked in some bed, the whereabouts of which I could not tell. There I lay, stenched by my own vomit, without a quarter or a friend. It was then, hitting rock bottom, that I admitted to myself that my life was not working. I reasoned that there must be a better way to live, and that I needed help. There was no other way but up, and it took that experience for me to realize it. I called out to God to help me find a new direction, and now I am a new man.

"What I want to share with you is that I had to hit rock bottom before I could bounce up. I was so stubborn that it was only when I had nothing, that I was willing to call for help. I feel that if I had had *anything* - a piece of clothing, a penny, a friend - I would have clung to that as a source of security in my old way. But because I had nothing, I had to start all over, and now as I look back on it I call it a blessing."

Embracing All of Life

Perception is not a fact; it is an interpretation. We do not see what is, but what we *choose* to see. We do not look upon the world as it is, but ourselves as we believe we are. The principle applies to *all* of our experiences, including joy as well as pain. This simple truth is the key to the transformation of our life, for if our pain has been chosen, we can make a new choice: We can transform the energy that we have used to torment and crucify ourselves, and redirect it to awaken, create, and share the good that is within us.

If we understand that everything that now seems to be working against us is actually the gift of a Force working *for* us - a power which we must discover how to use creatively - we can escape from a threatening, menacing world into a universe that is constantly flowing to lift us into greater joy.

When I visited a home for delinquent boys in upstate New York, I was deeply impressed by the enthusiasm and aliveness of the boys in residence. They did not seem at all like criminals to me. I observed an excellent, trusting rapport between the staff and the teenagers. When I complimented a counselor on this fine success, he offered me this account:

"The birth of the school was not easy. The members of the community, rather conservative folks by nature, felt threatened at the announcement that a reform school would be established in their quiet neighborhood, and they protested. In fact, they did all they could to stop us from establishing this school. They even came out and picketed in front of the site."

"So how did you deal with their protests?" I had to ask.

"We hired the picketers!" he laughed. "We gave them jobs on the staff, and you should have seen how quickly this school took off. That's been the way we've worked for twelve years, and that's why we've been successful - we don't make anyone our enemy, and we seek to take the teenagers and the community into our sense of self. As you can see, it works!"

Spirit versus Form

The ego judges events by their form, neatly lumping life into categories of good and bad. But the Holy Spirit teaches that no event is always good or bad; it is *how we look at it* that determines its worth; if we choose to find the light in it, we can consistently find the good.

At a healing workshop I attended one summer, the members of our class were given the assignment to stand and tell our individual stories of awakening. One man stood up and gave this report:

"My wife of twenty-three years recently left me, I lost my job, I don't know how the income is going to meet the outgo - and I am in utter bliss! I've never been so happy! These experiences have served to show me that happiness lies *within* me, and now that I have reclaimed my own power I am at peace."

It takes a great deal of trust to realize, as *A Course in Miracles* teaches, that *all* events, situations, and circumstances are helpful. "Trust remains the bedrock of the teacher of God's whole thought system"[5] explains the course. I attended a workshop given by Reverend Donald Curtis, a talented Unity Minister, who called the seminar *"How to Stop Whining and Start Winning"*. "That phrase pretty well sums up the fact that there are no tragedies except those of our own creation. Later I saw a book which gave me its whole contents simply by the title: *Stop Crying at Your Own Movies*.

Mud or Stars

Life is a gift from God, an unlimited series of opportunities to find the good in ourselves and each other. There is good in everything, if we are willing to see it. "Two men looked out through prison bars. One saw mud; the other, stars."

What are you choosing to see? It's all out there, whatever your mind can imagine. We attract to ourselves that which we think upon; this is how we are the engineers of our experience and the creators of our destiny. Destiny is not cast upon us from a capricious God seeking vengeance

---

[5] M, p. 1

through yellowed eyes, blood dripping from His lips. Destiny is a door opened before us, inviting us to walk into the light, or stand in the darkness. There are not even two paths to take. There is but one, and we choose either to walk it or stand still.

As we choose to walk, we go forward with mighty companions. No one walks the path to God alone, for as he takes a step toward the light he is joined by legions of others who gain strength from sharing it. The path to God is not travelled by the lonely or the meek; indeed no one who walks it need ever be lonely again. The path to God is as wide as all who choose to walk together, arm in arm, mind to mind, heart to heart.

Loneliness is nothing more than a fearful thought that leaves us the moment we are willing to look into the light and own our true radiance. There is no need for fear in a world of good, a world that is revealed by the simple willingness to trust. Would it not be astonishing to learn that the world has suffered for so long only because our faith in fear exceeded our courage to love? Who would have imagined that the light has always been with us, yet has gone unseen because so few have lifted their minds and opened their hearts to acknowledge it? And would it not be the most miraculous realization of all to understand that every tragedy that has ever been is really a blessing awaiting the awareness of triumph? *Love can triumph over anything.* There is no event that the light cannot make its own. Like a sun that shines from every part of the sky at once, radiantly removing all possibility of shadows, the power of God extends to *all* circumstances.

Children of Light, the time of shadows is over. There is no need to hide from reflections of evil. Evil has no power except what you give it by your belief. You who have eyes to see the light must now discover that the domain of God extends to all things. The Kingdom of Heaven is in your mind, and when you choose to enter the Kingdom everything you look upon will be a part of it. This is the awareness to which all of your experiences have led you, and the one you are now ready to accept. Step forward and become who you are by living in the world intended for you since the birth of your holy mind. You need not be afraid, afraid of your brethren, of life, of God, of yourself. *You were not born to live in fear.* You were created to live in the light, and as you step into your destiny you will find peace in the entire universe.

Life is good. All that is required for it to be so is for you to claim it in your daily activities. The healing of the your life and your world seeks not but for gods and angels, but for sincere souls like yourself to walk the earth with the sun of God shining from your eyes. Yes, there will be challenges, but none beyond your ability to conquer with the Holy Spirit as your guide. *The Holy Spirit never fails,* for it is of God, and God lives only to love.

There is one triumph in which there are no losers - the triumph of Spirit over emptiness. This is the triumph that you must seek, for it is the one victory of which you are assured. You will not gain it alone, for you are not alone. You are at peace and you are loved. Never forget how important you are to your Heavenly Father, and your heart shall always be filled with abundant blessings.

Up from Flatland

In the nineteenth century there appeared a book called *Flatland,** the story of a land in which all the citizens lived in only two dimensions. The book, written by "A Square," opens with this introduction:

> *To the inhabitants of space in general this work is dedicated by a humble native of Flatland in the hope that even as he was initiated into the mysteries of three dimensions, having been previously conversant with only two, so the citizens of that celestial region may aspire yet higher and higher to the secrets of four, five, or even six dimensions, thereby contributing to the enlargement of the imagination and the possible development of that most rare and excellent gift of modesty among the superior races of solid humanity.*
>
> -A Square

The Flatlanders lived their lives in one plane, seeing and knowing only what could be seen and known in that plane, and nothing above or below it. Flatland was populated by a large number of Squares and Circles, with a subculture of Triangles and an occasional Parallelogram.

The analogy of Flatland as a description of the world that we have been accustomed to inhabiting, and the pithy story of one Square's awakening is absolutely delicious. I would like to take the original notion of Flatland and imagine with you a scenario of the kind of leap of consciousness that we are all experiencing. So sit back, relax, and let us together enjoy a little excursion into a new dimension:

One sunny day in Flatland a little Square saw a Circle coming toward him. He carried on with his usual activities, but it soon became obvious that this Circle was not like any he had seen before. This Circle just kept getting larger and larger until it was clearly not just a Circle, but a Sphere. Square had heard about Spheres before, but he had always believed that they were

---

* Edwin A. Abbott, *Flatland: A Romance of Many Dimensions*, Dover Publications, 1952

just fairy tales or children's myths. This one, however, looked very real indeed. Frightened, Square began to run.

"Don't be afraid," called the Sphere, "I won't hurt you!"

The Square stopped and turned toward the stranger. Slowly backing away, he asked, "What are you, anyway?"

"I'm a Sphere."

"But there are no Spheres in Flatland," Square challenged.

"That may be so," gently replied the Sphere, "but Flatland is not all there is to life. There is more to life than the two dimensions with which you are familiar — much, much more, indeed. There is a actually another dimension of which most of the citizens of Flatland are not aware at all: *Spaceland.* Spaceland is a wonderful world with so much more freedom to see and move and play! But you cannot enjoy it because all of you in Flatland have gotten used to looking only forward, back, and to the sides. Hardly anyone in Flatland ever looks up! If you did, you would see many wondrous forms far more exciting and fascinating than you have found in Flatland."

"How can I see these lovely sights?" young Square wondered aloud.

"Simply look up and you will see the whole picture," the Sphere explained. "In fact," Sphere went on, "you will be surprised to know that what you see in Flatland is actually a part of the third dimension. Those you see as Circles are actually Spheres, but because you see only in two dimensions, all you see is one plane of a much greater reality!"

"You will be happy to know that you and your friends are not just Squares, but you are actually facets of a marvelous and very practical form called a "Cube." The Triangles belong to a mystical design called "Pyramid," and that funny-looking family down the street that you laugh at, Mr. and Mrs. Ellipse, are actually components of a most important configuration called "Egg."

"Alas, but you see none of these rich aspects of your life because you are so preoccupied with what is behind and in front of you — Oh, Square, if you only knew how much more there is to life, you would dance with joy!"

Sphere paused for a moment. She realized this was a lot for a little Square to absorb so quickly, and she wanted to give him time to awaken.

"My dear Square, the universe is so much greater than you have imagined — and now you are seeing things as they truly are, and indeed have always been. I am very happy for you."

The Square was astounded; yet somehow it made sense. Into his mind flashed some memories of having seen unusual shapes when he was just a few points old. He remembered seeing beautiful, dazzling configurations just before going to sleep or while travelling through the Park of Diamonds. Then he recalled that when he had told his mother about them she patted him on one of his sides and told him he had a vivid imagination. Eventually he stopped seeing them — he didn't want to be different from his friends.

The Sphere, shimmering before the young one, sensed he was ready to see more.

"Would you like to see your true self?" she asked.

The Square hesitated. He wasn't quite sure about his true self. It seemed that most of the inhabitants of Flatland were rather fearful of looking at their true self. Whenever someone would bring up the idea of their true self at a party, for example, someone would quickly make a joke or change the subject. Why were the Flatlanders so afraid of their own being? Even the Square could not understand why hardly anyone in Flatland loved himself.

"Yes," Square answered, "Yes, I would like to see my true self." The moment he said those words his fear went away.

"Very well, then — Look up!" Sphere commanded. "Look up and you will see who you really are!"

Square looked up and he could hardly believe his eyes. What a wondrous sight he did see! He saw that he was not just a small Polygon with four sides of equal length, as he had read in his Geometric Geneology textbook. He saw that his square self was just one part of his being, the part that could be seen in Flatland. Square saw that he was actually a great, glowing Cube, of which the lines that he thought limited him were but one aspect. How exciting to find that he was whole! So that was why he had felt so strangely incomplete as a little Square! Now he realized that there was nothing to be afraid of, nothing in his real self that could harm him. In fact, nothing had ever made him as happy as looking upon his real self and seeing all that he was.

That was just the beginning. As the Square became more and more comfortable looking up, he could see the real identity of everyone in Flatland! They were so beautiful! He saw marvelous Cones, sparkling Cylinders, and even a Great Sphere made up of Triangles. His guide told him this was a "Geodesic Dome" (but hardly anyone in Flatland was ready for that one). Square saw that what was happening in Flatland was such a little part of the whole picture. And he was afraid no more.

Just open your eyes, and realize the way it's always been.
                                                                    - The Moody Blues

The Spiral Mountain

Life does not go on in a circle...nor does it ever repeat itself. It always changes, and yet it evolves every moment to be constant. Life is all-encompassing and creates the next moment by virtue of its own being...

- Ramtha*

Sometimes it seems like we are getting nowhere, as if we are back at the same place we were months, years, or lifetimes ago. We may feel frustrated, unworthy, and confused, and we wonder if we are really getting anywhere in life.

Recently I heard a friend of mine, a thirty-eight year old woman moan, "I am stuck in a pattern in my relationship just like I was as a teenager! I can't believe it — I don't think I've gotten anywhere!"

Actually, we are always growing; the question is not whether or not we are getting anywhere, but how quickly we are moving along. Growth is *always* happening, even when we seem to be going down or moving backward. It is only the ego, seeking to keep us in the illusion of stuckness, that believes that nothing is happening. When such a smoke screen arises it is useful to remember that the ego is always wrong. We believe that we are getting nowhere because the ego interprets life as if it were against us, when in fact life is always working for us.

We discover a new high, we see a new vista of life from a mountain peak of truth that we have never scaled before, and then we feel that we cannot sustain it; we slip back into our old perception or way of acting. We may feel discouraged and want to give up.

At a point like this we must realize that we never slip back to the place we were at before we had the experience. It just *seems* that we are falling back because we are going down (in consciousness) *from the new height that we have discovered.* If we examine our path carefully we will see that we did

---

* Steven Lee Weinberg, ed., *Ramtha*, Sovereignty, Inc., 1986, p. 158

not fall all the way back into the valley — just to a plateau a little further down on the mountain. It is from here that we will begin our new ascent, which will take us to an even higher peak next time. The mountain of truth is scaled by taking three steps forward and two steps back. This process is perfect, and it is wonderful, for the going down gave us the momentum we needed to rise higher the next time, like a roller coaster or ski jump. One thing is certain on the spiritual path of the true aspirant: No step is ever wasted.

It is very helpful to consider our journey of awakening like the adventure of climbing a mountain by a spiral pathway. How compassionate is our Heavenly Father, who understands that a gentle, gradual ascent is much easier and more productive in the long run than a quick, steep climb! (Although some do choose the rugged path.) We can see this important process illustrated in diagram 1.

Let's take the apparent contrast of being in a relationship or out of one as an example. We start out on the bottom of the spiral not in a relationship. Here we feel a certain dissatisfaction, a need for more, a desire to be with another person. So we move across the bottom of the spiral into a relationship. We become deeply involved in the relationship; it becomes the all-important issue in our life as we devote most of our energy to participating in it, trying to make it work, and seeing if we can find happiness in it. Sometimes we seem to succeed, and sometimes it seems as if it is not worth it. Yet always we are thinking, feeling, learning, and growing.

Then at some point days, months, years, or lifetimes later we begin to feel that a relationship is not what we really want. Or perhaps we feel it is not really this person that we want to be in a relationship with. So we move toward being on our own once again.

We find being on our own is very freeing and rather satisfying — for a while. We feel relieved of the challenges and pressures of being in the relationship, and our life becomes more peaceful and more manageable.

Then, after a certain amount of time we start to feel lonely; that feeling of missing something in our life bubbles up, and once again we feel that we would like to be involved in a relationship.

Now, here is the point at which we might be inclined to throw our hands up and complain, "On no, I'm right back where I started! I haven't gotten anywhere — Will this go on forever?"

The truth is that you are *not* right back where you started, you *are* getting somewhere, and it will not go on forever. The only thing that goes on

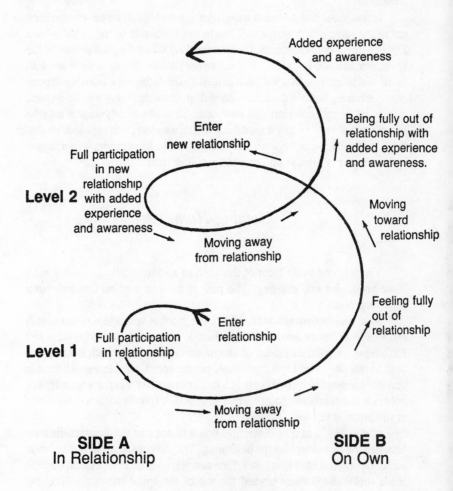

Added experience
and awareness

Being fully out of
relationship with
added experience
and awareness.

Enter
new relationship

Moving
toward
relationship

Full participation
in new
relationship
Level 2 with added
experience
and awareness

Moving away
from relationship

Feeling fully
out of
relationship

Enter
relationship

Level 1 Full participation
in relationship

Moving away
from relationship

SIDE A
In Relationship

SIDE B
On Own

The Spiral Mountain
Diagram 1

forever is God, and that is a very encouraging awareness to embrace and remember.

In this particular situation what has happened is that we have come back not to the same place we started, but to the same side of the spiral — *at a higher level of consciousness*. (See diagram 2.) While the *pattern* may be the same, our position is significantly improved because this time we bring with us all the awareness that we have gained through the very valuable experiences of having been in the first relationship, growing through it, being back on our own, and entering this new one. So while the dynamics may be similar, we are not by any means back where we were, although that is what the ego would have us believe. The truth is that we have grown — perhaps in inches, but it is always an upward-spiralling path.

Coming Home

There is one more facet of this path of awakening that makes it even more promising and exciting. The path is not just a spiral upward, but a spiralling *cone*.

As we move upward on the spiral, the gap that seems to separate side A and side B becomes smaller and smaller. We are not just moving back and forth between polarized sides of an emotional slinky; the path is actually a continuous one. The higher we move on the spiral, the clearer it becomes that what seemed to be two poles of a ladder that never meet, are actually *one* pole that winds around in a progressively smaller spiral until it resolves itself at the point at the top.

If you look again at diagram 2 you will see that the greatest distance between the two sides is at the beginning. This demonstrates why the elation and disappointment in first loves, for example, is much more radical than the more subtle oscillations toward the top of the spiral mountain. The gap between sides A and B on level 2 is less than it was on level 1, and even smaller on level 3. (Actually, to differentiate between levels at all is arbitrary and somewhat misleading, for all of the levels flow into one another; there is no real separation between them.) The amount of contrast between the sides gradually diminishes until at the top there is no difference at all. The process is like that of an unfolding flower, gradually releasing more petals from

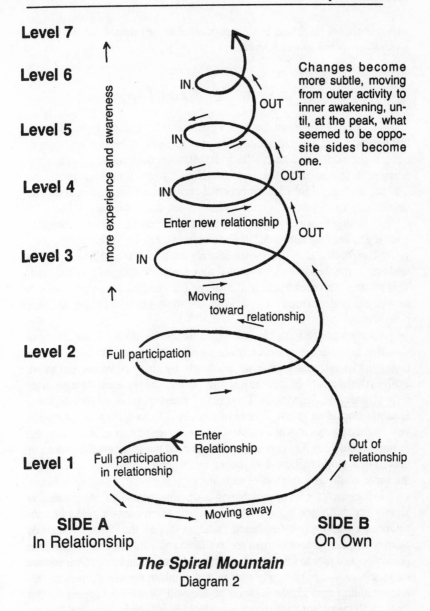

Level 7

Level 6

more experience and awareness

IN

OUT

Level 5

IN

Changes become more subtle, moving from outer activity to inner awakening, until, at the peak, what seemed to be opposite sides become one.

OUT

Level 4

IN

Enter new relationship

OUT

Level 3

IN

Moving toward relationship

Level 2

Full participation

Enter Relationship

Out of relationship

Level 1

Full participation in relationship

Moving away

SIDE A
In Relationship

SIDE B
On Own

The Spiral Mountain
Diagram 2

As we gain experience and awareness, the contrasts in our experience gradually diminish, and eventually both sides merge at one peaceful peak.

within itself; the final petal is quite connected to the original one. So are we always connected to our Source.

The View From The Top

The arena of relationships is just one example of all the types of issues that the spiral mountain illustrates. Other examples may be: dieting/binging; being in the world/retreating; selling real estate/renouncing money; accumulating possessions/letting them go; disciplining yourself/playing; and so on. You can probably think of many personal examples not considered here. The details may be different, but the dynamics are really the same.

Returning to our example of relationships (you can substitute another issue if you like) we notice that as you come closer to the top of the mountain you still go back and forth between desiring relationships and aloneness, but the oscillations become so subtle that they are *more internal than external*. This advanced level of learning allows you the freedom to stay pretty much in one external position as you work out these issues in a gentle inner process.

As we learn to recognize the voice of Spirit within us, we are more sensitive to guidance in the early stages of a step in any direction. At the beginning of spiritual growth we are taught by sharp contrasts; but as we evolve, the intensity of the contrast diminishes, and we learn through more refined inner transformations. There is still a movement of awareness, but it is subtle instead of gross. You have graduated from feeling like a human yoyo to accept more gentle lessons. Because your heart is attuned to the promptings of your inner spirit, you do not need the gross manifestations of the physical world to learn, and you are no longer required to bounce around the outer world as a method of training.

In the case of relationships/going-it-on-your-ownships, then, you may simply stay with one person while climbing the mountain peaks of consciousness within your own heart, realizing that all the lessons you could learn with other men or women are available and contained within this one perfect opportunity to find harmony with another human being. Or if you are on your own you may simply stay so and climb to the same mountaintop, understanding that all the lessons of life will be gently brought to you through all the persons and experiences Holy Spirit sends your way. It is not so important which route you take, just that you get to see the view from the top. Here you meet everyone who has traversed every route up the mountain, for here is the place where all the roads of learning converge at a spectacular viewing point. At this point you may see that all of us are always in relationship, and all of us are always alone. This point of paradox is a one of great power; here you get off the path to become the mountain.

Healing the Split Mind

The seeming polarities of the spiral mountain, not distant from one another at all, are like the two tribes in that marvelous motion picture, *The Dark Crystal*. In the story we find a divided world that began to die ages ago when the crystal that empowered the kingdom was split. Now there are two tribes in the realm: the gentle, loving, wise Mystics, and the villainous, vicious, vulture-like Skexies, ugly creatures ready to swoop upon and maim innocent victims for their own aggrandizement. The Mystics, saintly by comparison, are benign ones — but they have lost their power and they are dying.

A young boy, Jeb, the last survivor of a race that is neither Mystic nor Skexi, is given the task of healing the split world by finding the one piece of the original crystal that is missing and replacing it in the now dark crystal, held in the altar of the Skexies Castle. This he must accomplish before the prophecied conjunction of the three suns, the moment at which the world would be destroyed forever, unless the crystal is healed.

Instinctively the aged Mystics begin to make their way to the dark castle to meet the sordid Skexies before the suns conjunct. The Skexies prepare for war, while the Mystics step slowly and carefully to their appointed rendezvous (ooooommmming as they go). There is a strong sense that a cosmically-ordained event is at hand.

At the moment of conjunction — the very last opportunity for the world to be saved — the Mystics, Skexies, and Jeb find themselves at the altar of the Great Crystal. All have been drawn together like the stars aligned in the sky. At the perfect instant Jeb leaps to the top of the dark crystal and inserts the all-important piece. The dark crystal is healed.

As the crystal is made whole an astonishing event occurs: the Mystics and the Skexies step into one another, like two rivers flowing into one. At the moment the two become one, an explosion of light is created. Each of the joined pairs produces a great angelic light-filled being, emanating many times the power and magnitude of the little creatures from which they have sprung. These magnificent beings, representing the integration of apparent good and evil, grow in stature and intensity until the dark castle crumbles, light is restored to the kingdom, and a dying world grows green again. Finally we hear,

> *What was sundered and undone*
> *Now is whole, the two are one.*

There is a book by Hal Lindsay called *The Beautiful Side of Evil*. The title alone teaches the lesson of the dark crystal, restored to full power at the top of the spiral mountain. The healing of the dark crystal represents the unified consciousness that knows seeming evil to be the facet of the divine that it really is. It is therefore not evil at all — except relatively speaking. The world of the Mystics and the Skexies was dying because in it there was an unbridgeable separation of the energies of good and evil, the picture of a split mind that sees a difference where one does not really exist. Under no circumstances could such a world survive, for it is completely out of accord with the will of God, which is perfect and total unity. The evil Skexies were warfully annihilating their own race through lack of love, while the Mystics had lost their power because they had denied and cut themselves off from their seeming evil selves. As a result there was no communication, no strength, and no life in either camp, and subsequently their world was untraversably gapped and dying.

When the two groups merged, when the "negative" aspects of life were absorbed into the good, there was created a gestalt, a new being, all-encompassing and infinitely more alive than the separated parts. The Mystics and the Skexies *were* the split crystal — and the moment they owned, or accepted responsibility for *all* the parts of their self, the crystal of life was restored to its true nature and the realm was healed.

The Totality of Love

If we are to be healed — and we most surely are — we must enfold all aspects of ourself in love, understanding, and acceptance. This means *accepting everything that happens to us as part of God's plan for our good and our healing*. Every person, event, and experience that touches us contributes to the healing of our own dark crystal. We cannot cut off or deny anyone or anything as being outside our good or ourself. *Life is a process of ever-unfolding good.* We are constantly moving from strength to greater strength, from good to better to best. Sometimes it does not *seem* that way. But appearances are not the same as reality. Here we have the key to transforming all fear to perfect love: a time of seeing shadows is our best opportunity to deny appearances and look with spiritual x-ray vision into the truth. Bless your challenges, for they are your steppingstones home to the arms of Love. We are indeed on a journey of continually greater awakening. I do not believe it is possible to be reincarnated as a cockroach. It is possible to adopt a cockroach consciousness in a human body, but if a man could become a cockroach, Holy Spirit would have to run from aerosol bombs. And if there is one characteristic of Holy Spirit, it is that it never feels a need to hide from anything. Spirit simply enfolds everything that is brought to it with perfect love. Being created in the image and likeness of a whole and wholly loving God, the Spirit within us refuses to acknowledge anything unlike its holy self, and is therefore incapable of knowing evil, to say nothing of its perfect inability to fear it.

Therefore to my friend who feared that she was reverting to adolescence, I say "no way." I say the only culprit that makes us think we are going backwards is the ego, and that is because the ego is backwards, and it is incapable of seeing anything except itself. The game of the ego is to make us believe that we are not who we are, Children of Perfection, ever enjoying deeper healing through the peace that true love brings. Always we are becoming more like God, until finally we discover that we have always been divine. Indeed we are living in the heart of God all the time, and we need only open our eyes to recognize that we are already home.

To my friend I acknowledge that life is not rigidly stable, as the ploy for the ego's survival would have us believe. Life is a constant flow of newly blessed love energy. The only way to defeat the ego in the war that never was is to know with unshakable certainty that we are spiritual beings moving toward an invincible destiny of good. Like a river consummating its journey from the mountains to the shore, our love opens to complete itself as the ocean. The ocean toward which we flow is one of perfect healing, and I assure you, beloveds, that *there is nothing at all to fear.* What awaits us is all the peace that we have ever sought, and our only need is to open our arms and hearts wide, and let it come.

I say to my friend as I say to all who read this that we are on the most marvelous adventure of all, the most thrilling odyssey there could ever be. We are on the journey into Truth, and that voyage specifically includes the gentle dismantling of the illusions that stand between your self and the summit, which is your Self. Do not be deceived by the spiral way you walk. It is the way of everyone who has ever journeyed to the peak of consciousness, and it has been tread and conquered with love by all the great ones before you. You traverse this path in good company, Sons and Daughters of Majesty. You walk the way of the beloveds of God, of the family of the open-hearted, of the people of the truth. Walk in dignity, walk in reverence, walk in acceptance, and your journey shall be made light. This is the way of those who love.

The Power to Triumph

The Last Starfighter

*The responsibility for living harmoniously on Planet Earth
rests with each individual. As each person spiritually and cos-
mically comes of age, claiming his attunement and therefore his
involvement in the business of all mankind, a beautiful new
energy will be released which will gradually swing the earth into
alignment with the universal forces of harmony and peace. This
period of awareness will happen, but only when each man and
woman looks beyond the exterior to the interior of their being to
discover their own personal power through their connection to
the Ultimate of All Energies.*

- Agartha: A Journey to the Stars*

Somewhere between San Francisco and Honolulu, I changed my mind.
Not about the flight, about the movie. As the big iron bird hummed
gracefully above the wispy cotton Pacific clouds, my attention was drawn
from the window to the movie screen. *The Last Starfighter* looked more
interesting than I had anticipated, and now I wanted some headphones to
find out what it was all about.

It was about us. Alex Rogin was the champion of the trailer park video
game frontier. His skill in shooting alien spaceships out of the midnight
video sky was invincible, earning him the worship of every aspiring seven-
to-fourteen-year-old suburban defender of space invasion. The night he
broke the record on the machine the entire trailer park came out to cheer him
on to victory. Alex was a natural intergalactic marksman of the highest
calibre, and the amount of points he had amassed was exceeded only by the
number of quarters he had invested. Alex was good, he knew it, and he loved
it.

One starry night Alex was picked up by a slick stranger driving a sleek
sports car unlike any he had seen before. The driver, amiable enough, told
Alex he had to have a talk with the fellow who had achieved the *Starfighter*

---

* Meredith Lady Young, *Agartha: A Journey to the Stars*, Stillpoint Publishing, 1984 championship. Into the strange vehicle Alex went, curious, intrigued, and somewhat leery. He was surprised that this man knew him, and his eyes opened even wider, along with his jaw, when the sports car turned off the main road, not to the right or left, but up. Within seconds the roadster was transformed into a flashy starcraft propelling Alex and his mysterious host off to planets and dimensions far more romantic than the corner video parlor.

As a further test of Alex's resilience, the driver peels off his human face to reveal a reptilian visage straight from Iguana-land. Now Alex's host Centuri reveals the reason for this intergalactic kidnapping: The planet Rylos, from which he has come, is in serious danger. An evil force of space marauders from the starsystem of Ur is threatening the life of his species. The defending Starfighters have been all but wiped out. In a last-ditch attempt to save Rylos and its people, they have sought out someone who can singlehandedly stave off the invaders. For this reason they created a video game to simulate their starship control panel. They watched carefully to see who would emerge with the kind of skill needed to rescue them. Alex's expertise as the highest quality Starfighter drew them to seek his help in their cause. In short, they need him to save their planetary soul.

Hearing this incredible story, Alex's amazement changes to consternation. Him, save a starsystem? Him, take on a superhuman task? Him, have an entire life-form depend on him?

"I'm sorry," Alex blurts out, "I'm just a kid from a trailer park!"

Alex's extraterrestrial guru turns to him, finds his hesitating eyes, and speaks slowly and clearly to his young friend: *"If that's all you think you are, that's all you'll ever be."*

"If that's all you think you are, that's all you'll ever be." That one was for all of us.

The task of healing this planet seems monumental. The nuclear monster seems indomitably formidable. It appears as if the world is down to just a few lonely defenders of the truth, an unacknowledged band of lovers of light. Sometimes it even feels as if the burden of bearing the message of peace in a woeful world has fallen on our shoulders alone. At such a moment we may think, "How can a struggling little person like me accomplish the healing of our world?"

We *can* because we are powered by a Force far greater than "a struggling little person." We are not "just kids from a trailer park." *We are the last Starfighters.* If you are reading this, you are capable and ready to make a major contribution to the healing of the Planet Earth. If not you, then who?

Most of the greatest Starfighters have had to fight their way to the stars. Mahatma Gandhi, for example, was literally laughed out of a courtroom when he became tongue-tied while pleading his first case as a young lawyer. Later he was thrown off a train in the middle of a South African night because his skin was not the right color for that train. We know what Gandhi eventually made of himself, only because he was willing to change his mind about how powerfully Spirit would be willing to work through him.

Then Sir Richard Attenborough had a lifelong dream to honor Gandhi's work through a film about his life. Sir Richard worked diligently to raise funding for a major motion picture from non-major motion picture sources. After eighteen years of dedicated work, being unwilling to settle for setbacks, Sir Richard's dream was realized. The film startled the motion picture industry as it ran away with the Academy Awards, including Best Picture, Best Director, Best Actor, and a horde of other Oscars. In the beginning Sir Richard had to go it alone; in the end the world stood up to applaud him. When one steps forward with conviction, mighty companions — sometimes unseen — walk beside us. Sir Richard, like Gandhi, was never alone — God walked with both of them.

The Key to Transformation

Here is the key to the power to transform our lives and our planet: We can accomplish more with one breath of purposeful love than a thousand years of fearful attack. Gandhi said, "In a gentle way you can shake the world." The way of the planetary healer is marked by understanding, light-heartedness, and understanding, all of which begin by loving ourselves just as we are. For too long we have believed in changing ourselves to become worthy; now we need to believe in *being* ourselves to be worthy. If you feel that you cannot be a real force in healing our planet, or that you cannot even help yourself, do not despair. The devil (lack of awareness) is not the inability to heal, but the *thought* that we cannot. No challenge in life can stand when looked upon with true love. Every obstacle will dissolve in the presence of Truth, for there is only one power in the universe — the power of God's healing love. Hold any difficulty up to the light of love, and that wall must melt and be transformed into a gift of understanding, which will later be used in the service of healing. This is the real meaning of alchemy: The lead that once seemed to weigh us down and keep us from rising into joy is transmuted into the gold of good that reflects the light of

Heaven. Indeed true alchemy consists of the realization that we just *thought* it was lead, while actually it was golden all the time.

We have what it takes to make it. We just need to know the truth about our power and use it. *We can if we believe we can.* Not because belief makes it so, but because we can, and *belief lets our power manifest.* The word "believe" comes from two original words: "leave be." What we are willing to leave be, or let be, becomes real. We do not need to create good in our life, for *all of our good has already been created*—and it is waiting for us to claim it. All we have to do is *let it be.*

At a workshop in Erie, Pennsylvania a man told me that he had just gotten an excellent position with a large manufacturer of glass bottles. His job was to develop a design for a double-extruder bottle, a new product for their line.

"They called me a few weeks after the interview to tell me the job was mine," he explained, " — but the interesting thing was their explanation of why they chose me for the position. They told me that they had interviewed several candidates, all of whom had more credentials and experience with that kind of work than me. But here's the clincher: I was the only one who, when they asked, 'Can you invent this product?' answered, 'Yes.' I don't know exactly how I will do it, but there's one thing I do know: If you can think of a thing, you can bring it to life. Products are the results of thoughts, and what the mind can conceive, a man can achieve. You may have to invest some time, love, and money into a project, but all of that will come in the service of drawing that original idea into reality. If you are sufficiently dedicated and concentrated on any goal, it is only a matter of time until you see your dream crystallize into reality."

When I was a kid I used to like the Audie Murphy movies. I wonder if you remember him — he was a World War II infantryman who won the Purple Heart by accomplishing a phenomenal number of heroic victories. I remember one scene in which Audie maneuvered a flaming tank into the heart of an enemy nest. Amid exploding debris and sniper attack from all angles he saved a whole battalion and turned the tide of the battle. Now I am not supporting the kind of warfare from which Audie's heroism emerged; God knows we have had enough of that. But I am inspired by the singular willingness that Audie Murphy represents. To me he stands for the kind of fearlessness that comes with total commitment to a cause. He was willing to win the war singlehandedly if he had to, and he nearly did.

Now it is not a war between nations that we need to win, but the war of love, which is entirely different from any kind of war we have ever known.

This is the unstoppable campaign for the Light, and against nothing. We must realize that our love has infinite power. I know that this planet will survive by each of us being willing to do what we need to do to heal it — singlehandedly, if necessary. John Beaulieux said, "If I die, I'll die serving the Light." That's the kind of fearlessness we need to succeed. Actually that's a statement of victory, for no one with that strength of intention could ever be defeated.

We cannot afford to wait for someone out there to fix the world for us. That's how Hitlers, Anti-Christs, and boogeymen get born. We need to directly participate in our own salvation, allowing the savior to be born within our own being. God can do *for* us what He can do *through* us; we are the channels of our own transformation. And everyone and everything will be touched by the healing which begins in our own heart.

The miracle is that no one really has to do it singlehandedly. Everyone who is willing to do his or her part completely is joined by many others who are inspired by love to do their part completely. When we were born on earth, each of us was given a certain sphere of activity to influence — some larger, some smaller, all eventually touching all. No matter how great our personal domain of influence seems to be, that influence begins in the center of our own being and ripples out to touch the entire universe. Throughout our whole life our job is simply to exert the best possible influence on the part of the world we touch. This noble task requires little more of us than to keep our own little patch of the garden watered, weeded, and blessed. It is ego that tells us we must weed our neighbor's garden, while the Spirit within us gently reminds us that as we complete our own cultivation we will be guided to serve our neighbor in the perfect appropriate way. The flowers we cultivate in our own garden will drop their seeds in the patch next door. This is how, in our own gentle way, we transform the world.

The Starfighter's Creed

Perhaps an appropriate Starfighter to remember here would be Luke Skywalker. In *The Empire Strikes Back* Luke, in his headstrong way, defied Yoda's instructions to wait until he had mastered the Force before he went off to challenge Darth Vader. Luke set out before he was ready, and ended up losing a battle and his hand. Yet in *The Return of the Jedi* that followed, Luke patiently waited and practiced until he mastered the Force. This achievement gave him the power to walk right into the Emperor's lair and conquer the entire Empire.

Here is a message of the richest encouragement: Even if we fall down on our spiritual path, there is always a way to rise up, bounce back, and solve the problem. Indeed we must get up and walk in the light, for once we have set foot upon the path of Truth there is no turning back. Jesus fell three times on the way of the cross, and he accepted the help of those who came to comfort him. St. Francis of Assisi wrestled with all kinds of desires and challenges throughout his life. All the while the power of his soul marched steadily on, gaining strength as the spirit within him dissolved his fears. Gandhi struggled for years to be celibate, sometimes succeeding, sometimes not, yet ever continuing onward toward what he believed to be the highest truth his heart told him. Surely we can offer ourselves the patience and forgiveness that these great ones learned as a vital ingredient in spiritual success.

Hilda has offered some inspiring advice for Starfighters who find that they have veered from the plotted course. The affirmation she suggests is:

"I pick myself up, I dust myself off, and I march on!"

(You might like to repeat this affirmation to yourself now, three times mentally or aloud.)

It is no sin to make an error. In fact, it is a blessing to discover a mistake. Errors have power over us only as long as we do not realize what we have been doing. The moment we see that we have made a mistake we are free of it and its effects. Once we recognize that we have missed the mark, there is only one route that we can take: correct what we can, and do better next time. If you mistakenly drive off the road onto the shoulder, the only thing to do is get back on the road and carry on to your destination. You would not sit at the roadside bemoaning your lack of skill; you would turn the wheel back toward the road and step on the gas. To dwell on a past error keeps us tied to it, and releasing the error allows us to move forward instantly. *The only time we fail is when we don't try again.*

This world is actually a Starfighters' training school, a transformational forum for Jedi who are ready to return. That's all of us, at various stages of development. Sometimes it's a tough boot camp, and we learn from our errors as well as our successes. Sometimes we get a taste of how wonderful our life will be when we finish our lessons (indeed life already *is* wonderful; our lesson is simply to realize it!). This higher perspective keeps us shining through our challenges. Whether our lessons be difficult or easy, we gain tremendous strength from remembering that there is but one purpose to all of our living: *to see God in everything.* Starfighters need a target. If we remember that love is the goal, all of our learning becomes infinitely easier.

Mark Twain said, "When I was thirteen years old I thought my father was a complete dunce; by the time I was twenty-one, I was amazed at how much he had learned." Life is not about attempting to change people, conditions, or events. It is about changing our *perceptions and thoughts* about people, conditions, and events. We are here to discover the divinity that shines everywhere, all the time. That transformation of awareness begins within our own mind, with the happy understanding that we are not who we thought we were — We are Children of the Most High, heirs to all the power in the universe. *We can do as much as God can do, but we actually do as much as we think we can.* If you expect someone else to save the planet, the door to peace will remain barred. The key to the salvation of the world lies within *your* hands.

Once we are really willing to let God in, to let good come our way, and to know and act as if there is no order of difficulty in miracles, then we will be able to do as much for ourselves as Christ can do for us. *There is no limit to that.* All of your training, experience, and skills have led you to the point where now *you can change the course of destiny for everyone.* Our past has served us well, but now, like the first stage of a three-stage rocket which afforded the gross energy to push it beyond the immediate atmosphere, our past must fall away to allow us to soar to even greater heights of heavenly perspective. Here we discover rich and imaginative vistas beyond anything we have known or expected. All of our personal and group adventures have lifted us to the crest of a wave of love that is eternally breaking within our heart and blessing every person we touch.

No, no one is too small, no one comes from too obscure a trailer park to accomplish the defense of love in a small but ailing starsystem. Love knows no smallness, only the magnitude of impeccable intention. And because love has chosen you to accomplish its defense, there can be no doubt about how easily the light can and will remove all darkness. Like a movie about which we already know the happy outcome, we do not need to fear the plot. We can enjoy the adventure, knowing the story will somehow be resolved in our favor.

Perhaps we need to take our eyes off the window and return them to the screen. Maybe it is no accident that this particular movie is being shown on the flight we booked. And perhaps we would serve ourselves by purchasing the headphones to find out what's actually going on. As David Pomeranz so eloquently sings in *It's in Everyone of Us*, "I bought my ticket, but I've been seeing only half of the show." No longer can we afford to use unworthiness as an excuse to mask our magnitude. We are created in the image and likeness of a loving, caring, understanding, and most holy God Who is looking for a few good Starfighters to rescue a frightened planet from a long history of nightmares. This is the original salvation army, it's an all-volunteer force, and the price of admission is a little willingness to believe in yourself.

Oh, yes, by the way, the kid from the trailer park saved the starsystem.

The Ego Strikes Back

Have you ever noticed that just when you are about to take a step in a new and more positive direction in your life, something comes up to block it? Some people say, "This is too good to be true — I'm sure something will go wrong." And then, sure enough, it does.

Why would things go wrong? Things are not supposed to go wrong. Life is supposed to work, and work wonderfully. When it does not, we must look past the darkness to see the light.

When we experience a challenge to success, we have a marvelous opportunity to shine a healing ray of understanding upon the ego's thought system. In such a situation we can penetrate into the very bedrock of the wall of painful beliefs that have stood between you and your happiness for so much of your life. Are you willing to be free? Together let us be unafraid to look at the cause of our hardships and our hurts, that we may be released forever.

We must be willing to look fearlessly at what seems to be the source of our misery. In the *Star Wars* movie a small band of those living for the Force had to penetrate to the very core of the Death Star (how appropriately named!) to reach and destroy the reactor that was powering it. So, too, must we look deeply into our self to dismantle the sense of threat that seems always about to explode in our life. *There is no such bomb.* But we must have the courage to face what we *think* it is before we can truly be free of it.

Let us begin by sharing a powerful excerpt from John Price's *The Planetary Commission*:

As you move through the inner space of consciousness toward the union with Self, there is a bridge you must pass over...It is on this bridge that you shed the remaining particles of error thoughts and negative beliefs and go through the final cleansing. As the bridge comes into view, your world may seem to turn upside down, and the reason is because you are beginning the process of letting go of everything that seemed secure to you...

Your ego may choose to do battle as you step on to the bridge, and it will do WHATEVER IS NECESSARY to save itself. If that means creating an insufficiency of funds, it will do it, because this effect could very well cause you to step back... Another ego tantrum may give the appearance of a business failure, or the interruption of a successful career, or perhaps a physical ailment. The ego simply wants to show who is boss.

How do you navigate the last mile as the ego begins to fight for its life? You totally surrender to God...You turn everything in your life over to the indwelling Christ and give up all concern, knowing that your God-Self is the solution to every problem and the answer to every need, and that Spirit cannot let you down because it is against God's nature to do so![1]

This masterful advice is showing us that the ego perceives love, unity, and the peace of God as a threat, and defends itself — (quite insanely!) — against healing. The blessing is that the ego's rallying itself for defense against love is a *sure sign that healing is near.*

Here is a personal example of how the ego wages war on love, and how it can be overcome: A friend of mine began to feel afraid when she went into deep meditation. She asked Hilda about this, who told her, "That's wonderful, darling! That means you are really getting somewhere! When you are moving into a new and freer state of life the ego feels threatened, and it fights back by creating the feeling of fear. You can be sure that whenever you feel afraid the ego is trying to hold you back from enjoying your greater good.

"The ego believes that all change is threatening, and therefore defends against it, even — and especially — when the change is toward your happiness. That is why we can give thanks whenever the ego rails up — it is a sign that we are taking a step toward a better, brighter life. Do not be intimidated by the ego's cowardly roaring — once you have begun to initiate a step toward the light, it is only a matter of time until all ego resistance falls away."

---

[1]John Randolph Price, *The Planetary Commission*, The Quartus Foundation for Spiritual Research, Inc., P.O. Box 26683, Austin, TX 78755. Used by permission.

Through the Door

It may be said that we live in an invisible membrane of fear, encapsulating us like an imaginary bubble of boundaries. This illusory but tyrannical fence sets our limitations, decides who and what we like and don't like, and keeps us caged in a world of small thinking. We may feel safe, but this false sense of protection is quite meager in comparison to the security we feel when we know that *there is no real threat in the entire universe.* Wherever we go God goes with us, for God dwells within *us* as us.

The ego, like a vicious watchdog guarding the door of our cell, rests as long as we do not try to cross the imaginary threshold we believe is there. (I am told that if you draw a chalk circle around a chicken and spin the bird around a few times, it will not step over the line, believing that the chalk line represents a real and fearful boundary.) Many times we may step up to that doorway, and many times we may turn back, intimidated by the fierce growling monster that we ourselves have created by our agreement in a lie.

What we do not realize is that the watchdog has *no power* to hurt us. At best it merits a moment of laughter and a light brush aside. Yet we have imbued that beast with the strength that belongs to us, and we remain at the effect of its empty barking until we are willing to reclaim the power that we invested in it. We do not realize that our dragons are our own puppets because we have never looked long enough to see our own hand pulling their strings. We hold ourselves in bondage by our own mind alone.

The few who have taken the step past the threshold of seeming limitation have come back to tell us that there is indeed nothing at all to fear. Jesus returned after three days to tell us that death is not real, and that all of our trepidations about it are unfounded. In the garden outside the tomb an angel appeared so real to Mary Magdalene that she thought he was the gardener! And what did he tell her but, "Mary, why do you look for the living among the dead?"

The War That Never Was

The ego is totally insane in its frantic attempts to find peace through war. The ego's motto is "Attack before attack comes," but it has never paused long enough to rise to the high vantage point where it would see that there is no attack waiting. Its sense of attack comes entirely from itself. There is nothing outside the ego that has any concept of attack whatsoever. If fear would stop chasing its own tail, it would quickly see that nothing has been biting it but its own jaws.

The thirst for vengeance of Darth Vader, the Emperor of the Dark Empire, and the entire Klingon Armada is nothing compared to the ferocious mania of the ego in its effort to keep you small. In the *Star Wars* movies the Empire was overt in its quest to snuff out the light. In contrast, our ego operates in craftiness, subtlety, and the deepest viper pits of the subconscious. The snake scene in *Raiders of the Lost Ark*, in which Indiana Jones has to descend into a pit writhing with thousands of deadly snakes, doesn't even touch the chambers of horrors that the ego has conjured up in the prison of the part of your mind that fears. The ego is like a mad scientist maniacally concocting strange illusions in a laboratory in the basement of your thoughts. The only hope of this maker of distortion is to stay in the dark and keep you in the dark with it. It knows that, like the creepy little critters that hide under logs in the woods and scatter the moment they are exposed to light, the ego's fears are doomed to extinction the moment they are brought into the sunshine of loving truth.

It is important to understand that the ego will use *any means it can* to trick you into staying behind and keep you from **your** destiny of peace. It is completely unscrupulous and diabolically ingenious in its thirst to hold you hostage, and it will use the tactics to which you believe you are personally most vulnerable to stop you from accomplishing success. It will create disease, loss, and divisiveness to bar you from your good, and it will disguise itself as the opposite of what it is. The ego will tell you that you are not moving ahead because you are afraid to fail, when in truth it is the fear of *succeeding* that you have allowed to stop you. Every time I have made a step forward in my personal and spiritual evolution in the areas of health, success, or relationships, for example, I have had the feeling that I was about to be punished, die, or lose something. When I found the courage to go ahead despite the ego's gloomy counsel, I discovered deep peace, greater aliveness, and immeasurable gain. Now when pessimistic feelings arise I find cause for rejoicing, for I know that I am about to step not back, but forward. Remember that the ego is utterly insane in its quest for victory in the war that never was.

Moving Ahead

You must move ahead in the face of fear. The great metaphysician Emmet Fox said, "If you must tremble when taking your next step, then do it trembling — but do it." He also said, "Do the thing and you shall have the power."

Several years ago I learned an important lesson in how to disarm the ego by calling its bluff. As I was driving to the largest workshop I had ever organized — a hundred people were coming — I had some doubts about how well I could serve that many participants.

Driving up a mountain road in the Poconos, I began to sniffle and sneeze. I thought, "I must be coming down with some kind of flu. Maybe I'm getting the bug that Sally had." As I reached over to see if I had any tissues in my glove compartment, the train of thought followed, "I don't know if I'll be able to conduct this retreat. Maybe I should turn around and go home."

Then came another voice, like a cavalry rushing in with reinforcements: "No!" it told me, "Carry on. Don't go into agreement with that voice of fear and illness. Thoughts of limitation are not worthy of your attention. Acknowledge the reality of the Light within you, and remember that all is perfect."

Immediately I felt energized and uplifted. A force of enthusiasm surged through me. I saw myself in a brilliant white light. When doubts or thoughts of inability to conduct the workshop came up again, I affirmed, "I don't care how I feel. These people are coming to this workshop to be healed, and I'm going to trust Spirit to touch them through me — and I know God wants me to be healthy to do it."

Quickly the sneezing, sniffling, and runny nose stopped, and I felt better. I went on to deliver one of the best programs I have ever done, with many wonderful miracles of healing. It was not the flu that was attempting to hold me back, but *fear*. The sniffles were nothing more than an instrument of the ego, and as soon as my mind was corrected about its nature and its purpose, so the body corrected itself.

The body is the glove of the mind; as we move the fingers of our mind, so does our body follow the mental pattern. That is why our body is our best friend: it is always telling us what our mind is thinking. We can use it to discover where we are stuck and then practice remembering that we are not stuck at all. *We are unlimited free spirits.* We are Children of a Perfect God.

There is Only Love

You have nothing to lose. You cannot lose because all that you have is all that you are, and you are everything there is. Being everything, you cannot lose because you could never lose yourself. You can fall asleep and dream that you are losing, but dreams do not have the power to change the reality of your perfect invulnerability while your mind is turned away from it. Upon awakening you will find that you are still quite whole, and indeed always have been.

The only worthy response to the ego when it strikes back is love. To return vengeance for the ego's barking would ask you to enter into the thought system that believes that attack is effective. In that world you will never win. The ego's response to the Holy Spirit is to strike back, while the Holy Spirit's only response to the ego is to give more love. That should be your response, too, because you are not born of the ego, but of God.

There is a way to undo the mess the ego has appeared to have made: *Hold it up to the light!* Sharing is the way of Heaven, and hiding the way of hell. A problem is exacerbated when we feel that we cannot tell anyone about it. I tell you, there is nothing that the Children of Light cannot look upon and heal with love.

Because the ego is totally insecure, it will generate its biggest bluff when confronted with the simple fact that your protection lies not in it. The ego, in spite of all of its wild bravado and ability to produce some very scary movies, is actually nothing. *You, who are something, never need to be afraid of the ego, which is nothing.* The wilder the ego flails, the greater the potential for healing, for here is your sign that you are pushing up against the membrane of your illusory sense of boundaries. You are very close to discovering the truth.

The people, events, and situations that challenge you are angels. They have come to you with the key to your next step in your personal evolution.

Call them devil and you will find yourself in hell. See the angel in them, discover the blessing they bring, and you will live in Heaven — on earth. Everyone in this world is an angel. You do not have to fly up to the clouds to see their beauty. Just listen for the song of the harp concealed beneath the cloak of their seeming misdeeds.

Because the ego is based entirely on thoughts of hatred, you can be released from its nasty grip simply by giving it — and everything else — love. Here is how to love the ego into the light: Appreciate all of its attacks, panic, and flailings for what they are: gifts to you from God to learn that fear is never necessary, for *there is only love*. The Holy Spirit always takes a positive interpretation of an ego attack; no threat could fluster the light in the least. Your true Self knows that you are of God, and Spirit is invulnerable to all attack. It perceives only love everywhere in the universe. This is the truth that sets you free.

The Transfer Value of Courage

Everyone in this world feels that he or she is a sinner. As you are willing to accept your innocence you will heal everyone who comes into your mind by knowing that they are innocent too. Very few people in this world are willing to face their ego, their fears, and their sense of limitation. The few who have are hailed as saints, holy men and women, and gifted ones. Their gift, however, lies not in potential but in *expression*. It is crucial that you remember that you are capable of the same level and quality of expression. We are all gifted with the ability to be ourself, and this is the one gift that we can share with everyone we meet. *A Course in Miracles* tells us, "When I am healed I am not healed alone,"[2] and in the case of conquering our ego, this is surely so. All fear exists by agreement and by agreement only. When one of us breaks the agreement, watch how quickly the truth replaces misery in the hearts of all who would embrace it!

---

[2] W, p. 254

You are a Trailblazer

During recent years many persons have participated in firewalking workshops.[†] Thousands of people from many ways of life have learned how to walk unharmed over a bed of thousand-degree burning coals. I participated in such a workshop several years ago, and I gained much.

The leader began by giving us a powerfully inspiring lecture on the nature of fear and how to overcome it. He explained that the mind is the source of all of our physical experience, and that if one wants to change his physical experience he must change his belief system about what he can and cannot do. This idea registered within my soul as a truth. I was inspired to walk.

We walked outside to find an orange-red mound of glowing coals, the remnant of a huge pile of wood that had been set ablaze earlier that afternoon. Hearing about the bed of coals was one thing, but seeing it was another. Yet I knew I could walk. A voice inside my mind prompted me, "Go ahead — you can do it!" I felt that I could walk, but I still entertained some doubts. I wanted to walk, but I did not want to be the first one.

The turning point for me came when I saw one of my friends step onto the coals and walk across them without being burned. I was amazed, for I knew that he was no different than me, and he had no more training than I had. "If Neil can do it," I felt, "so can I."

I stood before the coals. The instructor, Tolly, had told us to take an affirmation or positive visualization before we walked. All I could hear in my mind was, "I believe in God." Those four words actually summed up a very profound and life-transforming thought process I was undergoing. I felt that I was standing not in front of a bed of burning coals, but at a crossroads: one path represented all of the "truths" I had ever learned from the ego — that I am a body which can be hurt, and I had better protect it, or I would be harmed. The other path shined with the knowledge that I am not a body, but a living spiritual being. It was founded on the awareness that the real me is not born of flesh and blood, but of Spirit. And that Spirit is not subject to fire or

---

[†] My experience is offered as an encouragement to others to follow their inner guidance. It is not an endorsement for firewalking. Anyone considering firewalking must make his or her choice based upon introspection and contemplation.

any other element in the material world.

I realized that I was not facing a physical threat, but *every fear I had ever run away from*. To turn back now would be to renounce my divinity and give fear power over my life by shrinking away from it. As I thought more about walking, I was confronted by sardonic images of all the woeful possibilities of what might happen to me if I walked. Pain, sorrow, and death were shrieking in my ears. Yet beneath their gruesome howls I could hear the whisper of that still, small voice, the gently loving guidance of the peaceful strength within me. "You can do it, Alan," the voice assured me.

I realized that I was not making a decision for one moment, but for all of my life. *"Do you want to continue to live in fear, or do you want to be free?"*

I reached the point where I would rather have been burnt up and die than live in fear. I decided to walk, and take my chances. If the voice that was telling me to step forward was a liar, there wasn't much left anyway.

So I walked. I affirmed to myself, "I believe in God," and I stepped onto the coals.

As I walked I experienced heat, but no pain. I continued for four or five paces over the coals, and still no pain. What a feeling of exhiliration I enjoyed as I completed my walk and stepped onto the grass! The exhortations of my ego were *not true*. I felt that I would not need to ever be afraid of anything again. I was the master of my destiny. My mind was more powerful than my body. I was not dead, but more alive than ever! I was free!

As I recall my moment of decision now, I see that all it took for me to conquer fear was for me to see one other person do what I thought I couldn't do. One person like myself broke through his membrane of limitation, and I followed along with many others. *"When I am healed I am not healed alone."*

We have the power to heal one another. The firewalk is a metaphor for all of the things in life that we have been told that we cannot do, but really can. When one of us gets out there in the jungle of fear with a machete and cuts down the weeds for himself, he clears a new road for the rest of us who want to walk with him. All of us still possess the machetes of courage with which we were born — but only some of us are willing to acknowledge that we do, lift them up, and whack away at the brush. Each of us has a piece of the jungle in front of us, a section that only *we* can clear. Glory be to us when we do clear it, for then all of us can walk hand in hand upon a new road with greater freedom to live as who we are and be who we were born to be.

The End of Nothing and
the Beginning of Everything

All that we have been resisting is pure love. Only love. Love is all there is in the entire universe. To fear anything in life is to resist the very Force we have been given to free us. Because we are spiritual beings, created in the image and likeness of an eternally perfect God, there is nothing anywhere that can hurt us. It is said,

"If God is with me, what could be against me?"

I assure you, God is most certainly with you. When you see Him not it is only because you are not looking with respect upon yourself. To look with respect upon yourself is to affirm all that God is and who you were created to be. Fear can cover over the awareness of our perfection, but it could never remove it. A sleeping child does not see his loving mother as she pulls the blanket up to his shoulders, gently kisses him goodnight on his forehead, and whispers a quiet prayer for his happy awakening. When the morning comes glistening with the brightness that ends all dark dreams, you know with perfect certainty that you never need fear again. No fearful dream can stand between you and the true Self you discover in the clarity of the morning light.

Fear, in the final vision, is wholly unjustified. You have been afraid of life because you have been afraid of yourself. And fear of yourself can be born only of not knowing who you truly are. Child of the Morning, the time has come for you to awaken! Delay your healing no more. All is well. How uselessly you have turned your back on your Father's love. And how easily is it regained! Come home, dear one, beloved one, beautiful one. Wander in the dark forest no longer. Your home awaits you. Each moment that you spend fighting yourself can be given instead to the celebration of your return to your Father's Home.

This is the time of the new beginning. This is the time of your release from all that held you from your freedom. This is the new morning. Fear it not, for here is the miracle you have awaited. All thanks be to the One who loves you as you come to love yourself.

The Power to Succeed

Until one is committed, there is hesitancy, the chance to draw back, always ineffectiveness. Concerning all acts of initiative (and creation) there is one elementary truth the ignorance of which kills countless ideas and splendid plans: That the moment one definitely commits oneself, then providence moves too.

All sorts of wonderful things occur to help one, that would never otherwise have occurred. A whole stream of events issues from the decision, raising in one's favor all manner of unforeseen incidents and meetings and material assistance which no one could have dreamed would come their way.

Whatever you can do or dream you can, begin it. Boldness has genius, power, and magic in it. Begin it now.

- Goethe

A number of years ago I put my Honda on the market, and I had a hard time selling it. The car was advertised in the newspaper for several weeks, and when I had received no more than a few half-interested nibbles I placed it at my mechanic's gas station with a big "For Sale" sign on the side window. Another week or two passed... still no takers. I rethought my asking price of a thousand dollars and recognized that in comparison to similar cars on the market, it was in the ball park. "Why isn't that car selling?" I wondered.

Around that time I attended a healing service by Reverend W. V. Grant, a most inspiring and dynamically gifted minister who literally works miracles before the eyes of astonished onlookers. During that thrilling service I saw Rev. Grant pray in the name of Jesus Christ, after which the blind saw, the lame arose and walked, and legs of unequal length were adjusted instantaneously. The reality of the healing power of God in that room was beyond any demonstration I had ever seen, and the strength of my faith increased dramatically as a result of my experience.

As part of his service that evening Rev. Grant collected several offerings for various causes, including orphanages he sponsors in Haiti, his television ministry, and, as he honestly admitted, his personal needs and those of his family. I and the entire audience gave generous amounts of money to support his work, which I believe is genuine, and I respect.

One characteristic that I noticed about Rev. Grant as he took up the offerings was his deep belief in his ministry. He was so confident in his purpose that he was willing to ask for very large amounts of money without any sense of apology, guilt, or self-doubt. For me this was a powerful teaching in the integrity of his ministry. The only way that he could heal so consistently was to have complete faith in God's ability to heal through him; if he had one percent of doubt he would not be the healer that he is. The transfer value of this faith to all of his work, including the financial prosperity of his ministry, was obvious and an important lesson for me.

Driving home from Rev. Grant's service that evening I considered the depth of his faith in God and in himself. The thought occured to me, "If Rev. Grant can collect $25,000 for his ministry in one evening, I can certainly sell my Honda for $1000." In contrast to his conviction I found in my mind some sense of guilt and unworthiness about selling that car for a thousand dollars. I realized that even though it was a fair price compared to similar sales, I felt guilty about asking that much for it, and I was also a little hesitant to part with an old friend which had served me so well for so long. I had already bought a new car, I had that bill and others to pay, and my guidance to sell the old car was clear. I saw that it was only my feeling of unworthiness that was standing before the sale.

That night, having caught the strength of Rev. Grant's confidence in his ability to be worthy of financial success, a sense of surety welled up within me and I felt that I deserved to sell the car and accept that amount of money for it. I went to sleep with a new sense of worthiness and freedom in my heart.

I was awakened early the next morning by the telephone. Clumsily I reached for the receiver and heard an unfamiliar voice:

"Hello, Alan?... This is Arnie."

"Arnie?" I scanned my memory bank. I did not know any Arnies.

The voice continued, "...I'll give you a thousand dollars for your Honda."

That woke me up. Or was I dreaming? Could a miracle happen that quickly? It was less than one waking hour since I had felt the worthiness and willingness to sell the car, and here was an immediate offer.

I met the fellow at the gas station and within three hours the car was sold for one thousand dollars, cash.

The Power to Succeed

The secret of all success is:

COMMITMENT.

No one has ever received, gained, or accomplished anything in life without first being deeply committed to it. Everything that has ever happened to anyone has occurred because he has held a commitment — consciously or subconsciously — to that result in his mind. No exceptions! All that we experience is a matter of willingness. The statement "I will" is not a future promise — it is an affirmation of what we choose to create *now*. We *are* the masters of our destiny.

A statement as bold as this one is likely to raise many questions in the thinking mind, for it certainly does seem that things happen to us that are beyond our choice or control. Here it is important to realize that the mind that makes the choices and commitments from which our experiences proceed is not the conscious mind. The real creator of our experience is the *subconscious* mind, which does not think in words, but in pictures, feelings, and intentions. In order to make any progress on the spiritual path we must understand without any doubt whatsoever that *we create our entire life* by the intentions that we hold in mind. We must see that nothing happens to us outside of our own choosing. The understanding and practice of this principle is the entire difference between a person who is the master of his life and one who sees himself as a victim of forces outside his control.

A Course in Miracles explains:

> *This is the only thing that you need do for vision, happiness, and release from pain and the complete escape from sin, all to be given you. Say only this, but mean it with no reservations, for here the power of salvation lies:*

"I *am* responsible for what I see.
I choose the feelings I experience, and
I decide upon the goal I would achieve.
And everything that seems to happen to me I ask for,
and receive as I have asked."[2]

The Formula For Healing

Mind is the progenitor of all of our experiences. We are told, "In the beginning was the word." This statement is not referring simply to an event that occurred at the beginning of time, but a principle that diagrams how we create each new moment of living. This idea calls our attention to the importance of the intention *within our heart*, the purpose behind the action, the goal we wish to accomplish. "Mind is the builder," taught Edgar Cayce. How correct he was!

The patterns in our life remain fixed only as long as our intention does. The moment we change our mind about what we want, *what comes to us must change* as well. If you feel that you are trapped in a repetitious pattern of disastrous relationships, financial setbacks, or ill health (I met one man who broke his right ankle seventeen times for seemingly different reasons), here is the way you can be released instantly:

1. Recognize the pattern.

2. Acknowledge that you have created it.

3. Learn the lesson it is bringing to you.

4. See, know, and affirm what you want instead.

5. Act on your goal with strength and mastery.

6. Allow God to help you.

I learned this lesson through a challenging relationship. The woman I was seeing did not seem to share my intention for a committed relationship. I struggled with the issue for a long time, and I could make no sense of the matter. I felt there were some dynamics operating that I could not see. Why was she not willing to go one hundred percent?

[2] T, p. 418

Around that time a psychic friend offered me a reading. I decided to ask about our relationship. "Why will she not commit herself?" I asked.

The answer came quickly, strongly, and concisely: "Because you are not willing to commit yourself."

The truth of the answer cut through my questioning like a sharp sword.

The counselor went on: "Within your own heart you have held fear and doubt about the relationship. Your partner picked up on this, and because she held some of the same fears and reservations, she mirrored them back to you."

That was it. That was the hidden dynamic of the relationship that I had been asking to understand. Although I wanted to blame her for not being there for me, it was me who was not fully willing to be there for her.

It felt cleaner, clearer, and much more peaceful to accept responsibility for creating the relationship as I experienced it, so much freer than being a victim. Amazingly, as I realized this my love and appreciation for my friend increased dramatically.

When we release our picture of others as victimizers, we free ourself from being a victim. The healing energy liberated in such a new vision will then transform the entire situation and manifest a positive, satisfying, and creative relationship.

A woman once asked me, "Why do men keep leaving me?"

My response was clear: "You attract men who leave you because you do not wholly want one who will stay. If and when you decide that you really want to be in a fully committed relationship, you are sure to attract a man who will reflect your intention."

Repetitious patterns in relationships are sure signs of an underlying pattern of subconscious intention. Like the needle of a phonograph stuck in a groove, we must lift up our mind and place it in a new course. The lifting up of our awareness to see more clearly is often sufficient to set a positive change into motion. We cannot change when we are unwilling to see. The moment we realize that we have been stuck and we ask for help, it must come. Recognizing we are stuck is not a misfortune, but a gift, for recognition is the first step of healing. Then we are free to see the way we must walk to be at peace.

Patricia Sun illustrated this principle in a refreshing way: "People tell me that they are now ready for a relationship, and wonder why can't they find one? I tell them, 'Saying "I'm ready" doesn't necessarily mean you are ready. Being ready is this:..." She stood with her arms, smile, and heart open wide, and invitingly smiled, "Hi!" She was demonstrating that there is no substitute for willingness; when we are truly ready and willing, we will surely attract the object of our desire.

The Commitment to Healing

No one who is committed to healing could remain ill, and no one whose intention is illness can be healthy. There is no middle ground, for there are no exceptions to choice. There is one question to ask about any illness, the answer to which can make the difference between disease and release: "Why have I chosen this?" Being willing to consider personal responsibility is the first step to undoing any kind of pain. *Every experience teaches us a lesson in the power of responsibility and commitment.* As you realize this truth you will become tremendously powerful in all aspects of your life.

We do not need to create an illness to get away from a job, a relationship, or a life. We just have to be lovingly honest about what we really want to do. Several years ago I was working on a building project involving long hours of pouring cement. Toward the end of that summer I came down with a cold and spent a couple of days in bed.

"Why have I created this cold?" I wondered.

As I reflected on my feelings, I realized that I had had enough of cement work for the summer. I was not sick from a disease — I was sick of pouring cement. When I admitted that to myself, I realized I did not have to create a cold to get out of work. I could have simply said, "I am taking a couple of days off." Then I could have relaxed in bed or walked in the woods or gone to visit a friend. *We are never just sick; when we are ill we are sick of something.* If we are willing to look at the thing we are sick of, deal with it, and tell the truth about it, we won't need our body to communicate what our mind wants to say. It hurts us to not tell the truth about what we are feeling. Every illness is a statement. Our goal — and birthright — is to be free of the illness, for indeed illness is not our natural state of being. Our object, however, should not just be to make the symptoms go away; our real purpose is to discover the statement we would like to make. There is a hidden truth we want to tell, and we are using our body to express it by means of those symptoms. The body is a wonderful metaphor. Illness can be a tool for awakening, which is what we came here for. The more we are willing to tell the truth about who we are and what is happening in our life, the less likely we will be to use illness to speak for us. *We don't have to get sick; all we have to do is tell the truth.*

We get sick because we fear that we would be hurt if we told the truth. But telling the truth is what would heal us. Dr. Jerry Jampolsky, the author of the popular book, *Love is Letting Go of Fear*,[3] uses this principle to accomplish wonderful healings with his clients. He asked a man who was dying, "What is it in your life that is so horrible that you would rather leave life than stay in it and face?" The man began to cry and he shared with Jerry for hours the experiences and feelings which he felt had hurt him and caused him to withdraw from fully celebrating his life. Jerry listened, understood, and loved the man. Before long the man had a reversal of his condition and was healed. Here we see that telling the truth has phenomenal power to heal and make us new. His illness was a call for truth. When he told the truth, he was free.

I was told, too, of a woman in a hospital being treated for cancer. A friend of mine, the hospital physiotherapist, was assigned to give her a massage. As my friend is a very loving and open person the woman began to speak of her life as she was being massaged. She told my friend that she had been angry at her sister and they had not spoken in twenty-five years. As she related the story she broke down and began to weep profusely, explaining that she felt terrible about the separation and she wanted to heal it. When the woman was taken into surgery the doctors could find no sign of the cancer. The woman was healed.

The Willing Way

As a counselor I find it interesting to see the different ways clients respond to suggestions for healing. Many people are actively resistant to being healed. All disease — physical, emotional, mental, and spiritual — requires a tremendous continuous investment of energy to be maintained. Our natural state is peaceful health, and the universe is always working to restore it to us. Holding on to any form of illness requires vigorous and sustained effort. What a dear price we pay to defend ourself against healing!

In a counseling session I may give two or three suggestions, openings, or simple reinforcements for the patient to align with a vision of their healing. Sometimes I find that these gifts are met with tremendous resistance by the patient. One psychologist calls this the game of *"Yes, but..."* No

---

[3] Gerald Jampolsky, *Love is Letting Go of Fear*, Bantam, 1981

matter what positive suggestions the therapist offers, the patient responds with a reason why the healing cannot happen. This rejection of help is like throwing a life preserver to a drowning person who immediately throws it back at you. In *Illusions*,[4] Richard Bach says, "Argue for your limitations, and sure enough, they're yours." No one is as unhealable as someone who is not willing to be healed.

When we are ready to make a commitment to healing, all of our past commitments to illness, along with their effects, go out the window instantly. This is the Law of Grace. No matter how deeply entrenched we have been in ideas, feelings, or thoughts that we deserve to be sick, the moment we are willing to be worthy of healing, the old patterns and their resulting symptoms evaporate like a bad dream.

A woman who regularly attends my classes is a good example of this willingness to accept forgiveness for her past and replace it with success now. Nearly every week she reports the wonderful miracles that have happened to her as a result of her putting the class lesson for the week into action. She tells of marvelous improvements in her job, her health, and her relationships. This woman is ready and willing to accept healing in all aspects of her life, and because she is committed to inner change, there is no force in the universe that can stop her. There is an ocean of healing energy available to all of us. We can come to that ocean with a thimble, a bucket, or a tanker; — it is all according to what we choose.

Responsibility Versus Guilt

Sometimes as we aspiring students of truth begin to see that we are responsible for everything that happens to use, we are apt to feel guilty for creating a disease. The contradiction in this approach is obvious when we realize that it was our sense of guilt, or feeling separated from God, that created the disease in the first place. Punishing ourselves for feeling punishable is no answer. The only remedy for lack of love is love.

There is no guilt or blame in not being healed, nor is it a matter of being good or bad, spiritual or unspiritual. A health challenge is an opportunity to replace our sense of power*less*ness with the awareness of our true power*full*ness. Quickly a crisis can be transformed from a curse to a blessing as we discover the vast healing power which has lied dormant within us. This way of looking at our potential acknowledges and celebrates the patient's inhe-

---

[4] Bach, *Illusions*, p. 100

rent ability to create his life as he chooses. If the patient had the power to create such an illness, then he must have the power to recreate perfect health. How strong is our mind!

The acknowledgement of our true strength offers us a much more managable way of handling an illness. Guilt keeps us stuck, while acceptance of responsibility leads us to healing. If you learn to become more responsible for your life through being healed, it may be said that you have extracted a valuable gift from the experience. This is in no way to imply that the illness was necessary for you to learn, for illness is *not* necessary. It is to say that the wise student of Truth finds a lesson in every step of his path, and joyfully gains from it.

The Call for Love

We may complicate matters further by projecting our own unresolved guilt onto our friends when they get sick. We feel guilty for our own illness, and not wanting to face our sense of guilt, we blame our friends when they get sick. In addition to removing us from the answer for our own recovery, this approach clearly does not serve our friend's healing. If someone is ill, the last thing they want to hear is a sermon on how they created the illness. What they need is love and understanding. At such a time a hug is usually much more healing than a metaphysical lecture.

As *A Course in Miracles* poignantly teaches, all illness is really a call for love. Our only truly productive response to illness in ourself or another is to give more love. Any form of blame represents a mistake in our own mind. To give any response other than more love only delays the moment of real healing. The instant the real call is heard and answered, the healing is accomplished.

I have seen this powerful principle successfully applied on many occasions. When a teacher of metaphysics who stuttered was asked by a student, "How should we view your stuttering?" the teacher replied, "Please see it as a call for love."

I learned this truth personally when one night I answered the telephone to hear the voice of a friend proclaiming, "Hello, Alan, this is Cary... I am just calling to tell you that I love you!"

"Why, that's really wonderful, Cary — I really appreciate that!"

"I'll tell you why I'm calling right now," he reported. "My foot was hurting me, and I know that the only way I can get healed is to give more love. I started to think of the people I love, and you came into my mind. I want to thank you for being a light in my life!''

It is said that all acts in life can be divided into one of two categories: clear expressions of love, and distorted expressions of love. All illness, anger, fear, and separation are actually calls for love in a form that is veiled. Longfellow said, ''If we could read the secret history of our enemies, we should find in each man's life, sorrow and suffering enough to disarm all hostility.'' Try responding to distorted calls for love as if the apparent victimizer is craving a vitamin (''L'' for love) that no one else has offered them. Such a one needs *more* love than someone who is expressing love more obviously. Give them the love they are really asking for, and quickly you will become a miracle worker. And you will wonder why you never before realized how simple is the key to living.

Know You Are Worthy

Our problem is not that we want the wrong things, but that we do not believe we are worthy of having the good that we desire. Why should it be so embarrassing to admit what we want? The courage to know what we want and then go for it will move us through life much more quickly and joyfully than sitting on the sidelines wondering if we deserve it. You have every right to ask for what you want. You deserve the best — do not settle for less!

True success is not a matter of capability, but of *worthability*. Do you know that you deserve good in *all* arenas of your life? Or do you hold some subconscious belief that you deserve to be sick, suffer, or sacrifice? *Now you can let go forever of any idea that God wants you to be ill or lose in any way*. Nothing could be farther from the truth. God wants you to experience complete health, happiness, abundance, and success in *everything* you do. At a workshop in Florida a man stood up and told the audience, ''I tried believing in myself once, but it didn't work — I realized I didn't have enough experience!'' Like this man, you have allowed your subconscious guilts and fears to run you into the dust for too long. It is about time you got out of the mud and made your way to the top of the mountain of life, where you belong.

Let me share with you an example of how we deny ourself prosperity by subconsciously sabotaging our own best interests:

One afternoon I received a telephone call from a friend who had been attempting to establish himself as an independent consultant in electronic engineering.

"I've been trying to get this business off the ground for six months," Gary explained with an air of frustration in his voice. "...yet I don't seem to be getting anywhere. I got one job, but the client called back to tell me he had changed his mind. What do you think is happening?"

Knowing that my friend is an adept engineer as well as a responsible person, it seemed to me that the crimp in the pipeline of his prosperity was being caused not by a circumstance, but a self-defeating mental program.

"Gary, is there any part of you that is resisting succeeding?" I felt guided to ask. "Do you have any thoughts that maybe you shouldn't be doing this?"

Gary took a moment to think. He hadn't thought of it in this way before.

"Well, now that you mention it," Gary thought out loud, "I do feel a little guilty about having an easy job that I like. When I was a child I was taught by example that a job is something you hate, which you slave at for forty hours a week, and at the end of the week the reward for your suffering is money. My idea for this business is to work out of my home for three or four days a week and to spend my free time studying massage and experimenting with photography. I guess part of me feels guilty for having a job that I love so much — it seems too easy!"

Gary was blocking his good from coming to him because he subconsciously felt that he didn't deserve it. Like many of us, Gary held himself in a state of lack because he was not willing to acknowledge that he deserved abundance. Similarly, many of us manifest our fear of success in the experience of failure. We sabotage good opportunities because we are afraid we will fail or we would have to take responsibility for their success.

I told Gary that we decide what we will accept in life on the basis of who we think are. If we believe we are sinful, unworthy people who deserve to suffer because we have done something bad, we will create illnesses, jobs, and relationships in which we lose and feel hurt. We will produce a personal movie in which we pay off the sins we *think* we have committed and for which we *believe* we deserve to suffer. THIS IS NOT THE TRUTH ABOUT WHO WE ARE. We are Sons and Daughters of a loving, forgiving God Who is well pleased in our joys and successes. The real God takes no pleasure whatsoever in anyone's suffering. The moment we know that God is a God of only love we begin to manifest a wonderful, healthy, and abundant life. Once we realize that God truly wants us to succeed and be happy at what we are doing, we step through the door of our destiny and serve many others in the process. You might like to know that Gary followed through on the guidance of his heart, and now he is a very successful teacher of massage, a livelihood in which he feels much more peaceful and satisfied.

The only decision we need to make is who we are. On the basis of that one thought will all of your experiences follow. If you remember that you are the heir to all of God's gifts, you will attract all the good your heart desires. You will prove this law by finding abundance in *every* aspect of your life.

God is Success

You can always tell what you want by what you are getting. The Law of Life, being a *law* and not a probability, is *always* working to give us what we are creating with our mind. This law is completely unbiased in its willing-ness to serve us — even if we go about creating experiences and events that we do not really want or need. We can and will have more of whatever we tell the universe with our thoughts. If we think abundance, we will get more abundance. If we think lack, we will see more lack. In this principle we realize that all is abundance — even abundant lack! We are always succeed-ing at being creators. We can even succeed at being a failure! And it is wonderful to recognize that we have succeeded at failing, for this means that *we are the masters of our destiny.* We can take the principle that we have unconsciously used to work against us, and harness the same power to work *for* us.

One of the most important elements of Goethe's brilliant elucidation of the power of commitment is this: *We do not have to know HOW we are going to get what we want. All we have to know is WHAT we want.* The "what" is our department — God will take care of the rest. When you have a clear perception of the goal, *the means for its accomplishment will be arranged for you.* If you are not getting what you want in life, it is not because the universe cannot provide good — it is because you are not sure of what you really want. Be sure, and life will lay all of its gifts at the door of your heart.

Our Real Desire

What we really want is the peace of God. Every dream, every aspira-tion, and every deed we undertake is an attempt to feel the peace that we remember deep within our heart. All of our striving seeks but to reclaim our birthright of inner contentment. We will stop at nothing short of true peace — this is a guarantee!

One of the pitfalls that many of us slip into in the early stages of spiritual awakening is becoming enamoured with the power of our mind to create material objects or events in our life. When this happens we clutter our consciousness with an overspiced goulash of transpersonal leftovers. We start to see that our mind is indeed a powerful tool to produce the movie of our life, and then we promiscuously manufacture a series of gospel bloopers. The result is that we end up with a lot of metaphysical footage on the cosmic cutting-room floor, a few good takes that we can splice into a sequel, and a fair amount of lessons in the cinematography of awakening.

Thus we have an early lesson in miracles:

"I do not perceive my own best interests."[5]

How many things have you asked God for, received, and then asked him to take back? You entreat our Heavenly Father for a certain car, home, or relationship, and then it is not long before you are standing at the celestial exchange counter begging for mercy because the garment you requested is not your size and you don't have your receipt. Then, of course, because God is a God of mercy, we get to trade it in for a new something, until sooner or later there we are at the counter again with a new reason. That etheric exchange department gets so much action that it makes K-Mart on December 26th seem like the Gobi Desert by comparison!

It is no wonder, then, that *A Course in Miracles* tells us, "You cannot be your guide to miracles, because it was you who made them necessary."[6] If you really knew what was good for you, you wouldn't be in the mess you're in!

How, then, do you integrate the fantastic creative power of your mind, and your phenomenal ability to subtly sabotage the full manifestation of your good? Once again the *Course* offers us a miracle:

Miracles are habits, and should be involuntary. They should not be under conscious control. Consciously selected miracles can be misguided.[7]

[5] W, p. 36
[6] T. p. 277
[7] T, p. 1

To illustrate: A friend of mine who liked to jog wished to live closer to the park so she could run there directly each day without driving to get to the jogging area. Every day she sat for twenty minutes and visualized living one hundred yards from the park. Clearly she gave God this message, with the feeling that He would fulfill it. And He did. God got her an apartment exactly a hundred yards from the park; unfortunately, it was on the other side of the river that bordered the park. She still had to drive fifteen minutes via the nearest bridge to get to the park!

Another friend, seeking to improve her financial situation, specifically visualized receiving checks in the mail. She spent long hours mentally seeing the mailman placing checks from a reputable source in her mailbox. Sure enough, that is what happened. What she forgot to tell God was that the checks be made out to her. When they came, the checks were social security payments to the former tenant. They did her no good. But checks did come in the mail.

Should these two people *not* have prayed to improve their situation? Certainly they should have prayed — but they should have prayed real prayers — not for circumstances, but for *peace*. Jesus said, "When you pray, you pray amiss." Instead of asking for an apartment or a check, which are but symbols of abundance or channels through which good is delivered, these students of truth would have done better to affirm their good as an *already-present reality*. Their desire for beauty of nature and prosperous living are perfectly aligned with who we are and what we deserve; but perhaps the most powerful visualization would have been one that saw all the beauty of nature and the abundance of the universe already residing *within* their hearts. We seek external riches only when we have forgotten the riches *inside* of us. Truly the only quest is for spiritual awakening, which reveals to us that what we sought is what we *are*.

When *A Course in Miracles* teaches, "Miracles are natural and involuntary, and should not be under conscious control," it is reminding us of the easy, natural way in which Spirit works. When something is right for us, useful for our awakening, and helpful to our peace of mind, the idea for the article or the experience will awaken spontaneously in our mind and heart. We will find ourself thinking about it, enjoying the possibilities of having this idea become a reality in our life, and contemplating all the good that it holds for us. This entire process happens *effortlessly*, without any force or struggle on our part. It is as if God plants a seed in our heart, and then we find ourself nurturing it with strength, shining our enthusiasm on it, and watering it with the spirit of our love. Our good springs forth out of peace and joy —

not a sense of duty or effort. We enjoy watching it unfold as we participate in it. And it will come to pass because it is of God.

When I came out of graduate school I began to look for a job as a counselor. While I was working at a Seven-Eleven grocery store, my heart was yearning to do some creative work with young people. One day I saw an advertisement in the newspaper for a coordinator for youth drop-in centers. Reading the job description, I knew that job was for me. Immediately I began to think about what I would do if I got the job. I envisioned setting up communications workshops for teenagers and their parents, establishing a telephone hotline, and participating with the teens in an informal recreational atmosphere. I did not in any way force myself to think about these projects; the ideas were so pleasing to my spirit that I found myself visualizing and thinking about them many times a day. I even wrote down an organizational outline.

By the time I went to the interview it was as if I had been doing the job for years. I had many of the details about the position worked out in my mind, and in a way I already felt successful at the job. The result was that I got the job and went on to see the fulfillment of all the ideas that I had thought about and jotted down — and more! Success flows easily when we are relaxed and creative in fantasizing about the things we would love to do.

The Peaceful Warrior

It should be noted here that we can be quite active and productive without any sense of strain. Absence of struggle does not mean absence of participation. You might be inclined to ask, "But if I gave up striving, how could I accomplish anything?" The answer is that *you are not the accomplisher* — God is. When you are working in attunement with the Voice of Spirit, it will tell you precisely what to do. Then it will clear the way for you to accomplish your dream and leave you with no strain at all, only a deep sense of peace and fulfillment.

> *Once you have accepted His plan as the one function that you would fulfill, there will be nothing that the Holy Spirit will not arrange for you. Without your effort He will go before you, making straight your path and leaving in your way no stone to trip on, no obstacle to bar your way.*[8]

---

[8] T, p. 404

To release struggle does not mean that you will become a blob; quite to the contrary! You will become a more efficient, creative, and productive human being, with a boundless resource of energy to use for the healing of yourself and others. The energy that you once invested in worry and self-protection will be available to be channeled into constructive, helpful, and rewarding projects. You will overflow with the talents and abilities that God created you to fulfill.

While I was writing *The Dragon Doesn't Live Here Anymore* I learned how to struggle less and accomplish more. When I was first inspired to write the book I worked almost non-stop for three solid months. I typed for eight to twelve hours a day, eating little, sleeping sometimes as few as three or four hours a night, putting nearly all other activities aside. My meditation and exercise program dropped away. It seemed as if all I was doing was living, eating, and breathing this book that felt as if it was being written through me.

To an observer it might have appeared that I was making a tremendous effort and sacrificing much. Yet during this period I had no sense of strain, struggle, or effort at all. I was neither pushing nor forcing myself to do anything about which I did not feel excited and enthusiastic. In fact, I had so much energy to work that I did not want to stop until I was finished. Afterwards, upon seeing the process from a grander perspective I realized that I was eating, sleeping, and meditating less because I was deriving my nourishment from the spiritual attunement I was enjoying in hearing and recording the ideas I was writing. "Man shall not live by bread alone, but by every word which proceeds from the mouth of God."[9] The spiritual insights I was receiving *were* my food, rest, and meditation. I did not need to do practices to put myself in touch with the Christ — I was already in His Presence. *A Course in Miracles* teaches, "Rest does not come from sleeping, but from waking."[10] It was the most intense work I have ever done — and at the same time the easiest!

I believe this experience is a model for how we can live our whole life: extremely creatively, while not laboriously. The more willing we are to engage in the creative activities that we enjoy, the more energy we will have to do them, and the more successful we will be in accomplishing them.

---

[9] Deuteronomy 8:3
[10] T, p. 71

Love is the Way

The real secret of success is love. We must love ourselves enough to know that we are worthy to succeed. We must believe that those around us want us to win at life, and that our winning can only support their winning. We must know God wants us to be happy in *all* the arenas of our life. We must understand that there is no need to struggle, strain, or live in pain or a state of lack. These hellish conditions are but signals that we must try another way. We must never settle for less than whole and holy abundance in our health, relationships, and livelihood. We were not born to scratch the dirt with chickens — we were born to soar with the eagles!

All of the conditions of material and spiritual success that you desire are within your power to create right now. You have the ability, courage, and support to mobilize your belief in yourself immediately. Your ideas are not products of a warped ego — they are given to you by God Itself. Your dreams have not been randomly learned from a chaotic outer world; these sparkling jewels have been imbued within your soul by the Mind that knows only your perfection and lives for its expression. You are here for a staggeringly important purpose; much — very much — hinges on you following through to complete your personal quest for the opening of your heart and the healing of all of your life.

To accomplish this noble mission you must know, without one hint or shadow of hesitation, that all of your most cherished visions will become a reality, bearing fruit in ways more miraculous than you can now imagine. You are not alone. You walk holding the hand of Spirit, and no one who walks this path can be stopped. Your destiny is broader than the oceans, wealthier than the coffers of King Solomon, and loftier than the farthest stars. You are destined to know yourself as a Child of the Living God, heir to the love that created the universe in all its radiant splendor. Child of the All that is Good, know who you are! Walk with dignity, majesty, and the wonder of the Beauty in which you were created. Thus shall you deliver Heaven to earth and live in both without fear. Love shall take you all the way home.

> *There are only two mistakes one can make along the road to truth:*
>
> *1. Not going all the way.*
> *2. Not starting.*
>
> — Buddha

The GRACE of GOD

As If the Nothing Never Was

*All of your past except its beauty is gone,
and nothing is left but a blessing.*

- A Course in Miracles[1]

One of my favorite tales is *The Neverending Story*, the magical adventure of a young boy who travels to the thrilling realm of Fantasia, a colorful world in which the rocks talk, there is a luck dragon, and a beautiful princess in need of help. As the hero, Atreyu, enters Fantasia he learns that it is being consumed by *The Nothing*, a mysteriously malevolent force which is rapidly eating away at the world. With increasing speed *The Nothing* is crumbling trees, houses, people, and everything in its path into emptiness, and the Fantasians have found no way to stop it.

Atreyu is summoned by the lovely princess of Fantasia to save the world from *The Nothing*. But to do this he must pass difficult tests and brave dangers that have never before been conquered. He must tread through a Swamp of Sadness, pass through the Portal of Mirrors through which no one who holds any doubt about himself can survive, and he must face the ferocious Wolf of Destruction which has been dispatched to devour all who confront *The Nothing*. Surely Atreyu's task is formidably set before him!

Our young knight courageously accepts the challenge and sets out upon his heroic mission. Trudging through the Swamp of Sadness he loses his faithful horse, but he emerges unscathed. Though he is frightened by the bones of those who have not succeeded through the Portal of Mirrors, Atreyu summons the strength of his belief in himself and what he is doing, and goes unaffected by the force field of death generated by the reflection of self-doubt. One by one all of his friends disappear into *The Nothing*, and Atreyu absorbs his biggest blow in the loss of his great cuddly friend and transporter, Falcor the Luck Dragon. Yet onward he marches, faithfully determined in his quest to save the princess and the kingdom.

Gradually more and more quickly *The Nothing* overtakes Fantasia until

---

[1] T, p. 76

it has devoured everything in the kingdom except the princess and her castle. As Atreyu reaches her she tells him that the only chance to save her, himself, and the kingdom is to call her name out loud. Atreyu resists, and it appears that this means the end. At one final moment the princess, with tears in her eyes, begs him to comply.

As Atreyu calls the name, we hear that it is the name of his mother whom he had recently lost. You see, in order for *The Nothing* to go away he had to be willing to believe that what appeared to be lost was still alive.

At the moment of his call the terrible Nothing is stilled. Atreyu draws nigh the princess and laments that though *The Nothing* has finally been stopped, there is pitiful little left of Fantasia to do anything with.

"Oh no," comforts the lovely maiden. "…There is much left. You can easily rebuild Fantasia!"

"But how?" the valiant one queries.

"By using your mind!" she explains. "Don't you see that everything in Fantasia lives according to the love and belief that you give it? All you need to do is think clearly upon what you love, and all that was lost can be regained!"

"You mean I can get Falcor and all of my friends back?!"

"Why, yes!…Just call them to you, and you will see how quickly they come!"

Soon Atreyu is delighted to find his beloved Falcor flying to him, lifting him up on the soft ridges of his furry back to take him home. Happily they fly over the mountains and oceans, laughing heartily as they soar. We see Atreyu's eyes and heart sparkle as from this high vantage point he witnesses the return of all of his friends, just as the princess promised.

"Wow, Falcor!" cries Atreyu, "It's as if *The Nothing* never was!" Falcor smiles as the two return to a world safe from the fear of nothing.

A child's fantasy?

In the late nineteenth century Baird J. Spaulding set off on a pilgrimage to find the living spiritual masters of the Himalayas. Years later he returned with a most amazing account of his journey called *The Life and Teachings of the Masters of the Far East.* Now a classic in metaphysical elucidation, this powerful work in five volumes recounts some of the most inspiring and enlightening experiences ever recorded, and provides spiritual seekers with answers and insights into the nature of the mind, healing, and the mastery of all life.

During these adventurous years the members of this expedition met saints and sages who performed astounding demonstrations of the power of the mind to control health and life. It was not unusual for them to be with a guide who would simply disappear before their eyes and then find him waiting for them at their destination three days later. They observed many miracles similar to the ones performed by Jesus, including the manifestation of food, instantaneous healing of the sick, and raising the dead. These feats, it was explained, were simply the results of a conscious use of the Laws of Mind, and anyone with the strength of belief could perform them easily.

On one particular occasion the group witnessed an invasion of a village by armed marauders. In contrast to their other uplifting experiences, this scenario involved conflict, bloodshed, and fear. Affected by the negative images they had seen, the troupe was downcast and discouraged. After tending to the wounds of the villagers the members of the expedition dejectedly began their climb up to the mountain retreat where they had their quarters. Ascending slowly, they noticed they had lost their regenerative powers.

> *We left the lodge and started to walk to the Temple as had been the custom on previous occasions. We had proceeded to the ladder that led to the entrance of the tunnel, when the one who was in advance stopped, with one foot on the first rung, and said: "What has come over us? Just a day or two ago we were in seventh heaven of delight, going from place to place at will and accomplishing things in three months that we had expected would take years to finish. Our food appears on the table, and all of this without the least exertion on our part. Now, suddenly, we have slumped back into our old habits. I want to know why this sudden slump? I can see only one thing. Every one of us has taken upon himself the condition of the experience through which we have passed. This is what is now hampering us and I for one am through with that thing, it is no part of me whatsoever. It is mine only as I worship it and hold to it and do not let it go. I step forth out of this condition into a higher and better condition and let go. I am entirely through with it." As we stood and stared at him, we realized he was gone, he had disappeared.[2]*

---

[2] Baird Spaulding, *The Life and Teachings of the Masters of the Far East*, Vol. III, p. 46 Devorss & Co., 1972. Used by permission.

"As you believe, so shall it be done unto you," taught the Master Jesus, and what a principle this is! Do you realize the implications of this idea, especially in light of the experience described in the expedition? This means that *any condition of body, mind, or spirit exists only because we hold it in mind, and the moment we release it from mind, the condition will disappear,* along with *all of its effects.* All that we see in our body and our entire life is a direct result of our thoughts. All that we need to do to change those conditions is to *change our mind.*

Let us look at our mind as a sort of electromagnet. As you've driven past a junkyard you may have seen a big crane with an electromagnet lifting and moving junk cars from one place to another. The cars are held to the magnet only by the current in the magnet which attracts the metal of the auto. Unplug the current for a moment, and the car quickly and easily drops off. It is a very simple principle.

That is exactly how the conditions of our life cling to us - and how they can leave us. In this case our mind is the magnet and the conditions of our life are the cars. We attract persons and events by our thoughts, and we free ourselves of them by not continuing to power them with the electricity of our attention. Just as the electromagnet releases the junk cars, we can be free of junk thoughts by refusing to invest emotional energy in them. When we turn our attention to the light of God within and around us, we empower *those* thoughts to create new and more positive conditions in our life.

This is the principle by which Jesus and all the other great ones have accomplished their healings. The power of their thoughts was so dynamic that the mind of the sick or the dead one began to vibrate in harmony with that of the master, and as the master gave *no reality* to thoughts or conditions of illness or death, instantly the negative circumstances disappeared.

Teaches *A Course in Miracles:*

> *Miracles enable you to heal the sick and raise the dead because you made sickness and death yourself, and therefore can abolish both.* You *are a miracle, capable of creating in the likeness of your Creator. Everything else is your own night-mare, and therefore does not exist. Only the creations of light are real.*[3]

---

[3] T, p. 2

112

Only the creations of light are real. This means that only the good in our life is true, and any form of guilt or error that we see is a misperception. We hurt ourselves by seeing the negative, which is not really seeing at all, but misperceiving. Our role, therefore, is not to correct conditions, which are *always good*, but to purify our perceptions to reflect the light.

Misperceiving is like looking at a distorted circus mirror and being horrified by our strange reflection. The error is not in the source, but in the faulty reflection of it. One of those mirrors is called "the past," another "the future," and both of them show you everything but what is here now. An appropriate reaction is perhaps a light-hearted giggle and a quick return to the joy of seeing life in its true radiance. There is tremendous spiritual power available to us when we are open to the now, and we can enjoy total healing simply by *letting it all be good now.*

Change Can Come in
the Twinkling of an Eye

During a powerful meditation Hilda guided, "Now let the conditions of your life drop away. In this moment you have no husband or wife, no business, no automobile. Leave everything that is temporary behind and rise into the light."

I felt myself lifting up like a balloon, and soon all of the painful dreams of life had no power to touch me or bring me down. I thought of the people and events in my life that were a source of discomfort to me, prefacing each one by a denial of its ability to remove my happiness in any way: "No body"…"No rent"…"No relationship." I was not attempting to get rid of these things by making them real and then trying to make them go away; instead I was transcending my belief in their reality and in the thought that they had power over me. Watching thoughts that had seemed so cumbersome dissolve, I experienced a freedom that nothing in this world can challenge. What a release!

In the hours and days after that meditation I found that many of those conditions were changed, or I found the peace and clarity to deal with them effectively, in such a way that they no longer were a problem.

Is this essentially any different than the man who disappeared when he affirmed that the seeming disaster had no power over him? I believe that the nature of the principle that helped both of us is the same. The Law of Mind is constant, and we are all free to use it for our healing.

113

Now is the Time for Release

Now is the only moment in which you can totally free yourself from the past. There is a beautiful key statement in the *Course* which tells us, "This course is not beyond immediate learning, unless you believe what God wills takes time."[4] *The Will of God is now*. You can be healed now if you are willing to completely let go of every idea that you were ever ill, mortal, or limited. You are a Child of a Perfect God, and no harm can ever befall the spiritual being that you truly are.

This moment, take your past and *throw it all away*. You will not be lost, but found, and deeply comforted by the blessings bestowed by the lessons of love that you have gained. The past does not exist - indeed it never existed - except as you choose to uphold it in your thoughts. As you release the past you release yourself. This past that seems a burden is but a raft that took you from one shore of the river to the other. You are on solid ground now and you are ready to go forward, and so you must loose your burden from your weary shoulders. You are done with it. You can leave it behind without fear or hesitation. All you will take with you is your appreciation for the gifts that you received along your journey. You are reborn into the freedom of the living present. You are free to claim your destiny as a Being of Pure Light. You are free to open the door to forever, which begins only now. So it is, and so shall it be forever in the hearts of those who love the light.

[4] T, p. 288

The Language of God

"Dibrai Torah B'loshan B'nai Adam."
"The Torah (Bible) speaks in the language of people."
                                    - The Talmud

I

There is a beautiful legend about an angel who sought admission to Heaven. To earn his place in the holy kingdom the elder angels gave him a mission: to find the person on earth who spoke the most powerful prayers.

For a long time the young angel was gone on his quest, and the overseeing angels wondered what had become of him.

When he finally returned he had with him a small boy.

"What took you so long?" his superiors inquired.

"I searched the earth," the aspiring angel told them. "I went to the synagogues and the churches, to the mosques and temples. There I found learned and revered men exhorting lengthy scriptures and rites — my mind boggled at the amount of knowledge their minds held. Yet when I looked into their hearts I saw their thoughts were wandering and they did not truly understand the words they were speaking.

"I found many people in all manner of houses of worship, dutifully reciting the delicate poetry of the psalms. But when I surveyed their souls, I found fear and hypocrisy darkening their love.

"I journeyed, too, to people kneeling at their bedside, and even in privacy I did not find complete sincerity in their prayer."

The elder angels listened attentively. "Why, then, did you not return and report this to us?" they asked him.

"So I was about to. I began to believe that there was no one on earth whose prayers had the power to reach Heaven. Then, as I flew homeward over a busy city, my heart was summoned by the sound of a child sobbing. As I drew close to find the cause of his tears, I heard him reciting the alphabet. Letter by letter he sobbed: 'A...B...C...' Then I heard him

115

whispering these words:

> *Dear God, I do not know how to read, and neither have I learned how to pray; the prayer book would do me no good. But I love you so much! And I want to thank you for all the wonderful blessings you are to me. So, if it is alright with you, I will simply recite the letters of the alphabet with love, and trust that you, my dear Friend, will put them together into the words that are pleasing to you.*"

This, agreed all the angels, was the most powerful prayer of all.

II
Communication, not Confusion

Delivering my opening address on "Balancing Our Planet with Love" at a large retreat in eastern Pennsylvania, I was about to tell the story of a healing that I had read about in a newspaper that I had discovered in a local Seven-Eleven store. As I began the anecdote I found myself reporting to the audience that I had gone into the store to buy some potato chips.

"Why am I telling them about the potato chips?" I wondered as I stood at the flowered podium. "That has nothing to do with the healing story," I thought to myself as I spoke. Slightly embarrassed, I went on, hoping I did not sound too foolish.

After the lecture a young man with a shining face came up to me at the side of the stage. Shaking my hand he told me, "I just want to thank you for telling that potato chip story! That really set me at ease. For years I've been on a very strict health food diet, and every time I have a craving for some junk food or binge out I feel guilty. To sit here and hear you, an author, a person who I respect as a spiritual being, delivering an address on healing the planet, telling that you eat potato chips — that really freed me of my sense of unworthiness! I was uptight until I heard that, but I enjoyed everything you said afterwards. I received the whole message of the lecture!"

At another workshop I found myself speaking of the transition between this life and the next. This was a five day workshop, and I was surprised to find myself discussing this subject for a while each day. "Why am I getting into this?" I wondered. " — This is not my usual lecture material."

116

The answer came after the last class of the week. Two women approached me to say good-by and wish me well, and as they did so they mentioned, "We want to tell you how much we appreciate the attention you gave to transition. Both of us have had persons dear to us pass on recently, and what you said gave us great comfort. We felt as if you gave those lectures just for us."

God speaks in the language of Her children. The function of spiritual teaching is communication, not confusion. *God speaks to us in terms with which we are comfortable and familiar.* Very genuine guidance may come to you in colloquial terms. In order to hear it and receive the blessing it is intended to bring to you, you must be open to accept it.

You may have been denying your guidance because it has not come in a form in which you expect to receive it, or in which other persons have received theirs. Just because others have received messages in "thee's," "thou's," or "burning bushes" does not mean this is the way you are to be guided. Such language may be appropriate for them, but if it is not *your* style, Spirit will most assuredly reach you in your own way. Accepting help requires trust, openness, and most of all the willingness to be helped. You must believe that God loves you so much that She is willing to reach you in a way that is peaceful for you.

After one of my yoga classes a young lady explained to me that she had received guidance in doing one of the postures. "As I was doing the bow, (the position in which you lay on your stomach and reach behind your back to grab your ankles) my body began to tremble," she explained. "I held on, but the longer I held the more my body shook. I didn't know whether to let go or try to push through, so I silently asked for guidance.

"Then in my mind I heard the voice of a man with a Scottish accent calling, "Cap'n, I c'nnot push these engines anymur, else the Enterprise'll blow us into the next galaxy!"

Another woman, seeking to know if it was time to conclude a long meditation that she had been forcing her way through, also asked for instruction. Her inner voice answered, "Over and out!"

And one evening Hilda was resting in her room, wondering if she should join some friends getting ready to go to a movie. Her guidance came in the form of the tune of "Alexander's Ragtime Band." She tells that she heard a rousing chorus of angelic voices singing, *"Get up and go!...Get up and go!"*

These voices are not those of possession, subconscious memories, or spirits outside ourself. They are forms of guidance from our superconscious mind, delivering lessons to our conscious mind in ways that we are able to hear. To a Frenchman inspiration would come in the French language, to an artist in pictures, to a musician in tones. Spirit is happy and willing to meet us on our own turf.

The Bridge to God

In many of the *Star Trek* episodes the crew of the Starship Enterprise would find themselves on a distant planet encountering some enigmatic creature who looked like a cross between Godzilla and Ronald McDonald, and spoke a language resembling a marriage of Yiddish and Swahili. At that point Captain Kirk would quickly call for *The Universal Translator*, a device which automatically translated the creature's language into English so the crew could communicate with it.

God has built a universal translator right into our mind as standard operating equipment. Like many of the marvelous concepts on Star Trek and other science-not-so-fiction movies, this idea represents a real and practical metaphysical principle. Universal translation is a psychic capability to which we already have access, and we use it more than we realize. There is a vast reservoir of wisdom living deep within us — Aldous Huxley called it the "Mind at Large" — and this knowledge is channelled to us according to our ability to receive, understand, and use it.

If we were in perfect communication with God, we would need no guidance. Yet because we have veered from truth in consciousness (and consciousness alone!) each of us receives direction and correction according to the way that we have strayed from the path of right thinking. Those who have veered to the left must turn right; to the right, left; those who have passed it must turn around; and those travelling on the correct path need but continue. That is why there is no one recipe, guru, diet, or spiritual practice that will work for everyone all of the time. Toilets north of the equator flush clockwise, while those south of it flush counterclockwise. You have to know which side of the line you are on before you can know which way your water is supposed to swirl (metaphorically speaking).

Each of us has our own toilet to flush, our own piece of the universe to purify. No one can know more about what you need to do than your own self. The problems of the world have arisen from northern flushers criticizing their southern counterparts, while the southerners feel guilty for flushing the wrong way. Meanwhile, all toilets are swirling perfectly according to plan. Well, I think it's about time we had faith in our own flushing! The universe functions much more smoothly when we keep our hands on our own handle.

Another way of viewing our way home is to describe our universe as a great jigsaw puzzle, with a unique shape cut out for every living being, a little space in the cosmos that only one special person can fill. The miracle comes when, as you find your place in the jigsaw puzzle, you form the pattern for me to find mine. We serve each other most powerfully simply by finding our own place.

The Meeting Place of Mystics

Several years ago I had the pleasure to introduce the marvelous dental healers Reverend Willard and Margaret Fuller at a series of their lectures in Toronto. On the third night of the series we were to speak at a church that we had not previously visited. The day before the presentation the minister of that church telephoned me and invited me to introduce the Fullers' program to his congregation.

As we entered the church the minister shook my hand, ushered me to a seat, and introduced the Fullers himself. Having anticipated doing the introduction, I felt somewhat disappointed, a little offended, and rather puzzled. As I sat and listened I wondered why he had chosen to introduce the Fullers instead of me.

The next day Rev. Fuller told me that the minister had informed him that he did not feel that I was dressed nicely enough to do the introduction. The standard attire of this church was jacket and tie, and I was dressed more casually. My ego felt hurt, but Rev. Fuller's response to me was a lesson far more valuable than a little ego wound.

"My brother Alan," Rev. Fuller began in a fatherly sort of way, "may I share with you something that I learned way back in the beginning of my ministry?"

"Sure...please."

"I don't believe that any way of dressing is any better or more spiritual than another. Jesus wore a robe, and as far as I'm concerned, that would do quite well. But somewhere along my way I learned that the goal of a preacher is to awaken peoples' hearts to God, and if there is anything that may stand in the way of that communication, it is not worth it. These days people wear suits and ties, so that's what I wear — not necessarily because I prefer it, but

119

because that is a commonly accepted format of dialogue in which the people in a public audience will comfortably hear what I have to say. Therefore it is worth it to me to meet on common ground. It is more important to me to communicate than for me to be personally comfortable. St. Paul said, 'I am all things to all people,' and I have learned the meaning of those words. If I were invited to preach the word of God at a clowns' convention, I would wear a clown's costume."

That got to me. You see, Rev. Fuller is a man who dresses impeccably; he wears stylish suits, his hair and beard are very respectably trimmed, and he always emanates a pleasant hint of cologne. For him to be flexible enough to trade that for a clown's costume to share the word of God, was inspiration enough for me.

Then I remembered what Ram Dass had described about his teacher Baghwan Dass, when he first met him in India. "We went to a Buddhist shrine and everyone welcomed him as if they knew him," Ram Dass tells. "There I noticed he was chanting their *mantra*. Then we went to a Hindu community where they took him in as their own. There I saw he was wearing an amulet like all of them. Later on we travelled to a mosque where he knelt down and prayed their prayers. Then they invited us to dinner and gave us a place to stay. He seemed to be a part of everyone's group, and sincerely so."

One Truth

In a way similar to Baghwan Dass I had to become a sort of undercover yogi when I was invited to give a series of lectures to employees at Bell Laboratories. Quickly I learned that "God" is a word that is not comfortable to many people in that environment, and it is rarely spoken. As I presented my first few lectures I noticed that whenever I would touch on any spiritual subject matter the audience would begin to squirm, wiggle, or raise objectioning questions. Gradually I cut back on spiritual lingo and tried to stay within a framework with which they were at peace.

I began to feel like a hypocrite. The language of spiritual terms, I felt, was my own; my heart loves God and I felt somewhat blasphemous in purposely avoiding His name. I spoke to Hilda about this, and here is the insightful counsel she gave me:

"Why, no, darling! That is not running away from truth -that's sharing truth in the way that it will most easily be heard. It is not necessary to use the word 'God' to feel, teach, and know God's presence. Just keep God in your heart, and then God will guide you to speak in just the right way that your message will be heard.''

That felt good. The next time I went back to the Labs I asked Spirit for guidance on how to teach about the power of thoughts to change and heal lives. In my mind's eye I saw the image of a crystal, the basis for a project on which the class's sponsor was working.

"Consider a crystal," I began (not really sure where I would end up). "A crystal has a seed shape around which larger crystals form. The larger crystals can assume only the basic pattern which the starter crystal gave it. So it is with our thoughts and our lives: Our feelings and experiences crystallize around the thoughts we think, which are like seed crystals. If we think positive, loving thoughts, so shall we attract positive, loving people, events, and experiences into our lives."

They got it. (I was more amazed than anyone, as I knew next to nothing about crystals or science!) But Holy Spirit, in answer to my prayer to be used as an instrument of peace for these people, knew everything they needed to hear.

God in Search of Man

There is one question, the answer to which will open all the doors of life unto you: *Does God love you enough to reach you in ways that you do not know how to reach Him?*

The Jewish mystic Abraham Heschel wrote a book called *God in Search of Man*. The title itself is a touching statement of our Father's deep desire for us to be reunited with Him. Over the ages many teachers and artists have conjured a picture of a wrathful, angry God who has turned His back on His evil children, or wishes to punish us for our sins against Him. Actually, the exact opposite is true: God is doing everything in His Power (and that's a lot of power!) to reach out to us. And He is eager and willing to use any means to do so.

Let us consider the movies, for example. It is getting a little harder for God to reach people in church on Sunday morning, basically because a lot of us are in bed around that time. It is difficult to give an experience of joy to someone who is absent from a house of worship because of feelings of guilt and fear. And why are people sleeping in on Sunday mornings? Because they stayed up late at the movies on Saturday night! There they found more relaxation, freedom, and aliveness than in coming to church the next morning. It is a fact that more people go to the movies on Saturday night than to church on Sunday morning.

But our Lord is not only intelligent, but adaptable as well. Instead of complaining, God does the next logical thing to reach His Children: Go to the movies on Saturday night. If you can't beat 'em, join 'em! And what a masterful job He has done! Consider the magnificent spiritual teachings that have been given through motion pictures to millions upon millions: the Force of *Star Wars*; the glowing heart of *E.T.*; the forgiveness and timeless wisdom of Mr. Miyagi of *The Karate Kid* — I tell you, God is a genius!

When I saw *The Karate Kid II*, I was moved between tears and laughter by the profound, touching lessons the sage offered his disciple — and every person in the audience. Nearly every line of that movie was worth an entire sermon. God *is* in search of man, and if He has to go into every theatre in America every Saturday night, He is happy and willing to do so.

An Apple for the Teacher

Another realm that we have eagerly patronized is the world of personal computers. PC's have gotten a lot of bad press from theologians who believe that they are the Anti-Christ. But the Anti-Christ is simply the part of our mind that believes that something could threaten the Christ. And because the Christ could never be in jeopardy, the Holy Spirit is delighted to work with and through computers to heal people.

I have been told of a computer program that does therapeutic counseling. It asks you simple questions, listens to your answers, and then rephrases them and mirrors them back to you in a way that encourages you to look more deeply into yourself to discover your own answers.

I met a woman who experienced a deep healing through this program. To this I say, "Wonderful!" I say, "Go for it!" I say that if this woman experienced a healing and her life is enriched because of it, it is real and I bless it with all my heart. Because I know that *God is the source of all healing*, if that woman was healed through that computer program, it was God who did it. And that must mean that God is willing to work through computers to heal His Children. Maybe God's idea of Who He is and how He can reach us is bigger than our idea. Indeed *everything* is God reaching out to love and heal us.

III
The Circle of Love

To really communicate, you must be willing to have a belief system that is so grand that you can include everyone and their beliefs. You must realize that everyone believes that what he believes is right, and it is not your job to convince them otherwise. Your only job is to love them and be with them in such a way that they feel forgiven, free, and loved. At that point you realize that belief systems mean very little in the grand scheme of things, while peace means a great deal.

It is important to realize that every war that has ever been fought on this planet has been a clash not between people, but because of our attachment to our own belief systems. It is ironic to me that more people have been killed in the name of religion than for any other reason. The tragic paradox of this history is clear when we realize that Jesus and the other cornerstones of the great religions were among the few who were willing to give up their bodies rather than hurt another. Yet, sadly, most of the conflicts on our planet have been religious wars in which each faction was firmly convinced that God was on their side. Meanwhile, God was on both sides — and neither.

Recently Prime Minister Margaret Thatcher of England was outraged when the Bishop of Westminster Abbey refused to hold a mass celebrating Britain's victory over Argentina in the Faulkland Islands dispute. "We cannot thank God for helping us kill our brothers," the clergyman told her. Beware believing that God is with you when someone else loses. The only sure sign that Spirit is with you is when everyone wins.

The Fruitless Argument

Perhaps the most fruitless battle is to argue about God. If you argue about God you have already lost God, for the peace of God is always accompanied by the absence of argument. You can be sure that any discrepancy over the nature of God is a folly of the ego. Spirit dwells where union is acknowledged.

One day I was passing through a building corridor when my eye was attracted by a custodian sitting and reading a book by J.R. Tolkien.

"How do you like that book?" I asked him, interested in drumming up a conversation.

"It's pretty good."

"Yes, I like Tolkien, too."

"That's great — say, I don't think I've seen you here before. Do you work here?" he inquired.

"Not regularly — I come here once a week to teach a yoga class to a group of the employees," I explained.

His brow dropped. "Yoga? — Are you aware that satan's hand is in yoga?"

Uh-oh.

"No, actually, I wasn't aware of that. I must say that I have seen the practice of yoga accomplish wonderful healings."

The conversation gradually turned from a convivial chat into a heated debate. This fellow believed that I was in the clutches of the devil, and it was his duty to save me. And I believed that it was my duty to convince him of what I believed.

"Do you believe that God is in this world?" he asked me.

"Sure," I responded. "If God is omnipresent, He must be everywhere."

"Then you must be a Pantheist," he suggested.

"What's a Pantheist?" I had to ask.

"A Pantheist is someone who believes that God is in this world," he explained.

"Well, I guess that's what I am, then." I was delighted to finally know. It sounded sort of cultured.

Then some of the other employees gathered 'round and began to take sides. It was not long before opinions were flying through the air like flak over London. I could hardly believe what had developed from a question about Tolkien.

After feeling frustrated and a little huffy, I decided I had had enough. I politely excused myself and, dusting off my shoulders, I made my way down the hall.

"What was that all about?" I wondered.

As I thought about our conversation I realized that my frustration came from trying to convince him that what I believed was right. I felt sorry for the guy, who believed that God is not in this world. I realized that I had been attempting to save him from his delusion.

Then it dawned on me that he, too, was trying to save me. In his perception I was this ignorant yogi who thought that God was in the world. That, according to his belief system — which was quite real to him — was reason enough to try to save me.

So there we were, two brothers attempting to correct one another, but actually we were entrenched in separation. We were trying to save one another, and neither of us succeeded.

As I continued down the hall I realized that the interaction would have been much more rewarding and healing for both of us if we had simply rapped about how the Mets were doing, or some other area of common interest.

That day after that conversation I vowed that I would never argue with anyone about God. Spiritual beliefs, I decided, are not a valid reason for dissension or any form of separation between brothers. I have held firmly to my vow, and I am deeply grateful. I have accepted the gift of joining, and I must say that its rewards go far beyond argument.

A Course in Miracles advises us that if we are emotionally attached to not doing something a brother asks of us, we have an important lesson to learn.

> *Recognize what does not matter, and if your brother asks you for something "outrageous" do it because it does not matter. Refuse, and your opposition establishes that it does matter to you. It is only you, therefore, who have made the request outrageous...[1]*

The poet has said, "He drew a circle that kept me out, but I had the wit to win. I drew a circle that kept him in."

Forgiveness Paves the Way

The door to real communication is opened only by true forgiveness. No communication is possible without an open mind and heart preceeding it.

Let me give you a personal example. Several years ago I had just completed the *est* training when I went to visit my mother. I was fired up by the training, and I decided that I was now ready to clean up my communication with her.

---

[1] T, p. 206

I sat my mom down at the table and began:

"Mom, I'm tired of playing this game with you."

"What game?"

"The game of mother and son."

"What are you talking about?"

"This game we've been playing, where you act like the mother and I act like the son."

"How else would you like me to act — like a beach ball?"

"You don't understand, Mom; this idea that you and I are mother and son is just an illusion."

"Not when I was in labor!"

"But Mom, we're really equals. I want to own my own power."

"Then how come you still bring me your laundry?"

She turned down the volume on the TV, looked at me and asked me, "Why are you acting so weird?"

"I learned a lot at the training, Mom, and I want to share it with you."

"Aha! So that's it! They brainwashed you in that crazy training! I knew there was something fishy when you came home the first day and wouldn't let me go to the bathroom! This is what you paid five hundred dollars for? — to tell me I'm not your mother? Is that what you learned there? They are right — you *are* an asshole! You didn't have to pay five hundred dollars for them to call you an asshole — I'll do it for a considerable discount!"

Well, that was about the end of that conversation. While I had intended to convert my mom, she helped me to learn a valuable lesson — worth far more than five hundred dollars — that it was more peaceful and powerful for me to enjoy her, and our relationship, in a way that was comfortable for her. In the long run it worked better for both of us to communicate about the things that joined, and not separated us.

At another time we had a similar interaction. One day I drove up to her apartment house to give her a ride. When she got into my car she noticed a picture of Jesus on my dashboard.

"What's he doing there?" she immediately asked.

"You mean Jesus?"

"You know who I mean — the guy with the beard and robe."

"I love him."

"You're Jewish — how did you come to fall in love with him?"

"Mom, he's one of our relatives."

"He's not in any of *my* family pictures."

"But I really like his picture there."

"Why can't you have dice, or baby shoes, or an air freshener like normal people?"

When I got home I thought about it. I felt that it was not worth having the picture on the dashboard if it upset her so much. I reasoned that it was more important to *live* his teachings than to force his picture on someone who was sensitive about it. So I put the picture in the glove compartment (when she was in the car). I also never flaunted Jesus or my love for him in front of her again. And she appreciated my respect for her feelings.

(I am reminded here of a couple who had one set of parents into born-again fundamentalism and another set into metaphysics. The couple had both kinds of books on their shelf, and when each set of parents came to visit, they would complain about finding the "other" kind of books on the shelf. So the couple bought a revolving bookcase and placed the fundamentalist books on one side of the bookcase and the metaphysical books on the other. Before the parents showed up they would simply rotate the bookcase. It made life a lot easier.)

My respect for my mom's feelings actually gave way to a miracle. Once when I went to visit her she went to her pocketbook and brought me an object. To my astonishment, it was a lovely picture of a Catholic saint.

"I saw this at a rummage sale, and I thought you would like it."

I gave her one of the biggest hugs ever, and I knew that we were healed. I learned that love and respectful understanding create miracles. Then I opened *A Course in Miracles* to find, "It is not up to you to change your brother, but merely to accept him as he is." [2]

Common Ground

Unconditional love means being willing to be with someone and love them just as they are, without asking them to change for you. It is said that *God sees us as we will be, but loves us as we are.* The love that I have most appreciated receiving is that which has seen me as beautiful just as I am. When I have received this quality of love, I want to return it and give it back many times over.

Barry Neil Kaufman and Suzi Lyte Kaufman are a couple who have become well-known for their experience in the power of real caring. They became famous through the miraculous healing of their son, Raun. This

---

[2] T, p. 156

inspiring story, documented in their book, *Son-Rise*[3], began when Raun was diagnosed as autistic at the age of eighteen months. With an IQ below thirty he was declared "retarded, incurable, and schizophrenic." Barry and Suzi set out on a search for help with Raun, but they were disappointed to find that most autistic children were being drugged, shocked, beaten, or restrained. The Kaufmans did not want to submit Raun to any of these methods, and so they sought to treat him with their love.

They began by agreeing that since Raun would not meet them on grounds of communication with which they were familiar (he would not speak words or make eye contact with them), they would meet him in ways that he would receive. They spent twelve hours a day, seven days a week, mostly in the bathroom with him (it was the only place where they could focus attention with him). During those periods of reaching out to their son, Barry and Suzi would imitate Raun, join him in the play that he enjoyed, and encourage him to reach out into the world.

One of the most important elements of the Kaufmans' work with their son was mirroring. If Raun flapped his hands, Barry and Suzi would flap theirs. If he would make a loud noise, so would they. Their philosophy was that they would not try to force him to be a part of their world if he was afraid to do so; instead they would do things to let him know that they wanted to be with him in his world, even if it was a foreign one to them. They trusted that if he recognized that they loved him he would want to share in their life, too.

It was a long and challenging process, but after six weeks the Kaufmans noticed that their son was making brief eye contact with them. The eye contact increased, and Raun began to say some words. Over a period of three years — a difficult time, yet not without reward — Raun was *completely healed* of autism. By the time he was in third grade Raun had achieved an IQ of 150, and he went on in later grades to become a straight-A student and the head of his class.

A miracle? Yes, but here we must realize that God does not work miracles just *for* us — He works them *through* us.

The Kaufmans have since gone on to accomplish similar miraculous healings with many other persons, children and adults alike. Their method is simple: you gain the grace to be yourself by allowing those around you to be themselves. Then we are all healed.

The value of the Atonement does not lie in the manner in which it

---

[3] Barry and Suzi Kaufman, *Son-Rise*, Harper and Row, 1976. The Kaufmans' work and teachings are offered by the Option Institute and Fellowship, R. D. #1, Sheffield, MA 01257

is expressed. In fact, if it is used truly, it will inevitably be expressed in whatever way is most helpful to the receiver... The whole aim of the miracle is to raise the level of communication...[4]

The Kaufman family. Barry and Suzi, right and center. Raun is at far left.

The Language of God

What is the language of God? The one you are reading. Where can God reach you? Right where you are. What can you do to find God? Let yourself be. Give yourself a break. Quit punishing and browbeating yourself. You are much harder on yourself than you need to be. Why not offer the same forgiveness to yourself that you would to others? When you do, you realize that God has never been aware of your sins, and you do not need to be concerned about them either. This is not heresy, but healing. See a forgiven world, and you can live in it. When we can see ourselves and one another as innocent, we have learned to love ourself as God loves us, and the Kingdom of Heaven is at hand.

---

[4] T, p. 20

The Laughter Of The Saints

Life is too important to be taken seriously.

In *The Life and Teachings of the Masters of the Far East*, Baird Spaulding describes his meeting with "the laughing disciple." Travelling with a group of pilgrims through extremely treacherous territory in the Himalayan Mountains, the author tells how the laughing disciple helped the group along their way:

> *In all, it was an arduous climb, but at the rough places, the chela (disciple) went ahead with laughter and song. At the more difficult places, his voice would ring out and it seemed as if it lifted us over them without an effort...*
>
> *We thought the trail on its flanks stony and perilous but now we labored over a trail much of the distance on hands and knees. Still, the song and laughter of the chela bore us onward as though on wings...*
>
> *Can you, dear reader, not see why the trail that day was not long and arduous? It all passed in an instant. The vibrations of strength, peace, power, and harmony that are always sent forth from the temples but serve to urge the travellers onward to these peaks.[1]*

We, too, are travellers over the mountain pathways of life. How valuable is the power of joy to enliven our soul as we go to meet our goal! Laughter lifts us over high ridges and lights up dark valleys in a way that makes life so much easier. It is a priceless gem, a gift of release and healing direct from Heaven. Laughter can help us through any difficulty and transform the most challenging situations. It is the doorway from misery to joy, from the dungeon to the peaks. Laughter is God's remedy for fear.

---

[1] Spaulding, Vol. III, p. 109-111

Turn Your Tragedy Into a Comedy

Life is a movie. As your own producer you can choose the type of movie you want it to be. You can make it a soap opera, a thrilling adventure, a touching romance, a boring documentary, a horror show, or a biblical epic, to name a few. My movie has been a musical comedy with some great romantic scenes. And it is clear to me that it is I who have produced it that way. Being an appreciator of comedy, I was quite impressed by Uncle Albert, a character (played by Ed Wynn) in the movie *Mary Poppins*. Uncle Albert spent a lot of time floating around his ceiling, laughing uncontrollably.

When the children in the story went to visit Uncle Albert, they found him sailing around the upper strata of his living room singing, "I love to laugh." When these serious children attempted to tether Uncle Albert back to ground level, they caught his infectious laughter. Soon the entire group rose together to enjoy a laughing party on the ceiling. The movie culminated when the skinflint bank president finally caught one of Uncle Albert's jokes, after which he died laughing. If we have to leave the stage, we might as well dance off in a chorus of chuckles instead of a dirge of doom.

Comic Relief

When I was at the funeral parlor arranging my mother's memorial service, the chapel director told me that the previous week they had hosted a funeral for a comedian. "It was one of the most original services we have had here," he told me. "The fellow who had passed on was a comedian, and for his service a number of his friends who were stand-up comics got up and did their routines for the audience. It was one of the greatest funerals we have had."

When the time came for my mom's service, I felt guided to speak. Every now and then as I spoke about her life I touched on something lovingly funny about my Jeane, such as how much I enjoyed her imitations of the romantic scenes in the soap operas she loved. I had to smile as I appreciated the unique and outrageous person she was, and the group assembled laughed with me.

At that point a little voice inside my mind chided, "This is terrible — you musn't laugh at your mother's funeral — that is disrespectful!"

But as I thought about it, I thought that my mom would probably want me to be happy. Jeane's sense of humor was one of her most endearing qualities; she could find a way to laugh at anything. She was one person who never fell prey to the disease of taking herself too seriously. Even during the last days of her sojourn in this world she was making outrageous jokes about her condition. Why, I reasoned, would she be any less jovial because she left her body? I should think her sense of humor would *improve* on the other side. I'll bet any eulogy she would have given herself would have included her delightful humor.

Several months after Jeane had passed, I was at a healing conference when I began to really miss my mom. I had been repressing a bunch of grief, and one afternoon it bubbled up to the surface. I went to my dormitory room and cried and cried for quite a while.

That evening during the healing service my friend Carla Gordan, a wonderful psychic and healer, approached me and whispered in my ear, "Your mom told me to tell you that she wants you to stop grieving, and that she promises not to ask you any more embarrassing questions."

Disarming Through Laughter

One summer while travelling in Colorado I found a toy that I thought my mom would enjoy. It was a little laughing machine, a funny-looking shaggy box with two button eyes, a cute felt tongue, and a tape recording in its tummy that howled a minute of deep belly laughter when you shook it. I brought it home for mom as a present, but she was only mildly impressed.

Then one evening she phoned me, giggling that she had found a perfect use for the doll: an obscene caller, she reported, had telephoned her. Upon realizing what he was up to, she asked him if he would mind holding on a minute. She went to the cupboard and returned to the telephone with the laughing doll, which she held up to the receiver in response to his colorful remarks. He never called again, she told me.

The Laughter of the Saints

Master Hilarion has said, "The halls of Heaven ring with the laughter of the saints."[2] Laughter is a mark of high spiritual evolution; indeed many holy people have laughed their way into Heaven!

I have had the pleasure to meet a good number of spiritual teachers, gurus, and perhaps saints. If there is one characteristic that I have found in all of them, it is joy. These truly holy persons light up any room they enter, for their lighthearted attitude is a refreshing contrast to the dreariness of mundane affairs. They win souls by the happiness that emanates from their innocent being.

I remember seeing a greatly revered Buddhist lama enter a great lecture hall and reach down to light an altar of incense. You may imagine the surprise of the assembled meditators when they saw that the incense sticks the guru had lit were actually Fourth-of-July sparklers.

When I travelled with Sri Swami Satchidananda in the Soviet Union, he won the hearts of the Russians with his childlike playfulness. One day the swami saw the driver's seat of our tour bus empty, and he jumped into it, acting as if he was stealing the bus. Swami confessed that he had always wanted to drive a bus, and here was his big chance! To see swami playing so comfortably eased all of us, and we went on our way a little freer.

---

[2] M.B. Cooke, *The Hilarion Series*, Marcus Books.

Later we went to visit a Russian Orthodox monastary. There our group was ushered into a great library, containing rare old original manuscripts of spiritual documents. Many of them were handwritten and bound in magnificent ornate covers. It was quite an experience to walk amid these stacks of ancient literature that spanned from floor to ceiling.

Swami walked calmly through the stacks, craning his neck to see the top. Finally he stopped, ran his fingers over a few books and exclaimed, "You mean I need to read all of these to find God?!"

Going for It

When our group had converged in Kennedy Airport to depart for the Soviet Union, one fellow stood out above all the rest. He was six feet-six inches tall and he was wearing a white tuxedo jacket with multi-colored paint spots decorating it. The ensemble was balanced by balloon pants, a yellow Mickey Mouse tie, a three-pointed beret, and a rubber nose. He also sported a handle-bar moustache, and his hair flowed from his towering crown all the way down to his waist. His outrageous outfit was topped with a colorful parasol that he held high above his head.

This was Dr. Hunter "Patch" Adams, a well-known and loved medical doctor who has attracted a great deal of attention for his use of humor as a healing tool. Patch has gone far beyond the usual parameters of the medical profession by having treated over twelve thousand people for free, without accepting direct or third-party payments, and holding no malpractice insurance. He is currently in the process of building a hospital for free medical service.

At his healing center, the *Gesundheit Institute*,[3] Dr. Adams combines fun and laughter with conventional and non-conventional medical practices. Between times of treating patients more formally, Patch performs juggling and teaches tightrope walking. The patients in residence live, eat, sleep, and socialize in the same facility as the doctors and ancillary medical staff. The patients are treated as family, and they are encouraged to relax and pay attention to healing the totality of their being instead of simply removing the symptoms of dis-ease. The new hospital is being built entirely on donations and grants from individuals and organizations supportive of the Institute's work.

I first met Patch a few years ago when both of us gave presentations at a holistic healing conference in Philadelphia. The brochure for the conference showed a picture of each presenter and included a potent quote by or about

---

[3] Gesundheit Institute, 404 Nelson Street, Arlington, Virginia 22203

him or her. Above Patch's picture was the quote, *"Tuck in your shirt; get a haircut; why don't you charge?"* The quote was attributed to Patch's mother.

At the opening of the conference I recognized Patch by the bright light shining around him. (His clown's outfit and rubber nose did also help me to identify him.) His aura was truly childlike and radiant. I introduced myself to him in the lobby after a lecture, where he gave me a hug, tricked me by thumbing his hand into the air when I went to shake it, and placed his knee in my hand *a la* Harpo Marx. I immediately loved this delightful soul, and we spent a good deal of the next day together sharing and laughing.

When the time for Patch's lecture came the next afternoon, he was nowhere to be found. I sat in the front row of the auditorium waiting for him to appear, when a handsome man in a white suit sat down next to me. I acknowledged the fellow, smiled, and went back to looking at my program. But there was something about the fellow that seemed familiar. Had I met him before? I looked at him again, and I admired how neatly he was dressed and how perfectly his hair was arranged. I looked again and he was smiling.

Could it be?

Nooooooo!

But it was. It was Patch. He had put on a suit, unwaxed his handlebar moustache, and bobby-pinned his long mane up under a stylish wig.

"It's for my lecture," he leaned over and whispered.

Oh.

Soon Patch was introduced as Dr. Hunter Adams, and he went up on stage to speak. The lecture was rather dry and relatively uncolorful compared to Patch's usual antics. I must admit that I was a little disappointed. "Has he sold out?" I wondered.

But my Patch did not let me down. After his description of the theory and practices of holistic health, he explained that the *Gesundheit Institute* had arranged for three speakers to represent itself today. The first was Dr. Hunter Adams, and the second was a Dr. Dizeldorf.

Then Patch reached behind his head and lifted off his wig, releasing three feet of thick locks to fall over his back and past his waist. A number of programs dropped from the hands of a number of spectators. Then, in high style, the doctor dropped his trousers, revealing some long, baggy, polka-dotted shorts. A larger number of programs dropped from a larger number of hands. Finally the man on stage put on a top hat and tuxedo, and introduced himself as Dr. Dizeldorf. The remainder of programs in the auditorium fell to the floor.

Dr. Dizeldorf had an excellent rap. He explained that in addition to the formal theories of holistic health which Dr. Adams had put forth, there was an entire other realm of healing, all too often ignored by traditional doctors, namely the essence of spirit. Dr. Dizeldorf walked to the other side of the stage where he drew the audience's attention to a large wooden cabinet which he opened to reveal a number of colorfully decorated glass vials. One said, "Essence of Giggles," another was marked "Tincture of Forgiveness," and yet another "Innocence Concentrate." Dr. Dizeldorf reached for the "Essence of Wonder" and opened it before the onlookers, who by now had, to put it in common language, had their minds blown.

"Let us experience the healing power of Wonder," the doctor announced. As he opened the bottle cap, strains of lovely music began to waft through the auditorium, the lights went down, and a colorful slide of an exquisite flower flashed on the screen just over Dr. Dizeldorf's top hat.

"Wonder is a most magnificent healer," he zestfully taught. "To allow your mind and heart to dance through the fields of Wonder will make you young and keep your spirit above all worldly troubles." Then he went on to tell some marvelous facts about how this one glorious creation, this flower, came into existence, how it is nourished by the sunlight, air, earth, and water, how it reproduces itself, and how it lives in harmony with all of the life around it. Truly it was a wonderful celebration of beauty, and my heart opened at the innocence of it.

After the Essence of Wonder, Dr. Dizeldorf opened several other tinctures and gave the audience doses of some very excellent medicine. We were touched.

The finale of this doctor's presentation sported two very large green animate objects rolling onto the stage. At the key moment two zippers opened and out from each sack popped several ladies dressed in round green costumes. After a little dance, they wiggled of the stage, singing "Give Peas a Chance."

What a mind.

Dr. Dizeldorf gave way to one final representative of *Gesundheit*, Dr. Patch Adams. Patch explained that there needs to be a connection, a bridge between formal medicine and informal fun. Thus he took the name "Patch" to symbolize the harmonious joining of the two equally important disciplines.

Then the rear stage curtain opened to reveal a tightrope stretched across the stage.

"Balance is a very important part of healing," Dr. Patch pointed out.

"Here we have a very good metaphor for balance."

He popped open a parasol (Mary Poppins would have been proud of him) and proceeded to step onto the tightrope and walk it across the stage. Then he invited two boys in the audience onto to the stage for a tightrope walking lesson, which they undertook to the delight and applause of the audience.

In Kennedy Airport en route to Russia, "conspicuous" would be a mild description for Patch's presentation. Our tour guide, Aime, (the third guide from the travel agency dispatched for our group — the first two had mysteriously dropped out at the last minute) approached Patch to confirm that he was actually a part of our citizen diplomacy group. When Patch assured him that he was, Aime's face shriveled like a football deflating under the weight of a three-hundred-pound tackle. A very white football, at that.

In that case, Aime told him, he would have to wear a suit when we crossed the Russian border and passed through Soviet customs. "The Russians are rather conservative and formal people," Aime explained, "and we do want to make a good impression on them."

Patch's response was brief and to the point: "This is my suit."

"Perhaps I didn't hear you correctly, Mr. Adams..."

"Really — I made up my mind that I want to go to Russia as a clown — all I brought are clown's outfits — my whole suitcase is full of stuff like this!"

Aime took a deep breath.

Then Patch reached into his rainbow-painted satchel and pulled out a fake passport called a "Laughport." It was issued by the *Gesundheit Institute*, and it bore a color photo of Dr. Adams sporting no less than seventeen rubber noses wrapped around his face. Beneath the photo was *Gesundheit's* diplomatic motto, *"Long Live Nasal Diplomacy!"*

Aime looked for the nearest bathroom.

When we arrived in Russia, we found that nasal diplomacy was indeed a powerful way to build bridges from heart to heart. Patch took to the streets, the subways, restaurants — anywhere an audience was available. He played with the Russian people, children and adults alike. He made friends with kids in the parks, he crashed a wedding, and he embraced Russian war heroes in Red Square. And it worked — the Russians loved him! Being very good judges of character, they appreciated the aliveness and sincerity of his way of reaching out. He even wore his outfit to our diplomatic meetings with the Soviet Peace Committees in Leningrad and Moscow.

(Patch's one disappointment was that the Soviet Peace Committee did not give him permission to wear his gorilla suit in Red Square, as he requested. "Personally, we have no objection," they explained — "but there is a rather strong chance that you may get arrested — or captured." Then the committee engaged in an informal debate as to whether Dr. Adams was more likely to be arrested or shot. After ample consideration they did, however, grant Dr. Adams permission to wear his costume in his hotel room, if he liked.)

Without exception the man with the funny outfit accomplished what many others could not.

At our final dinner, at which each of us shared what the trip had meant to us, Patch rose and thanked the group for "the greatest opportunity in my life to be nutty." He explained that "before this journey I thought about the way that I could most powerfully serve to make contact with the hearts of the

Russian people, as well the Americans on this trip. I realized that the greatest contribution I could make would be to be myself, and clowning is the way I most enjoy expressing myself. It felt like quite a risk for me to pack only clown clothing, but I felt that I had to go for expressing myself one hundred percent. I did, and I am very glad indeed.''

When Aime stood to speak, he confessed, ''I must admit that I had my considerations about going with this group; but after spending two weeks with all of you and feeling the purity of your intention, I feel sure that God assigned me to this group — and my life has changed so beautifully! Thank you for being yourselves!''

The Humor Potential Movement

There is a wonderful new *genre* of new age spiritual humorists, and I feel that the phenomenon is very healthy. One well-known guru of giggles goes by the name of Swami Beyondananda,[4] ''the Yogi from Muskogi.'' He wears a rainbow Bozo wig and offers enlightening discourses on such important topics as ''Teach Your Dog to Heal,'' ''How to Eliminate Ought-ism,'' and ''Tantrum Yoga.'' Guru Huggin'-Dazs[5] offers vital new age products, including the Chakra Shaver, The Buddha Beeper, and for persons who would like to improve their ability to channel spirits, Enti-tea. Pat Weeks, the Co-President of the Human Unity Institute,[6] has revealed his true identity as Da Free Lunch, founder of the Born-Yesterday Church of Occasional Clarity. The Church, Da explains, now meets on the Number 38 cross-town bus. This has been their home since they were barred from meeting in the laundromat after they emulated Jesus' example by ripping the money-changers off the walls. Way to go, Da.

Spirituality, Not Boredom

Let's face it: without laughter, the spiritual path would be boring. Spirituality was never intended to numb anyone into submission; its lofty purpose is to raise our spirits into Heaven. Peace is not the absence of liveliness, but the epitome of aliveness in expression. St. Ignasius stated that

---

[4] Swami Beyondananda, PO Box 1934, Ann Arbor, Michigan 48103
[5] Guru Huggin'-Dazs, PO Box 450, Kula, Hawaii 96790
[6] Human Unity Institute, PO Box 3431, San Clemente, California 92672

"the glory of God is humankind fully alive." If you are not fully alive you are not glorifying God. Deadbeats are the devil's spokesmen. Make your life an ode to joy and celebration! You will not only be an extremely happy and productive person, but you will be an inspiration to those around you. You will offer healing to everyone you meet, by virtue of the enthusiasm of your spirit.

I have discovered a great dynamic in public speaking. I have seen that audiences do not respond so much to the words or the information that a speaker is offering, but to the feeling he or she is imparting. Facts can be found in a book, but joy can be shared only from one person's heart to another. I have found that to stand before a group with happiness in my heart is a gift to myself as well as the group.

I have thus developed two goals upon which my lectures and work-shops are founded: (1) to inspire myself, and (2) to entertain myself. While this may at first seem to be self-centered, it is actually the greatest contribution I could make to an audience. Nothing is more boring than a speaker who is not interested in what he or she is talking about, and there is nothing more exciting that someone who is turned on by what they are discussing. I don't think I've ever given a totally serious lecture, and I hope I never will. God is not totally serious, and therefore neither do I have to be so. (A retreatant once told me that she likes my lectures because she enjoys watching me laugh at my own jokes. Well, at least I can always count on myself.)

Laughter as Prayer

I consider laughter to be a very high form of prayer. Church is something you can take with you wherever you go. It is supposed to be place of song and celebration, not duty and sleep. If you are in song and celebration you are in church, and you don't need a special building for that. All the world is a church, and if you are in the consciousness of love, you are praying with the joy of your being.

Ramtha has said,

> *The greatest prayer you could ever pray would be to laugh every day. For when you do, it elevates the vibratory frequency within your being such that you could heal your entire body.*[7]

---

[7] Ramtha, *I Am Ramtha*, Beyond Words Publishing, 1986, p. 80

My friend David prays very devoutly through laughter. His temple is the local movie theatre, and his rabbi is Woody Allen. I always enjoy going to the movies with him because I know that even if the movie isn't funny, David will be. David is the only person I know who goes into hysterics when the opening credits come on the screen. As he begins to howl, everyone in the audience turns and looks in our direction to see who is laughing so outrageously. Then I slide down into my seat so they won't think it is me. David is indeed an advanced soul; he really knows how to get his money's worth in a movie. He really knows how to pray.

Where Sin Ends

A Course in Miracles tells us that "the separation occurred when the Son of God (all of us) forgot to laugh." In other words, we kicked ourselves out of Heaven when we began to take ourselves too seriously. I am certain that we take ourselves more seriously than God takes us. God has a marvelous sense of humor. If we want to be Godly, we too must learn to laugh.

The *Course* also tells us that "all sin ends in laughter." If you cannot laugh about something, you can be sure you have not seen the whole truth about it. The truth always contains some element of humor. If you cannot see the lighter side of an issue, you can be certain that you have lost your way. And when you can laugh about it, you have found your way.

When you see the nothingness of something that you thought was a terrible sin, you will be able to laugh about it. Then you are free. Such a wonderful release should be honored as a sign of healing. This is a good way to gauge your healing: if you find you can laugh at something that was once a sensitive or fearful subject for you, you know that you have risen out of the swamp of self-pity and come to the high perspective of holy humor.

How the World Will End

While you have heard many maudlin theories about the end of the world, there is one that you may not have considered. Consider it now, for it is much closer to the truth than the sardonic tales to which you have been exposed.

The world you have known has been built on fear. And it is perpetuated through fear, and fear alone. Fighting fear with fear is like fighting alcoholism with another drink. The way out must be entirely different than the way in. To escape, you must go in a new direction, not the one by which you entered.

The only way that a fearful, dark world can end is in light. There is but one way to be liberated from the heavy oppression of dreams of death, and that is with a joyful heart. Throw away the case for condemnation and feel the freedom of your spirit! A happy heart generates a force field of love in which doubt, disaster, and dismay have no power to interrupt the flow of your good. Sages and mystics have known this important principle, and they have taught it with the illumination of their being. And those who have eyes to see and ears to hear have seen and heard.

A Course in Miracles gives us a very clear description of the end of the world, quite unlike any we have heard before:

> *The world will end in joy, because it is a place of sorrow...The world will end in peace, because it is a place of war...The world will end in laughter, because it is a place of tears. Where there is laughter, who can longer weep?*[8]

It is not your lot to weep, and you were not put here to suffer. To find value in suffering is to condemn yourself to hell. The Spirit that created you would not have Its Children in pain. Wake up, arise, and go on your way with laughter in your heart! Wipe away your tears, and live in love! You may explore every highway, byway, mountain, and valley of this world, and no matter how far you travel or how many years you search, you will come only to this very conclusion: life is for loving, joy, and celebration — *now.*

> *...Gladly will you walk the way of innocence together, singing as you behold the open door of Heaven and recognize the home that called to you. Give joyously to one another the freedom and the strength to lead you there.*[9]

---

[8] M, p. 36
[9] T, p. 399

Beyond Karma

I am under no laws but God's.
- A Course in Miracles[1]

One day while standing in line at a cafeteria in Newark Airport I saw a large sign with bold letters: *"It is impolite to pass persons in the cafeteria line while they are waiting to be served."* Alright, I figured, I can live with that.

The next week I was in the very same line when I looked at the sign again. To my astonishment I read this week, *"It is **polite** to pass persons in the cafeteria line while they are waiting to be served."*

The laws of politeness had been changed in one short week!

Who made those laws? Who did they bind? Who could change them?

It is clear that the laws of the world exist by agreement only, and it does not take a lot of experiences these days to cause a thinking person to begin to question what he has been taught to be true. Political, social, and even scientific laws have undergone unbelievable upheavals, and the degree of revolution in even the most conservative communities of thought has been enough to plunge anyone into a stymie.

If we are confused by looking to the outer world for answers, it is no wonder. I recently read that in 1957 the American Psychology Association declared that homosexuality was no longer a disease. This means that either every homosexual was healed when the declaration was issued, or that the description of homosexuality as a disease was incorrect before 1957. Or after 1957. No wonder homosexuals have been confused! The psychologists keep changing their mind about whether or not they are sick!

I also wonder what it must have been like to be a Catholic and be told that eating meat on Friday is no longer a sin. Was it a sin, and it stopped being sinful? If so, how could something be a sin against God one day and not a sin the next? And if it never was a sin, why and wherefore did the church say it was? And if the church changed its mind about that sin, what else might it change its mind about? And if the church made a mistake, who's

---

[1] W, p. 132

147

in charge anyway?

You might also be fascinated to know that until the sixth century A.D. reincarnation was an official doctrine of the Catholic Church. At that time the governors of the church body met at the famous Synod of Constantinople. There, by a vote of five to four, the board decided that reincarnation was no longer true. Five to four! That means that one man's vote determined that you get to come around only once instead of making a return trip. Just think: What if the man with the swing vote was hard of hearing and he was just scratching his ear when the vote was taken? Woody Allen would have a field day with that one!

In addition to being humorous, it can be quite startling and even scary to realize that so many — perhaps all — of the laws to which we have bowed are unfounded. This is what drives people to depression and despair. But seen in a higher light all of these contradictions and irresolutions can lead us nicely to a perfect position for learning the truth about who we are. Rapidly we are learning that we cannot look to the outer world for inner answers. We cannot depend on man-made laws to show us the way to peace. If are going to learn the truth of our own being, the only source that we can consult with confidence is *the integrity of our own being.*

A Higher Law

A friend of mine, a fellow student of *A Course in Miracles*, was about to undergo a biopsy to examine a thickening in her body. The morning before she was to undergo the surgery I was sitting in meditation when I was shown a vision.

In my mind's eyes I saw the edge of a photographic negative. I could see but a half an inch at the top and the bottom of the picture. Upon looking more closely, I saw that it was actually an x-ray. But why could I not see the entire x-ray? I looked again to see that the x-ray was covered by a book. It was a large book with its pages opened, and it obscured nearly the entire x-ray. Peering yet further, I recognized that the book was *A Course in Miracles.*

"What is the meaning of this vision?" I asked.

Immediately the message was made clear to me: the x-ray represented a picture of the body, and specifically an image of illness and the limitation of the body. In this case it represented a possible fearful result of my friend's examination.

A Course in Miracles, on the other hand, represented to me the power of God's healing love, forgiveness, and freedom from the laws of bodily limitation or retribution.

Quickly I realized the implications of this vision: The x-ray was obscured by the *Course* to show me that *The Law of Grace supercedes the laws of the body.* This woman's case had been turned over to a higher Doctor operating under a higher Law—the unfailing power of forgiving love. Healing took precedence over fear, forgiveness replaced retribution, and peace abided where suffering once ruled.

You can imagine my happiness when the next afternoon I received a telephone call from my friend informing me that the examination showed that there was nothing wrong with her; the doctor had given her a clean bill of health.

This vision is not concerned so much with a particular person or even with *A Course in Miracles,* but with a principle:

There is a Law higher than the laws of this world. It is a Law of total love, forgiveness, and healing.

Moreover,

You do not deserve to be ill. You do not deserve to be punished. You do not deserve to die. You deserve only to be totally at peace and completely happy. You are a Child of a Loving God, and your Father wants only perfect joy for you.

The Choice of Vision

Our happiness depends entirely on which picture we are willing to look at. In the inspiring motion picture *Resurrection,* the story of a woman who learned to use her healing power, there is a marvelous scene in which a woman with a degenerated spine comes to the healer for treatment. The woman's doctor tells them, "I don't know how you're going to help her — I've seen the pictures."

The healer proceeds to lay her hands on the patient, fervently intent in prayer for her release. Within a short time the woman arises and walks for the first time in years.

As the astonished doctor exclaims, "I'll be...!" the healer interrupts him and explains, "The difference, doctor, is that I didn't see the pictures."

Actually, she did see pictures, but they were not the same images the doctor saw. The healer did not recognize the patient's limitation; instead she focused on the woman's perfection and her reality as a whole being. She understood that the woman was born not of flesh, but of Spirit, and the rightful heritage of all spiritual beings is perfect health and peace of mind. The healer knew that the patient was not subject to physical laws, but Spiritual Principle. And her vision was strong and clear enough that the woman felt the truth and accepted it.

Here is a way to summarize the principle of all healing:

> *Spirit is in a state of grace forever.*
> *Your reality is only spirit.*
> *Therefore you are in a state of grace forever.*[2]

The Law of Endless Joy

You have reached the point in your life where you are ready to go beyond the laws that have kept you small, separate, and fearful. You are ready to accept your true identity as a Child of a loving God, and live in a way that reflects joy and celebration. As you step forward you will have a light shining around you that will cause those you meet to ask what good has come to you, and you will inspire them to awaken to the beauty of their own divinity. All because you realize that you live not under the limited laws of the world, but you are subject only to the Law of Eternal Love.

> *Think of the freedom in the recognition that you are not bound by all the strange and twisted laws you have set up to save you. You really think that you would starve unless you have stacks of green paper strips and piles of metal discs. You really think a small round pellet or some fluid pushed into your veins through a sharpened needle will ward off disease and death. You really think you are alone unless another body is with you...*
> *Think further; you believe in the "laws" of friendship, of "good" relationships and reciprocity...*

[2] T, p. 7

There are no laws but God's. Dismiss all foolish magical beliefs today, and hold your mind in silent readiness to hear the Voice That speaks the truth to you...About the Love your Father has for you. About the endless joy He offers you...[3]

To be healed we must experience a *complete reversal* of the way of thinking that we have known. While this may at first seem radical (and it is!) it must be apparent that if we have not been succeeding according to the laws that we have been taught, then *the laws that we have been taught must not be true.* Here we must reiterate the motto that a friend of mine sent me on his business card:

*If you always do what you've always done,
You'll always get what you've always gotten.*

— a disarmingly simple lesson! Another way of saying this is:

*If you always think the way you've always thought,
You'll always create what you've always created.*

The Reversal

The Apostle Paul understood this idea very well. He spoke of it as *"metanoia"* — the transformation of the thinking process to see divinity in all things. If you want to create more rewarding experiences in your life, you must start to think about who you are and what you deserve in a new and freer way. This is the critical leap of consciousness which enables you to be healed and then to become a miracle worker. The only requirement for Heaven is to *see only perfection.* The moment we are willing to accept complete forgiveness of ourself and the entire world, we realize that *all there has ever been is Heaven.* And if we have seen anything other than total beauty that opens our heart nearly to tears, we have been seeing something that was not there.

[3] W, p. 132-133

Truth or Appearances

Sometimes on summer days I enjoy sitting by the river behind my house and watching the jet planes fly overhead in their approach pattern to the metropolitan airport. One thing that I have puzzled over and learned a great deal from is the fact that the sight and sound of an airplane seem to be coming from two distinctly different locations. Because light travels much faster than sound, the visual appearance of the plane is in one place, while the sound of the plane seems to be coming from a location far behind the sight of the craft. This is why it sometimes appears that one plane is flying silently overhead, while the sound of what seems to be another unseen airplane travels behind it. Actually there is but one airplane, but the sight of it is reaching my eyes before the sound of it reaches my ears. One source has been divided into the appearance of two.

Sages have been exhorting us for centuries not to have faith in the messages of the senses, for they are deceptive. Here is a clear example that things are not what they appear to be. Where is the real airplane? Is it the one I see or the one I hear? A little logic will reveal that it is *neither*. By the time I see or hear it, the real airplane (if there is one at all!) has moved on from the position at which it generated the sights and sounds that my senses recorded. Therefore *none of what I am seeing or hearing is correct!* All that I am seeing is a reflection, a shadow, a phantom of the past.

Is it any wonder, then, that *A Course in Miracles* in the early lessons reminds us, *"I see only my past."*[4] and *"I see nothing as it is now."*[5]? We cannot afford to let our mind wander into the past or the future, which is just a projection of the past; (what evidence do we have that our future will be *anything at all* like our past?) When we leave the serenity of the present moment we find only anxiety, for we have strayed into pure illusion. Our only escape from anxiety is to find the peace available to us in the now, which is not threatening at all. As I have examined my anxieties I have found that every single one of them, without exception, is founded on a thought of guilt from the past or a fear of the future.

The world remains stuck only to the extent that we agree that appear-

---

[4] W, p.11

[5] W, p. 15

ances are true; the moment we withdraw the power of our agreement in error we are free to see what is really there.

I was told the story of an airplane that made a stop for refueling. As the passengers were stretching in the terminal while waiting for the next leg of their journey to commence, the pilot saw a blind passenger with a seeing-eye dog standing near the gate. The pilot asked the man if he would like to have his dog walked, and when the man appreciatively answered "Yes," the pilot decided he would like to get some exercise by walking the canine himself. The other passengers, however, not seeing what had transpired, saw the pilot walking with a seeing eye dog and quickly fled to the other airlines to exchange their tickets!

It is up to each of us to choose what we want to align with — love or fear. No one else can choose for us, and blessedly so. As we mobilize our willingness to know and see the truth, we shall surely find it. Several years ago I sent Richard Bach, the author of *Jonathan Livingston Seagull* and *Illusions*, a copy of one of my books. Several months later I received a post card from him, thanking me for the book and noting, "It seems as though the family of those of us who do not believe in appearances is a large one!"

Extra Strawberries: A Reversal in Practice

Several years ago when I was visiting some friends in Canada we went out one Saturday afternoon to buy some groceries for dinner. Riding in the back seat of the car on our way home I discovered some of the most succulent strawberries I had ever seen. Those juicy red morsels called to me from atop the grocery bag. I reached over and began to nibble on one. "Delicious!" I exclaimed to myself, and I took another.

The ride continued, our conversation deepened, and my strawberry-fest accelerated. Handful by handful I scooped the sweet fruits out of the sack and munched on them with savory pleasure. As we pulled into the driveway I noticed that I had lightened the load of strawberries by about half.

As we got out of the car I heard my hostess remark, "I can't wait to get inside and start on the strawberry shortcake I have planned for dessert. Yummy!"

"Which way to the bus station?" I wondered, seeking the nearest avenue of escape. Here my friends invited me for dinner, and I ate up their dessert! I reached for a tissue to wipe the red spots off my lips, but I quickly realized I would have to confess my transgression.

"I don't quite know how to tell you this, Carole," I blurted out, "but I just ate a significant amount of the strawberries." She turned her head to find a sheepish grin on my face. I knew she could see a melange of guilt and strawberries in my aura. Then the law of karma called to me as a way to expiate myself and atone for my sin. "I guess I'll have to have a piece of shortcake with no strawberries on it."

"No strawberries on your piece?!" she exclaimed. "The fact that you ate so many strawberries makes me happy to know you like them so much. Thank you for telling me! That means you get *extra* strawberries on your piece!"

We hugged.

That was a very quick and powerful lesson in how the Law of Love gently cancels the law of karma. Had my hostess been a teacher of limitation or fear, she would have agreed that I had done wrong, squandered my allotment, and now have me balance out my sin and pay my debt by experiencing a lack. But instead she was a teacher of abundance, demonstrating that her faith was not in error, but love.

Because Jesus knew the truth of the higher law of abundance he could feed thousands with a few baskets of fish. I cannot see him dividing a few baskets into thousands of tiny pieces or giving to some and not to all. Instead the master prayed over the food, affirmed total supply through the Law of Grace, and fed the multitudes. *The Christ knows no lack, restriction, or punishment.* When we act in the consciousness that all we ever need will be supplied of the Great God of All There Is, we step beyond the appearance of lack and affirm ever-present good.

The Way Out of Hell

I saw a cute cartoon showing a man pushing a wheelbarrow of rocks through hell. While those around him were sweating and suffering, this happy fellow was whistling along his way with a wide smile on his face. Standing behind a rock were two little devils with pitchforks, watching how happy this fellow was. Exasperated, one of the devils turns to the other and remarks, "I don't think we're getting to this guy!"

The fellow at the wheelbarrow was not in hell because he *chose* not to be. While the appearance of hell was all around him, his consciousness was not at all in hell, but in lightheartedness and laughter. He beat the devil not by anger or rebellion, but simply by being happy.

You and I can easily accomplish the same state of wholeness by taking refuge in the truth of love that abides within our hearts, and refusing to give agreement to the appearance of evil. Ramtha tells us that "...the only thing you have done wrong is to believe that you have done something wrong."[6] When you love who you truly are you accept *every moment* as an opportunity to rise higher into the open arms of joy. In this state of creative living the past, the future, and the notion of karma quickly disappear into delightful belly laughter. It is all quite perfect, and you are doing much better than you think.

Werner Erhard tells us, "If God told you exactly what it is you were to do, you would be happy doing it no matter what it was. What you're doing is what God wants you to do. Be happy."[7]

The Immediacy of Grace

How quickly and easily can the laws of limitation be overcome? I will tell you a story to illustrate:

A friend of mine was undergoing treatment for cancer. The doctors had been monitoring his condition, and he was asked to take some chest x-rays before surgery.

Standing behind the x-ray equipment my friend heard the lab technician tell him to take in a deep breath and hold it. As he did so he realized that this instruction was similar to that of his meditation class. In the class the teacher had instructed the students to visualize drawing white light into their hearts and then pouring it throughout their bodies.

Wanting to make the most of every opportunity to be healed, my friend decided to imagine that he was breathing in the breath of God and blessing himself with peace as he held his breath while the x-rays were being taken. He lifted his mind to God and visualized the pure light of Living Spirit filling him with each breath. Finally the technician dismissed him, and he felt relaxed.

The next day the doctor called him and told him that there was no sign of any disease on the x-ray and that no surgery would be necessary. "There is no medical explanation," the doctor reported, " — It must be a miracle."

---

[6] Weinberg, *Ramtha*, p. 133
[7] Werner Erhard, *If God Had Meant Man to Fly, He Would Have Given Him Wings*, Werner Erhard, 1973.

II

To become true miracle workers we must challenge every belief we have. If a belief is true it will stand up under any circumstances. And if it is false we are better off knowing that we have been wrong, that we may quickly go on to discover what is really true.

If the laws of the physical plane and time were true, they would apply to all of us. For one of us to rise above them means that *any of us* can be free of them. Jesus restored sight to the blind, raised the dead, and ascended himself. The master could perform these wondrous acts because he was *aware of the higher law* and he was willing to use it. That selfsame law is *equally and fully available to you and me,* and if we are willing to use it we shall surely be free of the hellish nightmare of limitations with which we have been hypnotized.

The Dreamer and the Dream

The idea of karma is nothing more or less than a belief system. It is nothing more because it exists only in the minds of those who believe in it, and it is nothing less because you have the power to create an entire world based upon a false belief and then live in it as if it were true. Yet even the blackest nightmare can be escaped instantly by realizing that you are the dreamer and not a prisoner of the dream.

Looking more closely at the belief system of karma, Ramtha tells us,

> What you term "karma" is not the law of God. It is the law of those who believe in it...The laws of karma are indeed a reality, but only for those who believe in them...The only laws that exist are those which you allow to be effective in your kingdom...If you choose to believe in karma you will certainly be in the hands of your own creation, for you have given power to that belief.[8]

---

[8] Weinberg, *Ramtha*, p. 129

To see God as punitive, wrathful, or remembering of our sins is to attribute human nearsightedness to a divinity that far transcends the ways that we have learned to hurt ourselves. The French Philosopher Rousseau said, "God created man in His image and likeness, and then man returned the compliment." In our madness we have seen an angry God, not realizing that we are but looking upon our own face reflected in a distorted mirror of cosmic proportions. Because we have not come to terms with our own sense of guilt, fear, and retaliation, we have projected those attributes onto a vengeful Deity who will swoop down upon us with His aweful will and in the Last Judgement condemn us to the hell that we deserve by our wretched sinfulness. We have butchered and perverted a God of only love to believe in a father that condemns us to hell rather than welcomes us to Heaven.

This picture of God was not painted by Him, but by fearful children who forgot who they were and believed they had sinned. We are told in *A Course in Miracles* that some of what is written in the New Testament is not the word of God, but the projection of fearful disciples who had not come to terms with their own sense of guilt, and projected it onto God in an effort to relieve themselves of what they *thought* they had done wrong.[9]

Clearly this God cannot be the One that created us in love, and has brought us to the point of awakening at which we now stand. Clearly we must be ready to learn of a God of Healing, of Peace, and of Joy. We are ready to know a wondrous and beauteous Father, for we are finally willing to find goodness within ourselves. And surely we will find in our Father what we find in ourself.

A New Heaven, A New Earth

In bowing to karma we have bound ourselves by small thinking and agreement in the notion that we are mortal creatures subject to time, separation, and punishment. We have used the idea of karma against ourselves to romanticize relationships, avoid living in the moment, and justify suffering. We have unconsciously created a parasitic monster of a belief system that denies to us the peace of God that is available to all of us at every moment.

We cannot afford to be spiritual mugwumps. (A mugwump is someone who sits with his mug on one side of the fence and his wump on the other.) Spiritual teachers have told us with one breath that all that exists is the eternal

---

[9] T, p. 87

now, and with the next breath that what is happening to us now is the result of our past. *Both cannot be true.* All that is happening to us now is the result not of our past, but our *current* thoughts. Change your current thoughts and all that is happening to you and around you will change quickly — even, as Saint Paul said, "in the twinkling of an eye."

Jesus was a teacher not of karma, but of Grace. When the adulterous woman was brought before him, about to be stoned, he told her, "Your sins are forgiven," and the people were astonished. Her sins were forgiven because in his eyes *she had never sinned.* We must learn to look at ourselves through those same forgiving eyes. When we see what the Christ sees, we become one with the Light of the World.

When the disciples asked Jesus, "Is this man blind because of the sins of his parents, or his own sins?" he answered, "Neither...but to demonstrate the power of God,"[10] and he proceeded to heal the man. Jesus' consciousness was not immersed in ideas of sin, but in the magnanimity of light. Had Jesus harbored any concept of condemnation, his efforts to undo the affliction would have been impotent. But Jesus knew the truth of total forgiveness. In *A Course in Miracles* Jesus tells us,

> *"I do not want you to allow any fear to enter into the thought system toward which I am guiding you. I do not call for martyrs but for teachers. No one is punished for sins, and the Sons of God are not sinners."*[11]

As Ramtha puts it,

> *"Know that you will never have to pay for anything that you have ever thought or done, in this life or any life, as long as you forgive yourself for it. Forgiveness of self is the divine act that removes from your soul the guilt and judgement of self that limit the expression of the God that you are."*[12]

The Test of Belief

There are a few questions which will reveal to you your readiness to go beyond the painful laws this world was created to preserve:

---

[10] John 9:2-3

[11] T, p. 88

[12] Weinberg, *Ramtha, p. 132*

1. Do you believe that you are being punished or that you deserve to be punished for any bad things you have done in the past?
2. Do you believe you must pay off any karma before you can be healed, free, or peaceful?
3. Do you believe that any suffering or sacrifice you undergo now will earn you happiness, peace, or a place in Heaven at a later date?

To answer yes to any of these questions is to deny that you are already forgiven, loved, and free. Moreover, you must realize that you have the power to create suffering, separation, and delay of healing *merely by your belief that you deserve pain.*

Imagine what it would feel like to know that none of what you believe is your karma can bind you in the least. The sense of exhiliration that must come from even the slightest consideration of this notion is phenomenal! And it is but a taste of the freedom that you will feel when you fully accept the grace in which your soul was created and in which you will always live.

You will burst out of your shell of fear and soar far above the petty limitations to which you have paid homage. The question is not "whether," but "when?" — and that is entirely up to you! Raise your head in dignity and walk the earth as a free soul, for *so you are. Dare to forgive yourself.* This is the leap of faith with which you will learn that it has been but your own mind that has stood between you and total freedom. Then you will demonstrate to the world that God has never condemned you or anyone.

Challenge your belief in a punishing Lord and you will see how awesomely the world is ruled by unnecessary guilt and fear. Make a stand for total forgiveness by starting with your own. You will wonder how you could have spent so many years looking down the barrel of a gun that was held by your own hand. And you will dance for joy at the freedom that awaits you the moment you are willing to release it.

You are destined not for suffering, pain, or hell, but to discover that you are forgiven, loved, and heir to the entire Kingdom of Love. You do not have to wait until you die to inherit it. Jesus said, "the Kingdom of Heaven is within you." He also told us, "Come, for all things are now ready."

All Good Karma

If there is any such thing as karma, it is all good. To divide karma into good and bad is to reenact the eating of the fruit of the knowledge of good and evil that threw our forebears into hell. You will be thrown into hell, too, if you see evil, for no one escapes the effects of what he chooses to see. And you will instantly be free of all fear the moment you choose again and allow your vision to rest on a gentle world.

The only way out of the maze of karma is to see all as perfect. Here is how you beat the devil, for satan has power only over those who believe he exists. God told Abraham, "Lift up your eyes"[13] and "Leave your country behind, leave your people behind, and go to the land I will guide you to."[14]

Metaphysically, Spirit was telling Abraham to raise his thoughts to a *new consciousness*; to let go of his old idea of who the people in his life were; to release his belief that he lived in a politically-defined country; and to go to the land that God would guide him to — not referring to a physical place, but a state of higher *awareness*, a consciousness of pure love, of abundance and joyful life.

Now you, too, must free yourself of the bondage of old thought patterns and habits of fear, unworthiness, and disease. You must step forward with dignity into the assumption of your true identity — a Child of Perfect Light. See everything that happens as a gift of God, and you will see the falsity of notions of bad karma.

Believe that every experience that comes to you is a blessing from God to help you learn that you are lovable, capable, and deserving of happiness. Given these gifts, could any experience be truly bad? Nothing can hurt you except your own mind. Be free of any notion that you are or have ever been outside of God's perfect love.

From Karma to Grace

There is only one way to escape the cycles of karma, and that is to *get off the wheel*. Forget about your blasted karma, and just start loving! Those who love truly can but laugh at the notion of checks and balances, for they have accepted a Law that far outshines those of this world. Even the most fleeting glimpse of such a Love must change a life forever. You have allowed your ego to have a field day indulging in reveries of the amount of judgement laid upon you and the penalty required. The notion of punishment is totally foreign to the One Who created you as perfect as Himself. He simply watches patiently as you play the game of limitation, knowing full

---

[13] *Genesis 13:14*
[14] *Genesis 12:1*

well that you will arise and run to His open arms when you have tired of the rules that you have created. Let go of your past, release your dreams of the future, and begin to celebrate the magnificence of your being this very moment!

Rise into the awareness that your true being is *totally beyond karma.* You are living Spirit, and Spirit cannot be determined by an idea that is smaller than itself. You have been told that you are created in the image and likeness of God, yea, even that you are God, and you have even mouthed or at least thought these noble ideas yourself. If that is so — and I assure you that it is — HOW COULD GOD HAVE KARMA? God is so far beyond karma that all He knows is perfect Grace. If you are willing to look at your life — yea, all life — from that lofty perspective, you shall be free of all that you believed bound you.

Masters, not Servants

There is one law to life, and that is the Law of Love. Because God is love, when we are loving we are at peace. In such a lofty state of awareness we can see that the entire universe exists only for the purpose of extending the love we already are. Every avenue we walk upon is a way to learn love, for "the healing of God's Son (all of us) is all the world is for."[15] Because love is the first and final lesson of all life, we can learn the truth of love through everything we do.

Sometimes while studying the esoteric or mystical sciences we may be sidetracked into becoming enamored with the mechanics of the science and we may lose sight of the truth that the science was given to teach. The purpose of all spiritual science is to help us become freer, lighter, and aware that we are forgiven. To the extent that we learn to reclaim our nature as whole beings, it may be said that our study is leading us to truth. If we lose sight of this, our only purpose, we take a detour from the highway home.

We fall prey to a sense of limitation when we see ourselves as determined by a source outside ourselves. Neither the stars nor past lives nor karma of any kind can rule us in the least when we realize that we are Children of a Creative God, and that we have the power to create our life in any way we choose, no matter what we have created in the past. At any moment it is our own mind, and only our own mind that determines what will happen to us.

---

[15] *T, p. 476*

The stars, card readings, books, or any other forms of divination are nothing more or less than a picture of your consciousness. You created them. Can something you created have power over you? Only if you believe it can. While these methods and thousands like them can serve as excellent tools to assist you in learning important principles of living, there comes a time — perhaps today — when you must claim your identity as the master of your life. Never again will anything outside of you have the power to influence you. At such a momentous point you may dismiss the charts you have written in the past and write a new one. Choose again and reclaim power over your life, your love, and your destiny.

The One Decision

You now have one, and only one decision to make. Actually this is the only decision you have ever had to make, but now it has risen to the surface for you to make it clearly. All other decisions are offspring of this one, and you will be able to easily answer every other question when you have answered this one truthfully. This question is:

> *Do you have power over your life, or*
> *does life have power over you?*

Are you a creator, or a slave? Are you a master, or a servant? Are you empty, or are you whole?

You have given your power away to people, circumstances, and ideas, and you have hurt yourself by it more than you know. You have made yourself small and weak by bestowing a crown of authority to that which is inert. When Pilate asked Jesus, "Don't you know I have the power to crucify you?" Jesus answered, "You have no power but that which is given you by my Father."

You can make that statement with the same authority. The stars, food, medicines, gurus, and all belief systems have absolutely no power but that which you invest in them. Realize this, and you are free in the flash of one correct thought. You created your gurus in various forms to tell you what you already knew. If you did not already know the Truth, how then would you know that they were correct? A guru, like a consultant of any kind, is someone who borrows your watch to tell you what time it is. And it is about time you started to tell time for yourself.

Wake up to your own magnificence! You shine brighter than all the stars in the heavens, your food is love, your medicine is forgiveness, your guru is your own self, and the only belief you need is that you deserve love. Remember this, mark this, know this, believe this, love this, practice this, and you will be lifted into exuberant joy in a twinkling of an eye. *There is nothing that this world can give you that is not already within you.* Learn this now and you save yourself eons of suffering!

God will not make you suffer — God has never made anyone suffer — but you can bring suffering upon yourself by looking outside yourself for peace. Look within, and there will all your answers be found. Your Father has imbued within you the Spark of the Divine, and you have come to earth to search for something that you brought with you. Find it, and you are absolved from further yearning.

There is but one position greater than a servant of the Lord, and that is to be His Child. The child of a king is heir to the entire kingdom, and when you are ready to let go of the idea that you are separate from your Father, you will rule your kingdom with the same authority with which He rules His. Decree your identity and all that you have denied will rightfully be restored to you.

Part II
THE HEALING

WALKING in LIGHT

Beaver's Truth

Only the whole truth will do
For me and you
The One dreamed it split in two
Now this part of your dream loves you
— Maitreya Stillwater, *"The Whole Truth"* [1]

It seems that the lessons I need to learn find me.

One morning as I was walking through my living room I noticed the TV rerunning an old *Leave It to Beaver* episode. Feeling that this was a delicacy too tasty to pass by, I sat down and watched.

In this mellow drama Beaver had gotten a "D" on his report card. While passing through the den that evening, Wally and — you guessed it — Eddie Haskell discovered the telltale report card on the desk, waiting for Ward to sign it.

"Hey, Wally, let's play a little trick on the Beave!" proposes Eddie, in the obnoxious manner for which he has become known and loved.

"What's that, Eddie?"

"Let's change the 'D' on the report card to a 'B.' Your Dad will be tickled that Beaver got all 'A's' and 'B's.' Then, when Beaver brings the report card back to school, his teacher will find it 'doctored' a bit. Then the fireworks will begin — it'll be the hottest show in town!"

"Gosh, Eddie," answers Wally, scratching his head, "I don't know...I don't think I want a part in this. If you want to do it, go right ahead, but you can count me out."

"Here, let me show you how easy it is...I used to do it all the time."

The next evening June Cleaver received a call from Beaver's teacher, Miss Landers (upon whom I had a crush).

"Mrs. Cleaver," the teacher began in a serious tone, "I would like to have a talk with you about young Theodore."

"Why, certainly, Miss Landers...What seems to be the matter?"

---

[1] Maitreya Stillwater and Layne Cutright, *"The Whole Truth,"* Heavensong, PO Box 450, Kula, Hawaii 96790

"Well, it appears that Theodore has changed one of the marks on his report card. He got a 'D' in arithmetic, and the report card came back signed with a 'B.' I'll send the report card back with him tomorrow. Would you please discuss this with him?"

"Why of course, Miss Landers! I'll take it up with Mr. Cleaver as soon as he comes home."

That evening Beaver found himself in the den having one of those talks with his dad.

"Beaver, Miss Landers called today and told us that you changed the 'D' on your report card to a 'B.' Now, son, you didn't have to do that. What made you think that you could get away with cheating like that?"

"Golly, Dad, I didn't change my report card!" responds the Beave, rotating his baseball cap in his hands.

"Now, Beaver, how can you sit there and tell me that? Here, just take a look...The ink isn't even the same color!"

"I can see that, Dad, but I didn't change it."

"Well, if you didn't, then who did?"

"Gosh, Dad, I don't know."

"Now, Beaver, it's one mistake to change your report card, but it's another one to deny it. I'll give you one more chance to tell me the truth, or I'm going to have to punish you. Are you going to stick with your story?"

After a moment's thought came the answer of a master, a teaching worthy of any holy book, a summary of the strength of all of humanity's heros:

"Gee, Dad, if you only have one story, I guess you have to stick with it."

One story. We, too, have but one story. Every moment of life asks us if we are willing to live it, or tell another one. It takes great courage to live in this world and stick to your story. But the word "courage" comes from the French word *coeur*, meaning "heart." If you come from your heart, you will have the strength to do whatever you need to do. You will walk without fear, for what Spirit guides you to do must easily be accomplished. And you will be at peace, for there will be no conflict between your internal feelings and your external actions. All this, because you have chosen to come from the heart. Courage.

To Follow Truth

Jesus had one story, from which he did not depart. When Jesus was brought before the *Sanhedrin* to face a kangaroo court in the middle of the night, the High Priest Caiphus asked him outright, "Are you the Son of God?" Without any hesitation, doubt, or vascillation, Jesus answered, *"I am."* He did not place his perfection in the future, he did not qualify it, and he did not deny it. He declared, *"I am."* And in that one simple statement he opened Heaven's doors for each of us to tell our story, which is the same as his.

Do you know who you are? Every question, challenge, and decision that you face is asking you if you know who you are, and if you are willing to act like it. Are you mortal, or divine? Are you limited, or magnanimous? Is guilt your guide, or do you place your trust in love, and love alone?

I meet many people who have decided to follow truth. I know a woman who almost singlehandedly established a Unity Church in a rural section of a northeastern state. I met a man who sold an empire of six successful businesses, bought a mobile home, and set out on a fascinating two-year journey to the tip of South America and back. I know presidents of companies who have resigned to go into the ministry. And I know ministers who gave up their pulpit to enter the business world. And what each of these people did was right for them.

I had the honor to meet Dr. Rodrigo Carazo, the former President of Costa Rica, who presided over a country that disbanded its standing army. There is now at least one country on the planet that has made a statement for peace that goes beyond words. Now Dr. Carazo is working to establish a United Nations World Peace University in Costa Rica.

Each of these courageous people experienced opposition to the fulfillment of their vision of truth. People around them called them fools, and at times they wondered if their friends were right. But when the heart calls, there is really no competition. Each of these people had their story to play out, and so they did. And they are stronger for it.

You, too, have a truth to live, and you must decide now if you are going to live it. The only alternative is to postpone your destiny. You may delay what you were born to do, but you cannot deny it. Sooner or later you will come to the same fork in the road, and you will have to choose again. And you will choose correctly. There is no alternative to Love.

The Empty Cornerstone

If you depart from truth, you may stray so far that you will have a hard time finding your way back. And you will find your way back. But you can make your journey much easier by being vigilant to keep the truth at the top of your priorities. "Brother, take not one step in the descent to hell," *A Course in Miracles* cautions, "for having taken one, you will not recognize the rest for what they are."[2] Hell is believing that you are separate from your brothers and sisters, and could therefore hide something from them without the expense of your peace. Heaven is remembering that you never needed to lie in the first place.

Have you ever told a lie for so long that you started to believe it yourself? I have. When I was in ninth grade I had a crush on a cute girl named Donna. She was from Milltown and she wore braces, and so I figured she was in my range. Around that time I went to see a live Beatles concert in Atlantic City, and Donna was eager to hear about it when I returned. Wanting to impress her, I created an incredibly exciting drama about how I had met the Beatles. I told her that a friend of ours knew the exit through which the Beatles were to make their getaway after the concert. As the story went, my friends and I hurried to the back door of the theatre to catch them on their way out. Sure enough, as soon as the music stopped, the door opened and John, Paul, George, and Ringo scurried to a long black limousine. But not before we intercepted them! We stretched out our hands to shake theirs, hoping to make some contact. While three of the Beatles slipped past us, Paul McCartney extended his hand to me. We had a quck handshake, after which he was gone. But when I looked into my palm, there I found a guitar pick!

Donna was in awe. Her jaw had dropped six inches and her eyes were open like two full moons. She was definitely impressed. The story was working.

Now, not only did he give me the pick, the story went, but I just happened to have it with me. Would Donna like to see it?

---

[2] T, p.460

You bet she would. The girl almost fainted.

I took the pick out of my wallet and showed it to her. To prove that it was real, there, etched into the plastic, were the initials, *"P.M."*

It was almost too much for her to handle. Of all the girls in the school, she was getting to see it!

As if that were not enough, I told her quite sincerely that I wanted her to have it.

"You really mean it?"

"Why, sure! You're special to me."

Donna held the pick next to her heart, swooned, and floated off to her next class. Ecstacy in the Junior High School!

The whole story was, of course, pure donkeydust. The pick was bought by me at the local music store, and I etched the initials into it that morning before I went to school. It was one whopper of a tale, skillfully fabricated by yours truly. I confess. (Donna, if you read this, please forgive me. You may want to read the chapter on forgiveness. You can return the pick if you like.)

But the story doesn't end here, folks. Donna told her friends, and mine, and before long the big news spread around the school. By the end of the school day lots of kids were asking me about the famous encounter. Not wanting to disappoint them, I gladly gave them a detailed recount of the exciting event. In fact, every time I told the story it included more details, and quickly the account grew in length and drama. I tell you, I should have been a fisherman!

After a while an interesting thing happened. I had told the story so much and colored it with such fascinating details that I began to believe it myself! The more I told it, the more real it seemed to me, and after awhile I forgot that it never really happened! As I look back on the story now, it seems as real in my memory as many things that *did* happen. Maybe it did happen! Or maybe the other things didn't happen. They all feel the same!

The point here is that I had practically convinced myself of something that wasn't true. And all of us have done the same, on a much deeper and broader level. All of us have convinced ourselves of lots of things that are not true.

The Power of Thought

Physiologists tell us that the central nervous system cannot distinguish between reality and imagination. This means that if you think about something enough, your body will respond as if it really happened. Hypnosis is a good example of this principle. If a person is a good hypnotic subject, he may be told that he is being burned by a *suggested* flame, and a blister will develop. Glove anesthesia is another example of the power of the mind to create physical reality. A subject can be told that his hand is numb, and if he accepts the suggestion a needle can pass through his skin and possibly through his whole hand, without any pain or bleeding. Surely this is a clear demonstration of the power of the mind to create physical experience. In these cases the mind manufactures an experience which overrides and replaces apparent physical law.

Be careful, then, of what truth you tell, for although you do not have the ability to change God's Truth, you have the free will to believe there is another version of reality and live in it as if it were so. And you will continue to find proofs of your truth, for along with your power to fabricate a truth is a propensity to substantiate it with evidence from your own warehouse of thought! And you will continue to do this until you realize that God's Truth is more rewarding than any you have substituted.

Ultimately, you will discover that *you* are the One who established the Original Law against which you believe you have rebelled. All of your experiences in attempting to substitute your will for God's leads you to the great awakening that your will *is* God's, and there is no other.

Truth in Action

Each of us reaches a point where we have the strength to recognize that original truth, acknowledge it, and live in it. When your memory of your own divinity is restored, you find no shortage of models for how powerfully you can live in the world. We can walk through our daily activities, even amid work, family, and play, holding and expressing the knowledge of who we are. We do not need to veer one hair's breadth from the reality of our beauty, for every departure from the truth is a moment of lost love, in the service of regaining it.

To sit in silence and meditate is a gift from God, and then to carry that peace into activity is to share that gift with all the world. Each day, go within to make contact with your God. Ask Him what He wants of you this day, and then go forth and glorify Love in all that you do. You are not asked to conquer nations or persons; you are asked simply to dispel illusions by acting on truth. There is no difference between what serves you and what will heal the world. You are never asked or expected to heal yourself or the world at the expense of the other. You *are* the world.

As you recognize the truth that leads you home, the road that it takes you by becomes ever wider. You must have the utter and unfailing conviction that the truth will never fail you as long as you do not fail it. No matter how many times you have fallen prey to lies born of fear, you must arise and say, "This time I lay my treasures in the storehouse of love." And though you may be able to see no further than one step in front of you, that is the step you must take. For then, and only then, will you see that the hand of truth has taken yours and extricated you from wandering in the fog.

Your days of loneliness and feelings of abandonment are over. How could you be alone when Love walks with you at every turn? Take refuge in the Truth, and the solace you feel will far surpass anything you have felt in the world. Be glad that Heaven is your home, and that you have never fully felt yourself to be a part of this world. Can that which is born of pure love find a home in a world of fear? No, no more than a diamond of truth could find a place in a rubble of deception.

You have a place in the universe, and you can be in it only by being totally committed to the truth. *You cannot be totally committed sometimes.*[3] This is your story, and the world needs you to tell it. Every ray of truth that you shine into a darkened world will illuminate a path for many to walk with you. It should be clear to you by now that you do not walk alone. When you bear witness to the Light that is you, you free millions from the shackles of their own fears. Such is your responsibility as a flame to warm a cold world in a dark and hungry night. And you will do it — indeed you *are* doing it — because that is what you came here for.

You, like Beaver, have but one story, and you will stick to it. The alternative to the truth is not lying, but *nothing*. And so there is no alternative to the truth. And be you glad, for your story is the only one that will take you all the way home.

You might have made a meaning of what isn't really real,
But no matter what you're dreaming, the truth can only heal.[4]

- Maitreya Stillwater

---

[3] T, p. 117
[4] Stillwater and Cutright, "The Whole Truth"

Good Lemonade

You can go a long way with some integrity.
- Lee Iacocca, President of Chrysler Corporation

One afternoon my friend Debbie and I were driving down a country road in northern New Jersey when we passed a large house with a huge number of cars bordering it. Automobiles filled the driveway, spilled onto the lawn, and overflowed onto both sides of the road for a considerable distance.

"Some party these people know how to throw!" I quipped as we passed the lot.

"Oh, don't you know what this place is?" returned Debbie.

"Looks like quite a bash to me."

"This is *Sammy's* Restaurant — It's really famous; people drive long distances to eat here."

"But I don't see any sign; where's the advertising?"

"They don't have any — mainly because they don't need it. The food is so good that everyone tells their friends, and they've become immensely successful just by word of mouth — you can hardly get a reservation."

I looked again. There was not one sign or word of advertising on the building. Yet the street was ribboned on both sides with long lines of cars. The food must have really been good.

What does it take to really be successful in this world? This is a question that we have all asked ourselves, indeed the question that we have all come here to answer. *Sammy's* is a wonderfully clear metaphor for the importance of placing integrity at the top of our list of personal priorities. If we have no integrity we may temporarily gain some symbols of success, but we will be empty inside. With integrity at our core, all the seeds that we plant must bear good fruit.

My friend Frank Asch is a bright and talented award-winning author of children's books. Frank and his wife Janani used to visit a country house I had where we would sit around the fire on blustery winter nights, sip tea, sing, and read enchanting stories aloud.

One night as he entered the house Frank placed a book in my hands. With a warm smile he told me, "Here's one of my favorite stories — I want you to have it; I think you'll enjoy it." I looked at the cover. In big bright yellow letters it shouted, *GOOD LEMONADE!*[1] Although it is written as a children's book, the lesson is for all of us:

One summer morning Hank decided to open up a lemonade stand. He found a wooden box in the garage, magic-marked a big oak-tag poster announcing, *"Lemonade — 10 Cents a Glass,"* and he set up shop on the sidewalk in front of his house. Hank went into the kitchen, mixed a packet of instant lemonade in a big glass pitcher, and skipped outside where he stood with his little brother Tommy. There the two of them waited for customers. Hank and Tommy waited...and waited...and waited. They stood there until five o'clock, when Hank had as many lemonades as he did when he began — except for one, which was bought by his little brother Tommy.

"Hmmm," pondered the little businessman, "I have to figure out some way to sell more lemonade," as he sat, chin in hand. "Let's see...Let's see..." The wheels of his young mind spun. "A sale!...That's it, I'll have a sale!...That'll pull in some business!"

The next morning Hank and Tommy set up the stand once again, but this time there was a new poster on the old crate. This sign was noticable for all of the different colored magic-markers that created it: *"Lemonade — Ten Cents a Glass...Three for Twenty-five Cents — Special — Today Only."* Anxiously Hank and Tommy sat waiting for customers to take advantage of the sale. Together the two boys waited...and waited...and waited, until five o'clock came once again too soon. Hank looked down into the cigar box to find but ten cents — the revenue from the glass of lemonade bought by: his little brother Tommy.

"This still isn't working!" complained our young entrepreneur, "I'll have to try another scheme!"

The next morning Hank broke open his piggy bank and hired Russell Wilcox, a boy down the street, to walk up and down Elm Street with a big sandwich board which Hank and Tommy had stayed up past their bedtime to make.

"Advertising is the key!" Hank explained to Tommy as they sat in anticipation of the crowd from Elm Street.

But the crowd never showed. When the welding plant down the street

---

[1] Frank Asch, *Good Lemonade*, Franklin Watts, 1976

blew the five o'clock whistle, Hank had recouped only ten cents of his investment — the income from the one glass of lemonade bought by his little brother Tommy.

"That does it!" popped Hank, "Now we bring out the heavy artillery!"

The next day persons driving on Elm Street were treated to a most unusual sight. Perched delicately atop two card tables, one on either side of the lemonade stand, were two dancing go-go lemons, bumping and grinding to the beat of some very funky rock music blaring from the boom box in front of the garage. (Closer inspection revealed the lemons to actually be two young ladies, about Hank's age, dressed in some rather elaborate outfits.)

"If this doesn't do it, nothing will!" Hank could be heard proclaiming to the little fellow sitting beside him, the mini-redhead nursing a misty glass of yellow cooler.

It was indeed fortunate that the little one had a propensity for lemonade (and supporting his big brother), for when Hank counted up the proceeds at the end of the day, there was but one ten-cent piece — with Tommy's fingerprints on it.

"I don't understand it," Hank quailed to his little group of employees; "I've done everything to get business: sales, advertising, go-go girls...Why aren't people buying my lemonade?"

Their brainstorming was interrupted by the shouting of Russell, who was running down Elm Street as fast as he could with a sandwich board over his shoulders.

"You should see the line of kids down at Artie's lemonade stand!" Russell reported. "...It must be half a block long!"

"Half a block long!" Hank reeled back. "I have to see what this kid has that I don't."

Hank grabbed a dime from the cigar box and ran down Elm Street as fast as he could. When he reached Artie's house, puffing heavily, there, sure enough, was a line of kids almost to Rosewood Avenue. Hank took a place in line, straining on the tips of his toes to see what Artie's gimmick was. The line moved slowly toward the stand where, to Hank's surprise, he found no go-go girls, no walking advertisements, not even a sale flyer.

"I don't get it," Hank puzzled; "How does he sell so much lemonade?"

After about twenty minutes Hank reached the counter. When he got there he saw just a simple sign, *"Artie's Lemonade — Ten Cents a Glass"* — not very different from his own original sign. Eagerly Hank plunked his ten cents down on the wooden box, his eyes spying behind the counter to see if Artie had discovered some new, scientifically efficient procedure for mass marketing.

The glass came presently, with a smile of thanks from Artie. Hank stepped to the side to drink it, still wondering how he did it. Hank lifted the cup to his mouth, tasted it, and then his eyes opened wide. His answer came as quickly as a taste of the truth.

"That's it!" Hank shouted; "That's the secret — **IT'S REALLY GOOD LEMONADE!**"

Hank zoomed back to his stand, unplugged the boom box, relieved the go-go lemons of their responsibilities, lifted the sandwich board off of Russell's tired shoulders, and ran into the kitchen. A little more slowly than usual he moved from the cabinet to the refrigerator, and then to the sink, where he began to mix a new batch of lemonade. This time, instead of just using the mix, Hank added the juice of two real lemons to the pitcher. He also spooned in one extra serving of sugar and brought a bucket of ice cubes out to the stand, so hot customers could feel a little more refreshed. Out to the stand Hank zipped with a new sign: *"Good Lemonade — Ten Cents a Glass."*

By one o'clock that afternoon there was a line of kids halfway to Rosewood Avenue — this time starting at Hank's house. All of them were smacking their lips and thanking Hank for some good lemonade. The afternoon flew by, and when the welding factory whistle sang through the streets of Honersville, Hank looked into the cigar box to find it nearly full of shiny dimes. His stock of thirst-quencher was down nearly to the bottom of the pitcher. Hank had sold all of his lemonade that day, except for one glass — the one he gave to his little brother Tommy, who drank it down with an extra twinkle in his eye.

Quality First

The story of Hank's lemonade stand is meaningful because his escapade in lemonade sales is symbolic of our lessons of integrity as we journey through the wondrous university of life. I recently saw a billboard advertisement for an automobile company which simply stated, *"Quality First."* This company, I thought, has discovered the secret of all success. To the extent that they practice their motto they can expect to enjoy the rewards of their intention.

Would it not be wonderful if all of us remembered and practiced this secret? I have been driving a Toyota for three years, with over sixty thousand miles on it. I want to testify that in those years and all of those miles the car has not required one repair. I have seen my mechanic but for oil changes and an occasional tune-up. I want to tell you how happy I have been to drive the car, recommend it to my friends, and feel confident about buying another Toyota somewhere down the road. The thing works, and I am grateful. I have seen lots of Toyota commercials, and none of them have meant anything to me. But the car is built well, and that means a great deal to me and all of the satisfied customers.

(I am not receiving a commission from Toyota for this testimony; it is simply a good example! I should also note that this is not to defame any other brand of automobile — every manufacturer can build a good car if they so choose.)

Your Divine Agent

Several years ago I began to feel that I wanted to teach yoga as a full-time profession. I decided to quit everything else I was doing and wage a huge publicity blitz toward drumming up business for myself as a yoga instructor. I had business cards printed, mimeographed letters of advertisement, and I called just about every YMCA, dance school, and health spa in the phone book. For weeks I was on the phone trying to sell myself. Most of the prospective clients offered me a polite "Thank you, it's a nice idea, send us your literature;" some said they weren't interested; and some said, "Come on over and let's set something up."

The net result of a fortnight of working anxiously to set something up was: one job at a YMHA which was cancelled before it began due to lack of sufficient enrollment, and another gig in a hotel health spa in which our class was put in the same room as people working on the *Nautilus* equipment. There the muscle-builders stepped over the yoga students (who were in deep relaxation) to get to the bathroom. We also received the added benefit of learning to be non-attached as the body builders snickered and made Don Rickles-like comments about the nature of yoga.

Actually, some lovely healings came of that course, but afterwards I realized that trying to sell myself was not something that I wanted to do. Self-promotion did not feel peaceful, and the work did not yield much in the way of success. Truly it was an excellent lesson, for from the experience I gleaned this idea: I would simply continue with the yoga courses I was already teaching, make the classes an offering to God, and give the students the best lemonade I could. In short, I decided to take care of God's business and trust God to take care of mine.

The results were phenomenal! I imbued those classes with such caring and excellence that the students begged for more, brought their friends, attended workshops I presented in other locations, and recommended me for courses to be set up in other schools.

An especially poignant lesson came as a result of a presentation that I was asked to do for a local B'nai Brith meeting. At this Sunday morning event I wasn't sure if the participants were more interested in the lecture I was giving or the bagels they were expecting afterward. When I looked into their auras during the meditation I did not see the cool streams and rolling mountain valleys I was suggesting, but dreamy drifts of cream cheese delicately set off by toasted onions on a balmy pumpernickel beach. When they returned from their gastronomic fantasy the participants challenged me, accused me of trying to hypnotize them, and I felt pretty much as if I had blown it. I was no match for brunch, I surmised. Why, I wondered, was I invited there anyway? It didn't seem as if I was received very well at all.

The next day the miracle came. I received a phone call from the director of a local adult education program who informed me, "We have been looking for a yoga instructor. Mr. Schwartz, who attended your lecture at B'nai Brith, said you gave an excellent presentation. We would like to have you work for us. Please come for an interview soon." I guess somebody liked it. That class led to another, and another, and to more after that. From those experiences I developed my workshops, which have blossomed so very beautifully. I am in awe of the process of the unfoldment of good.

Since that time I have pretty much let God be my publicity agent, and I have never been sorry. I rarely invite myself anywhere (unless I feel strong guidance to do so), I do not attempt to wedge my foot into any doors that God does not open, and I almost always accept invitations to speak or share my ideas, providing that I have the time available. I assume that if I am invited somewhere, the audience will have ears to hear what I have to say. This is a philosophy that has worked very well for me.

Letting Your Dreams Come Through

Spirit has an amazing and superbly efficient way of materializing our dreams. A minister friend of mine offers a workshop called, "Letting Your Dreams Come Through," and that is surely how our goals become a reality!

One evening in an adult school class I asked each student to share their dream, their idea of what they would most love to be doing with their life. One woman told that she has always wanted to return to Hawaii, for those islands have a deep and mystical home in her heart. A gentleman said he wanted to quit his administrative job and open up a kennel where he would breed show dogs. Another young lady wanted to have a fulfilling relationship with a man.

When all of the students had finished speaking, one turned to me and asked, "How about you, Alan? What would you most like to do?"

Feeling somewhat taken by surprise I had to think quickly and honestly. I felt that since I asked them to share intimately, I should be willing to do the same.

Into my mind flashed a picture that was imbedded in my heart, an image that meant more to me than anything else I had seen in a long time. The previous autumn I had seen a video tape of Dr. Leo Buscaglia delivering a lecture called "What is Essential is Invisible to the Eye." The lecture was based upon a quote from *The Little Prince*, the popular and beloved fable by de Saint Exupery. The message of the lecture was that the truth is not really what we see with our senses, but what we feel in our hearts.

Watching Dr. Buscaglia lecture was a marvelously inspiring experience for me. I became aware of something I had never seen before: although there were perhaps several thousand people in the audience, Leo had established a personally intimate relationship with each one. As the camera panned the audience while he spoke, I saw each listener on the edge of his or her chair, spellbound, as if Leo was having a tender, touching moment with him or her. That auditorium became a great cozy living room, and I know that there was no other place in the universe that each person in that audience would rather have been. It was a marvelous demonstration that what is essential *is* invisible to the eye.

Back to my class, it was time for me to give the answer. I told them, "I would like to travel around the world, speaking to groups of thousands of people, and bring them to tears for the love of God."

Did I say that? I don't think I had ever thought about that before, much less share it with a group of people I hardly knew. But I did say it, and it was true — that was my dream, the vision that I held in my heart of hearts, awaiting the opportunity to be brought out into the sunlight. I was glad I was asked, and even more pleased that I told the truth.

They say that you better be careful of what you ask for, because you just might get it.

Three months later I was sitting in my back yard on a delightfully warm spring day, when the mailman poked his head over the fence and handed me a letter. I read the return address: *"D. Hastings, Spokane, Washington."*

"D. Hastings? Spokane, Washington? Where's that?"

Curiously I opened it up. It was from a young lady who began her introduction with a lovely description of spring in the Northwest. She had just returned from picking strawberries at a mountain lake, and she wanted me to enjoy the beauty as she saw it through her appreciative eyes. She went on to explain that she had read and enjoyed *The Dragon Doesn't Live Here Anymore*. The minister of her Unity Church had based a series of lectures on the book, after which a good deal of the people in the church had read it too.

"So, dear Alan," Deneice concluded, "we'd love to have you come out here and share a week of workshops."

If thoughts are things, then I was certainly watching my most cherished seeds sprout. I thanked God for allowing me to be myself, and giving me the chance to serve Him in a way that I loved.

"Of course I would love to," I wrote back to Deneice. I felt like a pilot about to solo after years of dreaming about flying.

I didn't get a chance to mail the letter. The phone in the kitchen began to ring, but smugly I remained nestled in my lawn chair, intent on keeping my vow to act like a human being and not a slave to Ma Bell, a touch-tone yoyo. But it just kept ringing. "Man plans, and God laughs." I got up and answered.

"Hi Alan, this is Deneice...I didn't want to wait for you to answer my letter. There's a lot of interest here — Will you come?"

"Yes, of course, I would love to."

"Great! We're printing fifteen hundred tickets for each night. Will that be alright?"

That particular day I was glad that picture-phones had not yet been invented. I think I would have been a little embarrassed to have Deneice see me gulp across country. *Fifteen hundred tickets?* Did I hear her correctly? *Fifteen hundred?* Didn't she know I was just a Jewish boy from New Jersey who simply wrote down what he heard in his brain? Or maybe she knew more about who I was than I did.

"Why, sure, that'll be fine," I answered after a long moment's pause. Upon reflecting on it later I realized it was not really a moment — it was more like all of the years that it took me to learn to say "Yes" to who I am.

"Wonderful! We'll be looking forward to seeing you soon!"

The phone clicked on the Washington end, but I didn't hang up. My conversation with myself continued.

"Fifteen hundred tickets? For each night? God, what am I going to say to fifteen hundred people?"

The Voice answered quickly, with firm resolution: *"The same as you would say to fifteen."*

"No kidding?"

"Truth has nothing to do with numbers;" the Guide continued, *"It has only to do with being itself, which is the same as being yourself. The truth does not change according to how many people to whom you are telling it. Just go there, love them, be honest about your experience, and I will guide you exactly as to what to do and say — to fifteen hundred, or to one."*

Oh, I see.

I began to prepare my lecture. As I visualized standing before the audience, the question occurred to me, "Who should I be like?"

"I know," I thought, "I'll be like Leo Buscaglia...I'll wave my arms and sweat under the armpits and tell stories about my Italian mother."

"But you don't have an Italian mother," the Voice interrupted; *"You have a Jewish mother."*

Oh, yes; that's right. I can't be Buscaglia.

Well, then, I could be like Ram Dass. I could sit in lotus position and be mellow and cuddly and go into spontaneous meditation every now and then. That would really get them.

"No," the inner Counselor answered, *"that is not really your way."*

Well, that was true, too.

"I have it!" I got excited. "I'll be like Patricia Sun. I'll stand up there and glow and smile and make everyone tingle with my giggle."

But then, alas, my giggle is not especially cute. Forget that one.

Then into my mind came an absolutely amazing idea — one that I had not considered before.

"Why not try going as Alan Cohen?"

"That's it!" I got it. I realized that I would have the best chance of succeeding by being myself — an absolutely monumental discovery! I reasoned that if they had wanted Leo or Ram or Patricia, they would have invited them. But on this particular occasion they invited Alan Cohen, and that was the person I could best give them.

I followed my intuition and I went to that engagement as myself. And what a success it was! The audience enjoyed my presentation because I loved and believed in myself enough to be myself. The simplest answer proved to be the one that worked.

Selling and Serving

To really reap the benefits of good lemonade, you have to know what is the *real* lemonade you are selling. It is not the item before your eyes, the picture in the catalog, or the song on the tape — it is *the love within your heart*. If you believe that you are selling physical glasses of liquid lemonade to solid people, you will sooner or later be burnt out, bedraggled, and bankrupt. If, on the other hand, you realize that the lemonade is the vehicle, the vessel through which you can offer love, blessings, and healing to spiritual beings who truly live on "the waters that will never give thirst again," you will not only sell lots of lemonade, but you will be able to go to sleep each night with a contented heart.

All of life is spiritual, and spiritual only. To sell anything — a product, a service, an idea — you must believe that you are helping the person to whom you are selling. You can fudge your way to financial or social success, but unless you believe in what you are doing you will be a hollow shell of a person. "What shall it profit a man if he gains the whole world but loses his soul?" If you are feeling love in your work there is nothing that can stand between you and great success.

Wally Amos, founder and president of *Famous Amos* cookies, said, "I started selling cookies just to make a living. And when I let go of the concept of trying to make a lot of money, and just wanted to be happy and do something well, my whole life opened up."

I met a woman of similar orientation who was a very successful saleswoman. Here is what she told me:

"You know, *A Course in Miracles* has helped me phenomenally in my work. I've been selling photocopy machines for about six months, and my sales volume is double what the best salesman in the office is doing — and he's been there for six years."

"That's wonderful!" I enthusiastically responded. "What's your secret?"

"Actually, it's quite simple," she explained. "I never try to sell a photocopy machine; my most important goal is to help my client. If I feel that my machine can really help him accomplish what he wants, I tell him so with complete confidence that I have his best interest at heart. If I don't feel he can use what I have to offer, I tell him that, too. I believe that my clients know that I am loving them by telling them the truth, and this has developed a deep level of trust between my clients and myself. They know I would never hurt them, and they would rather buy from me than someone who was more interested in selling them something than helping them. The truth is that I really do want to make their life easier. That feels a lot better to me than trying to sell them a machine. The miracle is that the more I seek to serve them, the more machines I sell!''

Another friend of mine, an advertising representative, gave me this powerful insight into the dynamics of success:

"I keep my peace by turning my work over to God," Joan explained as she drove me home from a class one evening. "I don't feel that my sales are up to me alone. Once I have done my part of the business, I place the final decision in the hands of the Lord. I trust that if this deal will serve everyone's best interest, it will go through and we will all be satisfied. If it won't help everyone involved, then no good can come of it for anyone, and I don't want it. Somehow the more I turn the business over to God, the better it goes. My peers don't understand it, but it's very clear to me."

I knew exactly what Joan meant. When I was writing *The Dragon Doesn't Live Here Anymore*, I hardly thought at all about how the book would get published, where the money would come from, or how it would get into the hands of the readers. All I knew was that God gave me the book, and if He could do that, He could certainly find a way to get it published. My job, as I perceived it, was simply to write healing words. God, I reasoned, would be in a better position than me to know people in high places who could help me.

When the manuscript was finished, two people, independent of one another, offered me the money to publish it without my even asking them. Recognizing the offer came from God, I gratefully accepted.

Then, as I wondered how to advertise the book, I picked up a copy of Hugh Prather's inspiring *Notes to Myself*, his classic sharing of gentle reflections on the spiritual path. Inside the cover I found my answer. I read,

> *"This unique book was first published by a small unheard-of press in New Mexico. Without any advertising except word of mouth, it has sold over one million copies."*[2]

---

[2] Hugh Prather, *Notes to Myself*, Bantam, 1976

There was my answer. The statement confirmed to me that struggle and strain are *not* requirements for spiritual and material success. I let God be my agent, and in this matter and so many others I have never regretted it. The One who created me has never failed me.

Later, when I needed a national distributor to handle larger scale distribution of my books and tapes, once again I did not know where to turn. Remembering my earlier lessons, again I asked for Spirit's help. Within a few weeks I received a letter from New Leaf Distributors, a very professional and spiritually-attuned company in Atlanta. The president of the company was writing to let me know they had become familiar with my books, and their company was interested in handling national distribution. I accepted, and since that time they have done an excellent job for me.

A Living Lesson in Service

Perhaps the most powerful teaching for me in the benefits of serving good lemonade is Hilda, the spiritual teacher with whom I have had the honor of studying for many years. Hilda's ministry, health, happiness, and aliveness are marvelous demonstrations of abundant living. She strives with all of her heart to serve well all who come to her for friendship and guidance, and she radiates the kind of contentment owned only by those who truly love.

In all the time that I have known Hilda she has not required one penny from me or anyone for some of the highest teachings I have ever received, nor has she charged for any of the classes she teaches or the healings she so generously channels. During the fifteen years I have known her, Hilda has never lacked for money, material goods, or sustenance. She does not advertise her teachings, yet three to five hundred persons come weekly to participate in her classes. She has never required any student to take an oath of allegience or join an organization, yet those who love her teachings number in the thousands, her spiritual family circles the globe, and her friendships last for a lifetime and more. In short, Hilda has done everything exactly the opposite the way the world dictates one should go about manipulating to get what one wants, and she enjoys the kind of peace of mind, love of friends, and success for which the world pines. Here is a true teacher of God, demonstrating that one who holds God in her heart holds the world in the palm of her hand.

The Gift of Quality

Perhaps it is in the very intention to fill our work with the light of love that we are fulfilled in doing it, and blessed by the positive response it generates.

On a recent tour through the cathedrals of Europe I was deeply impressed by the quality of the craftsmanship that was imbued in the stone and wood work in those sacred places. It seems that each pillar and buttress was the result of long and caring hours of delicate artistry; that the beauty of the work far outshined the speed or economy of the job; that the artisan saw inspiration as the means as well as the end of his work. I felt that the artistry was a blessing to look at because it was a joy to create.

Could it be that love, caring, and the desire to truly be of service has captured the breath of the divine in such artistry, and consecrated it to bless all who look upon it? Could it be that the art of loving what we do and making it a gift to those we serve, is the lost art of our civilization? And might it also be that those who seek for their work to reflect the divine have discovered the secret to satisfaction in human vocation?

A Zen master once taught, "If you can serve a cup of tea correctly, you can do anything." The key to mastering any skill is to know that it is not the tea that we are serving that is important, but our brother to whom we deliver it. If we can only remember that the things of this world are cups in which the love of God can be given, all of our questions about human activity will be answered. Such an awareness brings healing because it acknowledges that we are dependent only on the divine for our sustenance. Love is a gift that we make real by offering it to one another.

The Greatest Baker

Why would you do something you do not love? Our purpose in life is not to labor begrudgingly, but to be joyful. The real function of a vocation is to feel creative, alive, and enthusiastic, and to serve those you touch. Your service is not limited to the product, but it emanates from your attitude. The famous psychiatrist Karl Menninger said, "Attitude is more important than facts."

189

The values of the world are inside out, and thus we have reversed the importance of effects (products) with their source (creative love). The real joy of any profession is the love we feel in doing it. Ramtha has said, "When you eat, it is not the food that nourishes you, but the love that you feel when feeding yourself." This is why a diet that you hate cannot work. No matter how effective the diet is advertised to be, if you hate it you are feeding yourself poison. On the other hand, you are sure to be healed by any diet you love.

The same principle is true for professions. If you love what you do, you are sure to succeed. The amount of aliveness you feel is the real yardstick for aptitude and success in any endeavor.

I saw a television interview with several of the most financially successful people in the world. On the panel were Ray Kroc, the founder and president of *McDonald's*, Mrs. Hilton of the hotel chain, and several other fabulously successful moguls and magnates.

When the interviewer asked them, "What advice would you give to a young person starting out in a career?" all of them agreed on the answer: "Go for your dream. Do the thing you love. Do not strive simply for material success, but for inner fulfillment. The wealth will follow from your dedication to fulfilling your heart's desire. Real success is being who you are and doing what you love to do well."

When you are bored or unfulfilled, look at the why of it. At that time you must either recreate the way you are looking at what you are doing, or do the thing that you would really love to do. When the author Jack London went to his father, a baker, and asked him the secret of success in a profession, his dad answered, "The day I don't love baking bread, I quit."

An earlier baker advised us, "Man does not live by bread alone, but by every word that proceeds from the mouth of God." Because God is love and only love, every word (idea or intention) must be an attribute of love. Therefore the real bread is the spiritual substance that nourishes your heart when you work with love.

We are Good Lemonade

Life works. Life is miracle. There is indeed a Loving Presence that cares for all of our needs, if we are but willing to entrust them to a Higher Power. We do not have to fight to get what we want in life. Love is the most practical force in all of our affairs. Our greatest strength lies in allowing the earthly to be guided by the divine.

We must *be* what we want before we can have it. No amount of outer manipulation will quench our thirst for good lemonade unless we first realize that we *are* good lemonade. The universe is the biggest lemonade stand in history. God has taken all of the lemons we have given Him and cranked them into the sweetest of beverages, free without measure to all who thirst. The knowledge that we are beautiful, worthy, and lovable will quickly and automatically attract to us all in life that is wonderful, while the thought that we are not enough will keep us striving for the things that we are as if they were out there, instead of already within us. Success is simply knowing who you are while you enjoy watching the universe confirm your vision of yourself.

"Seek ye first the Kingdom of Heaven, and all will be added."
                                                            - Jesus, the Christ

The Creed of the Dauntless

Luke Skywalker: *How will I know the good from the bad?*
Yoda: *You will know through calm and peace. This is the way of the Force; a Jedi does not need to attack; the Force will work for him.*

- The Empire Strikes Back

During the nineteenth-century tenure of Edward Everett as President of Harvard University, a Black man applied for admission. As such an admission was unheard of at that time, the application raised quite a few hackles on the Harvard campus. Mr. Everett, however, was committed to a Higher Law than the admissions policy of Harvard. "If this boy passes the examinations, he will be admitted," Mr. Everett guaranteed; "and if the White students choose to withdraw, all the income of the college will be devoted to his education."

Of course it would. What other route could a person of integrity take? When you are committed to personal integrity, you do not need to fear the consequences of any of your actions, for your deeds bring peace as you contemplate their results. Your brow is smooth, your patience is deep, and, you can sleep at night with a satisfied heart. These are the gifts of Spirit earned by those who live in harmony with their personal truth.

What is integrity? What kind of creed would the dauntless follow? Why is honesty a source of real strength?

Integrity is the way to ensure that you will feel the peace of God while living in this world. Because there is nothing more important than feeling peace, there is nothing that is worth doing that would cause you to lose it. While living the truth may at times be challenging, in the long run it is far easier than hiding.

The opposite of integrity is lying. I am not referring so much to verbal lying, but to living as something or someone other than who and what you are. To live as someone or something else is a great loss. Your life is like a photograph, and where you were supposed to be seen smiling, there is an empty outline. You cannot be someone else and yourself at the same time. If you are not you, both you and the world have missed a great gift.

To Honor Truth

Life continually puts us into positions where we have to tell the truth. This is wonderful, because in our heart we really want to tell the truth, and every time we are true to our self we are strengthened. The fear and the struggle and the pain of being something we're not, or not being something we are, is overwhelming, and sooner or later we come to the point where it feels more peaceful to simply tell the truth than to continue to hide. And then we wonder why we ever hid in the first place.

I was at a Patricia Sun workshop[1] when a man stood up and explained that he had come to a point in his career where he was facing a tremendous challenge of integrity. In order for him to be at peace with himself, he would have to tell the truth at work. But he feared that telling that truth may cost him his job. But he couldn't live with himself without telling that truth.

"It sounds like the universe is forcing you to tell the truth!" Patricia replied. "And you may, in fact, lose your job — but that may put you in the perfect position to get a job in which you may retain your integrity and sleep well at night."

I don't believe that God would punish any of Her children for making a stand for integrity. We may experience some temporary setbacks, but in the long run, with faith, Spirit *must* support those who are courageous to be what their heart calls to them to be.

The Free Man

When I was in the Soviet Union I met a beautiful fellow named Sorin. Sorin was a *refusenik* — he had applied to leave the country and he was turned down. As a result he lost his job as a Ph.D chemist, and the only job he could get was as a chess coach for a high school, at about one-tenth of his original salary.

But Sorin was not a beaten man. Because his mind was free and he refused to make believe he was something he was not, he was a free soul. Sorin spoke beautiful English which he had taught himself. He showed me a

---

[1] Patricia Sun, PO Box 7065, Berkeley, California 94707

personal dictionary that he had created. In his notebook he had listed about a dozen English novels and self-help books that he had gotten his hands on. Under a heading with the title of each book, he had printed a list of words he needed to learn, with their pronunciations and definitions next to them.

As Sorin proudly leafed through the pages to show me his little booklet, I felt a tremendous enthusiasm and aliveness in his spirit. He had a zest for knowledge, and he was devoted to expanding his mind. He was excited to break into a new world of awareness. His body may have been restricted, but his mind was soaring. His mind was free, and therefore so was he.

A Course in Miracles asks us, "Would you rather have freedom of the body or freedom of the mind? You cannot have both." To me this means that if we believe that we are a body, we will equate our freedom with what the body is doing, and we will deny the truth that our thoughts really determine our freedom. But if we know that our life springs from our thoughts, we can rise to lofty heights no matter what our body is doing. One who is free in spirit is truly free.

The Power of Defenselessness

It cannot be overemphasized that the dauntless hearken to an *inner* call, trusting Spirit to confirm their faith, observable in the events of the outer world.

A woman who attends some of my workshops has made wonderful changes in her life in the past few years. As her mind and heart have opened to the reality of Spirit, her work, her creativity, and her relationships have developed in miraculous ways.

One of the areas that has been amazing to watch unfold, she reports, is in her marriage. She explains that her husband was not very supportive of the spiritual path she had taken. When she began he casually wrote off her interest as a fad that she was going through. She began to defend herself, but then she realized that the best way to proceed would be simply to carry on in peace and trust that if her path was true, only good could come in her family and her entire life.

She describes a scene that was a turning point:

"One night my husband and I were reading in bed before retiring," she shared. "He was sitting on his side of the bed sifting through the pages of *Playboy*, and I was on my side, reading *Jonathan Livingston Seagull*. Every now and then he would look up and make a wisecrack about "that sappy spiritual stuff." I would just smile and go back to my book.

More and more he started to look over at me reading. Finally he said, "Say, let me take a look at that." Gladly I handed him the book, and he started to get into it. He actually liked it, and now I share more of my spiritual life with him."

I love this vignette as a metaphor for how spirituality works. Truth is firm within itself, and it trusts that anything that is good will share itself in just the right way and timing. No defense is necessary, and neither any proselytizing. Defense and proselytizing are signs of insecurity. The truth is anchored in the firmest of ground, and it does not require allies or fear destruction. Truth attracts friends by the compelling quality of its presence. Those who live in the truth can rest in the power of their being. Being is the most powerful form of living. It is the strongest form of doing, for without trying to do anything, all gets done.

> *Therefore the sage says:*
> *I take no action and people are reformed.*
> *I enjoy peace and people become honest.*
> *I do nothing and people become rich.*
> *I have no desires and people return to*
> *the good and simple life.*[2]

The Mirror's Gift

We have said many times that the world is but a reflection of our own consciousness. When we learn to recognize that *all* events we experience are demonstrations of our will, the world will become our friend and our most worthy teacher. If we want to know more about what we are thinking or feeling at any given moment, we can simply look at what is happening to us. In issues of integrity, the universe will be quick to reflect our integrity — or lack of it.

For example, some friends of mine were sitting in a car, about to leave for a seminar. When the driver turned the key, the car engine groaned and cranked, but it did not turn over. The driver repeated her efforts several times, to no avail.

After her third attempt, she turned to the others in the car and stated, "I

---

[2] Lao Tsu, *Tao Te Ching*, Gia-Fu Feng and Jane English, translators, Vintage Books, 1972

have never had this problem before, and the car is in good shape. There must be a lie in the space.''

After a long moment of uncomfortable silence, one of the ladies in the group spoke up: ''You're right — I don't really want to go to this seminar tonight. I just came because I was afraid to say no. My presence here is a kind of a lie — I'd rather be home.''

''Thank you very much,'' said the driver, ''I appreciate you telling me the truth.''

With that she turned the key, the car started, and off to the seminar they went. (I wouldn't be surprised if it was a seminar on integrity.)

This scene illustrates some very important lessons for us:

First, the world is a reflection of our attitude. Most of the time the attitude that creates our experience is functioning on an unconscious level. We see but the tip of the iceberg of our consciousness, and the universe is always giving us clues about what we are willing. This is always helpful, as it is of the utmost importance for our will to be conscious, integrated, and chosen at all times.

Second, the world can and will change as we change our attitude about it. When we shift our thoughts from fear to love, or from deception to honesty, the world will reflect our clarity and our path will be made clear. We are speaking now in a very physical, material, practical sense. Since the world is but consciousness, every change you make in your consciousness must create a change in the world.

Finally, we see that integrity is not simply about being perfect, looking good, or always winning in a storybook sense. It is about telling the truth about where you are. It is more important to tell the truth about where you are than to lie in an attempt to act like where you would like to be. You may not be able to get where you want to be until you master where you are.

When You Tell the Truth, Everyone Wins

One day I received a telephone call from a friend inviting me to give an evening workshop at her church. ''It sounds good,'' I told her. ''Please tell me the details.''

When she told me that the church was approximately a two-hour drive from my home, I began to have some reservations. I felt that four hours was more than I wanted to drive for a workshop on a weeknight evening.

"I would love to come," I told her, "but I have made a commitment to myself to relax the pace of my life somewhat. I feel that I would rather not drive that distance for an evening weeknight workshop."

It felt good to tell the truth.

"I understand," she told me; "I am disappointed, but I do know how busy you have been, and I support your decision."

The next morning I received a telephone call from the same lady.

"How would you like us to send a limo for you?" she asked.

Now she was talking.

"Well, that would certainly be much easier than me driving all that distance. But I wouldn't want you to overstep your means."

"Oh, it's no problem," she assured me. "One of the members of our church has a limousine service. He has read and enjoyed your books, and he said he would be happy to send his limousine for you at no charge to you or the church."

It was an offer I couldn't refuse. You can imagine my neighbors' surprise when a long grey limousine pulled into my driveway and a dashing uniformed young man opened the door for me with a formal salute. I didn't feel comfortable saluting him in return; it felt nicer just to put my hand on his shoulder and tell him, "Thank you for coming."

Two friends and I slid into the plush back seat, where we sat back and enjoyed the ride, drinking apple juice from the bar and watching Terry Cole-Whittaker videos on the VCR. We also had a lovely conversation with the driver. The workshop turned out to be a great success, and I returned home that night relaxed and energized.

In this particular situation, everyone won. I got to give a workshop, be with loving people, get paid for it, and share my books, all of which I love. The church had a strong and uplifting workshop which brought new and old congregants together. The limousine owners, a lovely couple who had wanted to meet me, invited me to their home for refreshments afterwards. I gave the driver some of my books, and learned some great ideas from Terry Cole-Whittaker.

All because I was willing to tell the truth. If I had said a flat "no" or made up an excuse about why I couldn't come, the church would not have been able to respond in the way they did. But I was willing to trust that telling the truth would work for everyone, and it did.

The Truth Gets Results

One very powerful and valuable benefit of telling the truth is that it gets results. It moves life along more quickly and more effectively than lying, beating around the burning bush, or procrastinating. And it elicits direct responses. Honest questions call forth honest answers.

A while back I received a telephone call from a woman asking me for a date. She had met me at a workshop and she wanted to see me again. "I really liked being with you," she told me. "I felt attracted to you, and I would like to get together with you again. Is that something that you would like to do?"

Her honesty hit me right between the eyes. She was so straightforward that I felt I had to give her an answer of the same quality, integrity, and forthrightness with which she asked.

"Thank you for telling me that," I told her. "I enjoyed meeting and sharing with you at the workshop. I must tell you that I am in a committed relationship, and I would rather not see anyone else," I had to tell her. "And I want you to know how much I appreciate your being so open and honest with me."

That was the end of it. Honest question asked, honest response given. A complete communication. No fooling around. No guessing. And no hurt feelings. Honesty requires great love, and for someone to be honest with you means that they respect and honor you a great deal. In this case perhaps it meant more than a date.

I really admired this woman for coming right out and declaring where she was at. I respected her willingness to go for what she wanted. No dinner invitations; no discussions of the news, weather, or current meditation techniques. No questions about semi-related subjects. Just the subject at hand: "Would you like to go out?" And that was a great teaching of integrity for me.

And she got results. One may say that she did not get results because in effect I said "no." But "no" is a result. It is more of a result than not knowing, and it definitely moves things along to the next step. Perhaps there is someone else she would like to see, someone who would work out better for her than me, and my being out of the picture would clear the way for that to happen more quickly and easily. She was definitely ahead of where she was before she called. And so was I. I had the chance to examine my feelings, my relationship, my commitment, and my willingness to tell the truth. I had to make choices in the brief time between the question and the answer. And everytime we make choices, we grow. So we both won.

On a deeper lever, I really didn't say "no" to her. The outer "no" was just the drama level, the story line, the obvious plot. On a deeper level I was joining with her in a commitment with her to have an open and honest relationship. If I never saw or spoke with her again, my heart could rest satisfied that in that relationship, even if it was in the space of a short conversation, we were both straight with each other. Even though we didn't date, I will remember her as someone who loved me enough to tell me the truth, as I loved her in my honesty. That's a pretty good relationship, a wonderful gift to share.

Ask for What You Want

The Children of God receive good because they know they are worthy of it. Life is a series of opportunities to learn that you are lovable. The situations that you create demonstrate what you believe you deserve. Do not stop until you have created what you really want. Every failure is an encouragement to choose to accept better the next time. You will always have the opportunity to choose again until you choose to be lovable. And indeed you are.

You must trust the desires of your heart. Some philosophical systems decry desires as evil, needful of being purged or annihilated. There is another way of looking at desires, as there is another way of seeing everything. Seen in the correct light, the world can become new instantly. You need but know that it is possible to have all the blessings of Heaven, even while in this world.

To have what you want, you must ask for it. To avoid asking for what you really want always comes from a sense of guilt, for who that was not guilty would be denied what he wanted? You do deserve to receive what you want, and the most powerful way to ask for it is by knowing that you deserve it.

A man went to Heaven, where he was taken on an orientation tour by God. When they passed a closed door, the man asked God what was behind it.

"Oh, it would make you very sad to see what is in that room," God explained.

But the man was curious, and he asked God to show him.

"Very well," God acceded. God opened the door, and there the man saw many gifts and treasures. The man was astonished at the great wealth of objects his eyes beheld. Many were wrapped in elegant paper and adorned with lovely bows and decorations.

"This looks like a great treasurehouse!" the man exclaimed. "Why would it make me sad to see this?"

"These are the gifts that I have offered people, but they have not accepted them." God explained. "If I offer someone a gift and they do not accept it, I have no choice but to take the gift back and hold it here in this great storehouse until they or someone else is willing to have it."

"This is amazing!" the man exclaimed. "Why would anyone not accept these beautiful presents? Here is a wide-screen color television set...a huge hot tub, and...isn't that a Rolls Royce over there?"

"Yes, Joe," God answered. "Go look at the tag on it."

Joe walked over to the gleaming car, turned the tag over, read it, and his eyes opened wide.

"Why, that's my name on this tag!" he shouted. "This car was meant for me! But why didn't I get it? You know how much I would have loved to have a car like this! And I prayed to You every night!"

There was a pregnant moment of silence. If it is true that you get what you pray for, what reason could God possibly offer for not giving Joe the car of his dreams?

"You did not get the Rolls Royce, Joe," God explained, " — even though that's what you wanted — because every night you prayed to me to send you a Ford."

Why would Joe have prayed for a Ford if he really wanted a Rolls? Only because he didn't believe he could get one, or he didn't feel he deserved it. While he wanted it all, he asked only for what he believed he could get. And so he got what he believed he could get — no more, no less.

Prayer is not so much asking God to give us what we want, but an exercise in our knowing what we deserve. If you pray for something, you must believe that you deserve it. If you truly believe that you deserve it, by the time you have prayed for it, it is already yours, by right of consciousness. You will attract what belongs to you.

The goal of prayer, then, is not to supplicate God to give us something that we don't deserve, but to remind ourself that we deserve the best. There is enough of everything for everyone, and if you remember that God is the Source of infinite, abundant, unfailing supply, you have placed your faith where it is truly merited.

On Eagle's Wings

A Course in Miracles asks us, "Who would attempt to fly with the tiny wings of a sparrow when the mighty power of an eagle has been given him?"[3]

A friend of mine had a sign up on her wall:

Ask for what you want, but don't demand it.

You can wrestle what you want from the hands of creation, for it is within your power to do so. But there is an easier way, a lighter way, a more peaceful way. Our good comes to us much more fluently when we do not try to force it. We don't need to yell at God to get Spirit's attention. The One Who created us lives within us, and She can hear our whispers as easily as our shouts. We can conserve our energy.

If you have to demand something in order to get it, you may be forcing the universe to give you something that you do not really need. I have found that demanding things from others, from myself, or from the universe does not work as well as asking. I can ask, and ask with firmness and surety, knowing that if I am to have this thing, I will receive it. In that consciousness, if I do receive it, it will be because God gave it to me, not because I forced it by my ego's dictate. If you try to pick a fruit before it is ripe, the process will be a struggle, the tree will bleed, and the fruit will not taste good. There are even some fruits which are poisonous if you eat them before they are ripe. But if you pick the fruit when it is ready, it comes gently into your hand (sometimes it falls on the ground at your feet!), it tastes deliciously sweet, and it is nourishing.

If I feel I have to threaten, cajole, or manipulate, I must have allowed some fear to intrude upon the holiness of my thoughts and tempt me into believing that there is a way that would work better than peace. At such a point I would do well to consider why my request may not be materializing. Perhaps I don't really need the thing, or maybe the timing is not just right

---

[3] M, p. 8

now. Or perhaps someone else needs to make a choice that I cannot make for them by attempting to persuade them to do what I would like them to do. Perhaps I have been resisting my good by a fear of love or healing. There might be a thousand different reasons why a request is not answered immediately. But demanding is a sure sign that you are heading in a direction that will not take you to peace.

The real way to change what you are getting is to change your mind. You can go through all kinds of physical or metaphysical gymnastics and gyrations to manipulate the outer world to give you what you want, but if there is no change in your inner world, all of your efforts are very weak and ineffective indeed. Ah! But once your mind is changed, you have the strength of the universe behind you! To see a new world you must see with new eyes. You already have those eyes, but you need to look through them. And what a beauteous universe they will show you! You will see all about you as a gift and a blessing. You will see persons and events not to be corrected, but appreciated. And best of all, you will be in love with yourself. You will find wonder in your own being, and let your ideas of sin and fault fly to the wind to be scattered like flowers among the breezes. You will be able to look in the mirror and love what you see. You will arise in the morning and go forth with enthusiasm, knowing that the entire universe is alive with love, and the blessing of Spirit goes with you everywhere. You will see yourself as you are, and you will weep blessed tears of joy at the beauty which has been bestowed upon you, with nothing asked of you in return except your hearing the madrigal of your heart singing gentle praises to all the universe in the silver light of a moonlit evening. And you will be happy. All this, without a single care or anxious struggle on your part.

Is this not preferable to a life of worry and woe? I assure you that all is quite well taken care of. Your purpose is not to improve upon it, but to celebrate it. This realization is the simplest one, and yet you may find it to be the hardest, for you have been trained to not be enough, and consequently you see your world through the same clouded vision. But you are quite enough, because you are all there is, and what more could there be? It would be a blasphemy to attempt to improve on your holiness, but it is a sacrament to honor it by knowing it. And so once again we come to the point and purpose of your existence: to know yourself.

Everything and Nothing

By focusing on accepting the blessings in your life, you may find that you actually have a lot more than you thought you did. You may discover that Spirit's plan for you is taking you Home much more easily and effectively than if you were left to your own designs. The universe gives us much more by accepting than by criticizing. One thing is for sure — if you lose your peace, you have nothing.

To ask means to allow the answer to be what it is. If you have a preconceived notion of what the answer should be, you are not asking, but telling. When you ask something of God or a another person, leave room for the answer to be what it is. A Catholic priest was asked, "Does God answer all prayers?" He answered, "Yes, He does — but sometimes the answer is 'No.'" But a "no" to what would hurt you is actually a "yes" to what will help you. God would not be a very good parent if He/She gave you what would hurt you.

Are you absolutely sure that what you are asking for is in your best interests? If you are not certain, it would be wise indeed to allow Spirit to give you what will help you, especially if that would serve you better than what you believe you need. And it surely will.

The most powerful prayer is one that acknowledges peace of mind as the crowning joy of life. To look upon yourself and your fellows with a happy heart is exactly God's will for you, and therefore we cannot fail if we pray for this. A loving heart and rewarding relationships will far outshine any symbols of love. Why settle for a symbol when you can have the real thing? If you are not sure what to pray for, pray for peace, and the entire universe will support you in finding the object of your heart.

To Give is to Receive: The Integrity of Support

One of the ways that we can strengthen our own integrity is to support others in living their truth. It is not for you to judge another's truth, but to empower them to live it. It is very difficult for any of us to know what is right for another person. They may need an experience that you judge as bad or unnecessary. Encourage your brother to follow his heart, and support him in doing it. If he fails, he will learn why he has failed, and he will be ahead of where he is now. But no matter whether he wins or loses, he will know that he has a friend in you. Then he really wins.

Two of my friends, a married couple, were popular ministers at a very successful church in the Northwest. After years of building the ministry at this church, they were offered a position at a church in Hawaii, which they felt guided to accept. When they announced to the church that they were leaving, the congregants were disappointed, but they chose to congratulate the ministers and wish them well. Although I believe that most of the people in the church would have liked the couple to stay, the congregants supported them in doing what they felt would make them happy. The church people came out and gave them a huge congratulations and going-away Aloha party. A number of people showed up in flowered Aloha shirts and mu-mus. How loved and blessed the ministers felt to be supported in following their heart! Now the ministers are doing well in their new position, and the original church has an excellent new minister who is popular and appreciated by the members. Love does attract miracles.

If you give your friends the permission to follow their truth, you will find the permission to follow your own. When you rejoice in the good that others find, you will rejoice in your own, and others will stand behind you when you have an opportunity to succeed. And even if others do not seem to be there when you feel that you need them, you have One Friend inside your heart Whose strength and support you may *always* count on. When your heart is open, so are the gates of Heaven.

Be a giver, a supporter, a nourisher. Jesus told Peter, "If you love me, then feed my sheep." He meant that we are to nurture and protect and enfold one another with support for spiritual growth. I have had people tell me that at times I was the only person in their life who believed in them enough to encourage them to follow their dream. And that, they said, made all the difference. They went ahead and their life was richer for it. I cannot think of a greater gift that I would like to offer someone, for I cannot imagine a greater gift that I would like to receive. This world *can* be like Heaven. Our love is what makes it so.

The FLOW of GOOD

What to Do
in a Raging River

I am committed to truth, not consistency.

- Mahatma Gandhi

Two men were walking to a neighboring town when both of them fell in a raging river. One man panicked and feverishly attempted to buck the torrents in a struggle to make his way back to shore. In his resistance the river overcame him and he drowned. The other man decided not to fight the flow, and so he relaxed, laid back to the best of his ability, and allowed the river to carry him. Eventually the river deposited him on a calm shore, where he found himself in the town toward which he had been walking.

We are boatmen on the river of life, learning to navigate and enjoy the trip from the source to the ocean. At times it may seem that we do not have much choice about where or how swiftly the river is flowing. But we always have the power to steer our boat. We can direct our vessel in opposition to the current, or we can go with the power of the tide and use it to our advantage. The choice is ours.

The chief characteristic of the river is that it is always alive in the moment. If we are flowing with it, we are one with the force that empowers it. "You must become one with the Force," Yoda told Luke Skywalker. Another skywalker, Richard Bach tells our story:

> *Once there lived a village of creatures along the bottom of a great crystal river...Each creature in its own manner clung tightly to the twigs and rocks of the river bottom, for clinging was their way of life, and resisting the current was what each had learned from birth. But one creature said at last, "I am tired of clinging. Though I cannot see it with my eyes, I trust that the current knows where it is going. I shall let go, and let it take*

209

me where it will.''

The other creatures laughed and said, ''Fool...Let go and that current you worship will throw you tumbled and smashed across the rocks.''

Yet in time, as the creature refused to cling again, the current lifted him free from the bottom, and he was bruised and hurt no more.[1]

Getting the Point

At some point in your soul's evolution, you must decide if you are going to live for your own heart's calling or for the dictates of the masses. The world functions according to error, and to be truly happy you must learn to honor and follow the truth that you feel in your own heart. This is especially important when your inner guidance nudges you in a direction other than the one to which most people subscribe. But you must do what you do because it is true for you, regardless of what seems to be true for others.

When I was thirteen years old I celebrated my *bar mitzvah*, one of the most time-honored traditions in the Jewish religion. For years I prepared by learning the Hebrew language, history, and the significant rituals associated with this rite of passage from youth to manhood.

Sitting with my friends in the temple one sabbath morning, I heard my name called to step up to the altar to recite a blessing over the Torah, the great scrolled Bible.

''What should I do when I get up there?'' I whispered to a big brother.

''Just watch what they do, and do as they do,'' he answered.

Soon I found myself standing in the center of the house of worship on a platform with the rabbi, the cantor, and the president of the synagogue, all elders of the temple. Anxiously I recited the blessing and then watched the cantor read from the ancient text. I noticed that he used an ornately carved pointer, a silver tool with a small hand figured into the end. He used this instrument to follow the lettering of the Torah from which he chanted in a haunting melody. When he finished reading he lifted the Torah high above his head, at the sight of which the congregation rose and joined in a traditional chant of praise. Hearkening to my friend's advice, I followed the cantor's lead in word and movement.

The cantor turned his attention to the soft velour cloth upon which the

---

[1] Bach, *Illusions*, p. 6

Torah had lain. Then he began to stroke the table in horizontal movements. The president took his hand and did the same. Then the rabbi came over and performed a like movement over the cloth.

Remembering my friend's advice to watch their cues, and not wanting to be remiss in performing the appropriate rituals, I stepped up to the altar and began to stroke the cloth in exactly the same fashion. I watched the elders' faces to see if I was doing it correctly, and they were pleased.

"Well?" the cantor whispered to me as I finished.

"Well, what?" I whispered back, hoping I hadn't unknowingly committed a sacreligious act.

"Did you find it?" he inquired.

"Find what?"

"The pointer."

The congregation chanted in the background.

"What pointer?"

"The pointer I was using to read from the Torah."

"I didn't know it was missing."

"Of course it is missing. Why do you think we were rubbing the cloth?"

"I thought it was part of the ceremony."

"What, 'part of the ceremony'? We lost the pointer. We thought you were helping us find it."

"I thought I was performing a religious act."

"Only if you believe in pointers."

Now I do believe in pointers — but I am starting to see that they are within my heart, and not on a table.

To Live in the Moment

It takes courage, clarity, and light-heartedness to live fully in the moment. This world is founded on trying to live in the last moment or the next, and very few people very rarely live in the present moment. Have you ever noticed that when you try to repeat an experience that is really great, it usually doesn't work? You have a spontaneous party that knocks everyone's socks off, or you do an inspired impromptu dance for a class, or you come up with an off-the-cuff joke that makes everyone laugh. The next time you tell the joke it sort of works, but not really as well as the first time. That is because it is not really the first time. It is a repeat of the first time, which is called the second time, and unless the energy is just right for it, it will not be as alive as the first time. There is, however, something that will work this time, and that is what the energy, the flow calls for this time. If you can tune into what the current moment wants to express, the energy will *always* be the first time. Life is an ever-expanding flow of first times. This is the secret of eternal youth.

Trusting the Process

I deeply admire people who are willing to trust the process of living as they play at the adventure of learning what this world is all about. Such persons are unafraid to look silly, fail, or be accused of changing their mind. It is no sin to make a mistake. The word "sin" comes from a Greek archery term meaning "to miss the mark." Notice that the definition does not include any sense of fear, eternal damnation, or losing the love of God (which is the only sure thing in all the universe!). All the word says is that you missed the mark. And when you miss the mark all you need to do is take another shot. It's that simple! But we have taken that light notion and made it heavy by our beliefs in heaviness. That is why the letters SIN actually stand for "Self-Inflicted Nonsense."

Life is a game of awakening in which we learn equally from our successes and errors. And all of the errors are worth it when you get it right. The way the game is designed we must keep trying until we get it right. Don't ever worry about making a mistake—you will always get another chance! Everyone who has ever lived on this planet has made plenty of errors, including Jesus. He fell three times under the cross, and he was not ashamed. In *A Course in Miracles* Jesus explains that he has faced, failed under, and overcome every earthly temptation that we face. If he hadn't encountered and risen above the same obstacles that we meet, he would not be in a position to help us overcome them. But he has, and so he stands beside us, happy to walk with us to make our way light. Thank you, our elder brother.

Patricia Sun calls this process "the wobbles:" Imagine you are a kid and you see someone zipping by on a snazzy ten-speed bike. "Wow!" you exclaim, "That sure looks like fun! I wish I could do that!" So you go out and a get a bike, but soon you discover that riding is not as easy as it looks. You get on the bike and immediately you flop on the ground to your right.

---

[2] T, p. 51

212

"I'm not doing that again!" you vow as you remount.

You start to ride again, and immediately you fall to the ground again, this time to the left.

"That's not it, either!" you discover, a little frustrated, yet still motivated.

On the next try you fall halfway to the right, but this time you catch yourself and shift your weight. But you shift it a little too much, and so you fall halfway to the left before you shift back. Still not perfect, but you're starting to get the idea.

The next time you fall a quarter-way to the right, then to the left, and so on, until after a series of ostensibly clumsy movements you somehow learn the art of balancing and, incidentally, riding a bike.

It is important to understand that *every one of those falls contributed to your ultimate success.* Yes, you may incur some bruises and scrapes in the process, but they are gone after a few days, while the knowledge of how to ride a bike lasts a lifetime. Not a bad deal.

Being Real

What some of us do when we get frustrated and don't seem to be making any progress is to discover that we can put the kickstand down and sit on the bike so that other people will think that we are riding it. It's called "looking cool." This works for a while, but sooner or later it gets very boring — and besides, we are not getting anywhere.

So we look cool in our relationships, our bodies, our families, our jobs, our religions, our nations. We say the right words, know the right people, wear the attractive clothes, utter the current catch-phrases, espouse the popular philosophies — except meanwhile we are dying inside. Sooner or later we realize that we are not really getting anywhere, and we decide that we'd rather be real than look cool. We want to learn to ride so much that we are willing to tell the truth about our not being able to ride now, if that will help us get where we are going. So, with the loving assistance of those who have already ridden, we pull up the kickstand and really go for it — not just make believe we are going for it, but we really make up our mind that riding is what we want.

Then something really miraculous happens. Somehow, through some process bigger then ourself, we learn. We learn to get from one place to the next by being honest about where we are. We see that falling down and getting up again and keeping trying is more satisfying than sitting in a seat going nowhere. And we wonder why we ever tried to kid ourselves. We discover that life is about learning to pull up the kickstand and we ride.

The Courage to Change

Flowing with the river of life gives us the freedom to be who we are and do what we feel guided to do in any given moment, unshackled by the past, expectations, or fear. It is only when we crawl out on the skinny branches that we can see how far the tree goes and we can grab the fruit that no one else can reach.

I knew a wonderful man who had the courage to change his life and his name as he went along. When I first heard of him he was called "Baba Gil." He sat in Central Park in New York City as a silent yogi, communicating only in a language of hand signals that he had devised. He and his friends slept on rooftops, lived simply, and served freely all who came to them for love and guidance.

Several years later Gil renounced the life of a yogi and became a Christian. It was at his retreat land in Ithaca, New York that I first met Gil, who by then had changed his name to "Freedom." He had given all the people in his community colorful names like "Precious," "Fountain," and "Praise." How melodic it was to hear those names being called throughout the day at this peaceful community! At this retreat site Freedom taught the power of following the life of Christ, living humbly in sharing and service. It was a marvelous, life-changing experience for me to be with him for one weekend.

Later I learned that Freedom had moved to Israel and become an Orthodox Jew, and he was studying the Torah with learned rabbis.

Now some might say that this young man couldn't make up his mind, but I would say that he had the courage to be whatever he was with the richest involvement. Whatever he was, it was not phony; his motive was sincerely to know and share God in the highest form that he knew. Why should it matter if he changed roles as he grew? If one accepts the idea of reincarnation, we are told that we go through different roles in different lives, wearing different hats according to what our soul needs to learn and teach. Why, then, should it be surprising for one man to go through several different experiences in one lifetime?

We are living in times of rapid change. Many metaphysical teachers tell us that life experiences have been speeded up so that we can learn many lessons in a short time. If we are not aware of this important process we may believe that something is wrong with us for going through dramatic changes, while in fact all we are doing is learning quickly.

Many of us in this generation, for example, have gone through two or three marriages or significant relationships, and we wonder why this is happening. We may even begin to doubt our sanity or self-worth. We experience these changes not because there is something wrong with us; to the contrary, we have had the courage to learn and grow a great deal in a short time. Praise be to us for being willing to open to greater love!

Hilda has explained it this way: "Lessons that in the past would have taken a lifetime to learn, now are being learned in just a few years. In past lives it took a whole lifetime to be married to someone, learn the appropriate lessons, and work out a relationship. Now that is happening in a small portion of that time. It is like going through two or three lifetimes in one."

Adopting this view of the changes in our life is not to support running away from a relationship before it is complete, but it is to offer the possibility that if a relationship is indeed complete, the universe will move us naturally on to our next experience, and we need not harbor guilt feelings about having moved through the lessons in a shorter time than we expected. To know whether you are running scared or are complete, you must look within your own heart and ask the indwelling Spirit for your personal answer. As the Yaqui Indian mentor Don Juan told Carlos Casteneda, "You can leave only when you are free of fear or ambition."[3]

To further illuminate this lesson, Ramtha tells us, *"Love yourself...And listen to what self says, what it needs to feel, and then pursue it, heartily, until you're bored with it. Boredom is a sign from your soul that you have learned all there is to learn from an experience, and that it is time to go on to another adventure. When you listen only to the feelings within you, then you are free to become in this moment whatever you choose to become."[4]*

Great Love Relationships

This is perhaps a fertile juncture at which to discuss the "'til death do us part" clause in the traditional marriage ceremony. This is, of course, a

---

[3] Carlos Casteneda, *The Teachings of Don Juan, A Yaqui Way of Knowledge*, Ballentine Books, 1968

[4] Weinberg, *Ramtha*, p. 133

commonly applied sanction against divorce. But we need to acknowledge that there are many forms of death: physical death, emotional death, and spiritual death, for example, all equally real in our experience. It seems to me to be a rather arbitrary delineation to choose physical death alone as the one that is legal to do us part. Relationships are born and relationships die, and a relationship can be dead long before one of the physical bodies is. In fact, physical death doesn't have much power to change a relationship at all, for the realm in which relationships exist is that of the mind, and minds always outlive bodies.

The death of a partner is no guarantee of the completion of a relationship. Just because someone leaves this world does not mean that the relationship is ended. Because relationships are spiritual lessons, they are complete only when our spirit is at peace. The fact that a body is gone does not mean that the lesson has been learned. In fact, I wonder if the "'til the death do us part" clause may actually encourage people to leave their body instead of heal the relationship! Someone once said that death is one way out of a bad marriage, chosen as an avenue that seems easier than confronting the issues in life. Now this certainly does not mean that anyone who dies is doing so just to get out of a marriage, but it may mean that some of us have chosen disease rather than discussion. Perhaps, just perhaps, if we were willing to face the relationship and bring it into the light, or to leave the relationship in dignity in life, we would not feel that we had to escape into death. As *A Course in Miracles* tells us, death is not to be equated with peace; only love can be equated with peace.

There have been many, many great love relationships that have *increased* in power after the physical parting of the pair; many relationships have been healed after one of the partners has passed on, because the surviving mate had a change in his or her consciousness. In such a wonderful awakening there grows *more* love after the other person has left this world. Bodies actually have very little to do with real relationships.

No Real Separation

Sometimes physical separation can be a very viable avenue for healing a relationship. In fact, if the temporary or permanent distancing of two bodies contributes to the emotional healing of one or both of the couple, separation is actually a misnomer, for the end result is greater spiritual *union*. Once again we see that it is not what bodies do that makes love, but what the spirit in those bodies is feeling.

If one or both persons are dying emotionally in the relationship, it is no longer a relationship, but a litany to sacrifice. Destructiveness is not a worthy goal of the Children of God. A relationship in which one or both partners are suffering must be brought quickly to the One who can heal it. At such a time it is extremely important to remember that God's will for your relationship is only joy, and that if you are feeling anything less than peace you have forgotten that you deserve only love.

It is certainly possible that the relationship has offered both of you all that you can receive at this level of your understanding, and struggling to keep it alive would be as futile and heartbreaking as attempting to keep a loved one on earth when they have chosen to pass on to the next life.

The ending of a marriage or relationship has very often *improved* the relationship. Many persons have reported to me that the official breaking up of a relationship was actually a step toward the beginning of a deeper and more productive friendship with their now ex-husband, -friend, or -lover! At any given moment we do not know the true purpose of any experience. Temporary separation can often lead to a long-term healing of the spirit.

Of what use to God is a relationship in which two people live under one roof harboring deep feelings of loneliness, fear, and separation? These are not the feelings that the Children of Light were born to know. Though we can become accustomed to alienation, we will never be satisfied with it. What seems to be the death of a relationship may just be a sleep. Like the trees in the winter that have lost their leaves and appear dead though they are not, relationships appearing to be dead are simply going through a season of transformation, a temporary period of apparent darkness that will ultimately culminate in deeper bonding. *A Course In Miracles* tells us that it is the destiny of all relationships to become holy.[5]

All possible attempts should be made to find harmony and healing with your mate. This was, and remains the purpose of your sharing your path. Your healing always involves releasing the expectations and projections that you have brought into the relationship. At some point you must acknowledge that your mate is not your mother or father, and rejoice in the awareness that your partner is a beautiful being in his or her own light.

In times of challenge in a relationship it is advisable for each or both of the partners to do what they need to do to regain the true function of relationship, which is to bring greater and greater creativity into the activities of their life. A physical separation may renew the spirit of the relationship in the direction of re-joining physically, or it may renew the self toward moving in a new direction. Or, after taking the issue into meditation, it may be revealed that no separation is necessary. The important change is that the goal of supporting one another in greater aliveness has replaced the goal of deepened fear, and this is the key that opens the door to healing.

The spiritual path calls for an extremely keen sense of intuition and stark honesty. At a point of crisis or confusion you must turn to the Voice of the Holy Spirit within you, and ask for help. But you must be willing to hear His answer, and not the one you brought before you asked the question. Be assured that His answer will bring far greater peace than yours. If your answer brought you peace you would not need to turn to Him for His. And be you glad that He does have the answer in which everyone involved will win. You will go on from here with the realization that the One who has shown you the way walks with you always.

The Psychic Integrity of Children

Almost always there is a fear to end a marriage or relationship out of concern for the children. This is a most valid concern. Loving and supporting our children is one of the most liberating and healing lessons of a lifetime. It is true that our children are gifts from God.

One of the questions that we may overlook when becoming anxious about the future is, "What is it like for the kids *now?*" Children, like all of us, are very psychic, often moreso than adults. We can be sure that they are well aware of all the feelings and dynamics of a strained (or wonderful) relationship, though we may never say a word out loud about it. Making believe that nothing is wrong can create more confusion and distress for the child than openly discussing the situation. When efforts are made to conceal the difficulties, the child is learning that what is happening is so bad that it needs to be hidden. This can be a much more painful and confusing lesson than that mommy and daddy are not getting along well and they are having a hard time being together. Believe me, they know it anyway.

At such a time of strain, there are two actions that will carry you through all kinds of flak: *forgiveness* and *vision.* You must forgive yourself and your partner for what you perceive to be your errors. Do not berate yourself or your partner for not being totally enlightened saints. If you were, you would not be here in the first place. Remember that earth is a school, and you came here to master your lessons. When a challenging lesson comes up we should give thanks, for this means that we are ready to master it and become even grander in spirit.

Second, you must have the *vision* to see how beautiful you, your partner, and your family are, no matter what the outer circumstances would indicate. Outer circumstances are deceptive, and you will not win by judging the situation as what it seems to be. Remember that the children as well as the parents are whole and wise beings. To treat any of you like you are small, fearful, or unaware is to ignore the truth of your wisdom. Remember that all of you know the way out of the forest and into peace, and you are here to support and empower one another in drawing that wisdom into action.

Love is the Guide

A piece of paper does not make a marriage, a divorce, a parent, a teacher, or an expert. The only proof of a person being born is that he is alive, and no amount of documentation or lack of it could prove otherwise. Such is the impotence of a parchment in marriage or divorce. In all of these situations the truth in the heart of the relationship far supercedes a signature, and in the case of marriage it is clear that many persons are not married even though they hold a certificate saying they are. At the same time many persons who have never gone to a justice of the peace have much justice of peace in their relationship, being deeply married by virtue of the commitment they hold toward one another in their hearts. It is also obvious that a relationship can continue, for better or worse, long after a judge says it is over. Marriage is a state of mind and heart, and as we honor the truth that lives within our being we move into greater clarity about who we are and what we are to do.

I hope you will not read that I am encouraging marriage, divorce, separation, or any particular form of relationship. I am encouraging whatever will bring real peace to the soul in any given circumstance. The Holy Spirit does not have a fixed position on anything except to support whatever creates happiness and harmony in one's inner and outer life. It is the rational, linear mind that believes that one way always produces one result, while the Holy Spirit knows that results are quite particular to the situation. Love alone sees that each act is to be judged not by the form that it takes, but by the peace that we feel.

The End of Pain

All pain is born of resistance. Wherever there is pain, whether it is physical, emotional, mental, or spiritual, you can be sure that there is a resistance behind it. To know this is to understand that the way to be free of pain is to let go of resistance. Mahatma Gandhi underwent a surgical operation without anesthesia; he had no pain because his whole life was an ode to non-resistance. Skydivers are taught to land in a crouch and roll to ride with the energy of the impact. The same truth is demonstrated in the martial arts, which are based upon taking the force delivered by the opponent and using it to one's own advantage instead of fighting back. What flows, goes; what resists, persists.

One afternoon I attended a meeting at which there was a man who had hurt himself in a bicycle fall on his way there. His knee was hurting him, and so we invited him to lie down on the floor for a group healing. All of us surrounded him, placed our hands gently upon him, and visualized him filled and surrounded by healing white light. As we did so he began to relax. I could see a change beginning to happen in his body. I watched his face become softer and lighter, until the tension and discomfort left him completely. I must say he looked quite beatific! It was an amazing transformation to watch, and a powerful lesson to learn.

As he was resting quietly, these words came into my awareness: *"No mind, no pain."* In other words, when his mind had removed itself from the pain, by placing his attention on a healing light, the pain was gone.

We always get more of what we think about, and we are psychically tied to what we resist. When we hate someone we carry them with us wherever we go, for our mind draws them to us like a big fishing line. *A Course in Miracles* tells us that if we keep someone in prison (in our thoughts) we must stay there with them to make sure they don't escape. We imprison *ourself* with thoughts of hatred. Every judgement we hold is a bar of our cell, and our desire to be right is the lock. Here it is easy to see that forgiveness is the key to our freedom. When you release someone from the prison of your angry thoughts about them, it is actually yourself that you are pardoning. Then both of you are free. By the same principle we can liberate ourself from any kind of pain simply by releasing it from our mind and turning the entire situation over to Spirit.

It is never our job to punish anyone. When we punish anyone physically or mentally we punish ourself, for in doing so we teach ourself that punishment is an effective way to heal, which it never is. And more harmfully, we reinforce the idea in our mind that we and the other person deserve punishment. You can be sure that the next time you commit the crime for which you would have the other punished (and you most certainly will commit it, for you are attempting to punish him for your sense of sin) you will feel guilty, and then both of you have lost. Here the *Course* tells us, *"Do not teach your brother that he is anything you would not want to be."* For your own peace of mind free the world, and you will be free with it.

With All Your Heart

Forms, rituals, and institutions are born of high intention, but they can be perpetuated by fear. We invent rituals to help us remember a beautiful feeling of connectedness with God, but unless our hearts are turned to Heaven as we enter into them, they become empty shells. Jesus said, "Do not pray with long exhortations. Pray with all your heart." If we trusted our hearts enough we would be in a constant state of prayer, for we would feel the aliveness of every moment and we would want to give thanks for it. True prayer is not invoked by one's lips, but through one's being. Those truly in love need no coercion to say, "I love you," and those truly in prayer do not need a plan to make love with God in every activity of their day. To call one activity "prayer" and another activity something else would blaspheme the truth that every moment is an invitation to live in Paradise. Those who have found their way back to the Garden realize they have never left It. And now they walk consciously. The gentleness of their being is a blessing to God, and they glorify Spirit by shining His love into the world as they pass through it. They know that Heaven is already present on earth, and they teach it simply by being happy here.

The Coming of Age of Strength

We were not meant to live in pain. We have not realized this because we have never experimented with letting go of our pain long enough to learn that there is no value in it. We cannot have strength and pain at the same time.

There is no virtue in suffering.

Many of us are experiencing a growing up of the soul, an awakening to our own strength, a celebration of the integrity of our own perfect being. We are being loosed from the path of recipes, external gurus, and standard formats, and turning toward the wisdom of our own inner knowing. To one accustomed to finding cues from without, this can be very disconcerting, harrowing, and even terrifying. Yet the plan is wrought with full wisdom, for God seeks to nurture Children who find full divinity and happiness within their own self.

The one truth about life is that it is alive, and this means it is constantly becoming something new and better. The universe never moves backward. Perception of backwardness is a sign of fear of forwardness. Anyone who has ever advanced in life has learned the joy and the adventure of launching into new territory. It is said that "a ship in the harbor is safe, but that is not what ships are for." There is wisdom in flexibility, and greatness in innocent acceptance. When you accept life, you will have accepted yourself, because life is what you are.

Don't stop now. You will advance if you let go of the twigs and rocks you are hanging on to, and let the river take you home.

> *When you have learned how to decide with God, all decisions become as easy and as right as breathing. There is no effort, and you will be led as gently as if you were being carried down a quiet path in summer.*[6]

---

[6] T, p. 260

The Pig of God

Trust would settle every problem now.
                                     - *A Course in Miracles*[1]

A man was driving up a winding mountain road, ever cautious of the twists and turns on the narrow precipice. Approaching a hairpin curve at the steepest point, he was startled by the unexpected *vrummm!* of a little red sports car as it whizzed past him from the hidden side of the bend. The speeding roadster cut him off, missing his vehicle by inches, and caused him to veer toward the mountain, where he came to a halt just short of the rocks.

As if that were not enough of an insult, the driver of the other car, a portly woman with a tense face, raised her arm toward him and shouted, *"Pig!"* as she passed.

Infuriated, the man shook his fist at her, called her *"Sow!"* and rounded the turn from which she had come, where he ran headlong into a pig sitting on his side of the road.

How quick we are to assume that someone is trying to hurt us, when actually they are attempting to help. You can probably identify with the driver who mistook a blessing for an attack. Indeed much of our lives has been steeped in fear that others have been out to get us, when actually they were serving us in ways that were not obvious to us at the time. One might say that we have suffered from a deep sense of paranoia, the fear that the world is out to get us.

But our challenging experiences are actually opportunities for us to choose again. If we are willing to see the good in a situation, we will be less likely to be afraid the next time that circumstance arises.

A friend of mine was driving home late one night in New York City. When she stopped at a red light she noticed a man in the car next to her trying to get her attention. He was driving a big red Cadillac convertible with a playboy bunny symbol hanging from the rear view mirror, and loud music

---

[1] T, p. 519

blaring from several speakers. He leaned over his velour seat cover, smiled through his sunglasses, and waved to her.

"I can do without this tonight," my friend thought to herself. She ignored him, waited for the light to turn green, and stepped on the gas.

When she reached the next red light, there he was again. Again he tapped on the window and tried to get her to look at him. Once again she looked the other way and drove on.

At the next light the scene repeated itself, but this time she decided she had to do something about this annoying man. She locked her door, rolled down her window, and asked what he wanted.

"Your lights are off!" was his message.

"Thank you!" was hers, and gratefully she drove home.

Do you believe that life is *for* you, or *against* you? This is the basic question that you must answer. But answer it honestly, for in so doing you will discover the perceptions in your mind from which your whole world has arisen. Your thoughts do not spring from your experiences; your experiences spring from your thoughts. Beware what thoughts you allow to root in your holy mind, Child of God. You have the power to create an entire life from the tiniest thoughts. Be vigilant, and think with God.

Creative Investment

Trust is like a muscle. You must exercise it to enjoy its benefits. *"Use it or lose it"* is a principle that applies to the psychic world as well as the physical. When you open your mind to the greatest possibilities of every situation, you will grow younger and more alive with each experience. Joy is the natural consequence of trusting, and those who practice faith are rewarded with success to match their vision.

If you do not exercise your capacity to trust, you will find yourself sealed in a little ball of protectiveness, and you will wonder why life has treated you so harshly. When we close ourself down to trusting, we shrivel up and become crabby. In fear, we attempt to wall other people away from us, but the net effect is that we seal ourself in. Hugh Prather said, "Letting other people in is pretty much a matter of not spending the energy to keep them out."[2] Defensiveness requires a tremendous investment of energy to push other people away and maintain our lonely outpost of isolation. That

[2]Prather, *Notes to Myself*

energy could be used for contacting hearts, healing yourself and others, and celebrating your whole life. The choice of what you do with your energy is up to you. That is what free will is. You are not free to determine how it will all turn out, for God has promised a happy outcome to all situations. But you are free to grump and groan and delay your awakening. As *A Course in Miracles* asks us, "Why wait for Heaven?"[3]

We hurt ourself when we decide about a person or situation beforehand. "Prejudice" means "pre-judgement," or assuming that you know the outcome of a situation before it happens. What guarantee do you have that anything will turn out like it did before? You judge the present on the basis of the past, and there is no basis for this. We continually recreate the past not because the present is like the past, but because we expect it to be, and so we set up situations and recreate events. Then we complain that the universe is working against us — when all the while we were working against ourselves!

But it doesn't have to be that way. We can allow each moment to be fresh and new and different than ever before. Just think: *you can end any destructive pattern of your relationships right now!* You can start over and have your relationships be fresh and alive, totally untainted by your history. Your history is not your destiny. When you place your well-being in the hands of God, you will find your future miraculously different than the past. All of this is within your power to create right now.

The Inner Guardian

Trusting does not imply that you must trust, agree to, or do everything that anyone asks or tells you to do. Nor does it mean that you should do anything that would hurt you or make you or anyone else unhappy; that would indeed be foolish, and it is not necessary. Trust means honoring the voice of the Holy Spirit *within* you. Every "should I?" question can be answered by turning within. The Holy Spirit will tell you quite clearly what book to read, which job to take, where to live, what teacher to study with, who to marry or not marry, what school to enroll your children in, and any other question the thinking mind can conjure up. But you must be willing to listen. If you do not hearken unto the Voice of Peace, you cannot blame God for your errors. "If you cannot hear the Voice for God, it is because you do

---

[3] W, p. 347

not choose to listen."[4] And once you do choose to listen, all of Heaven and earth will rush to fill your every need, for you have chosen to take the hand of the One who knows the way to peace.

Jesus said, "Be as clever as serpents and as gentle as doves." If your mind is peaceful and relaxed through trusting the process of living, you will be open to guidance from the divine mind *within* you. This inner voice is always available to light your way safely in the presence of unscrupulous persons or dangerous situations.

One afternoon I went out to lunch with my friend Denise Cooney, a free-spirited healer who channels excellent psychic writing and counseling. Outside the restaurant I met a fellow who asked me if I wanted to buy a car stereo. Ironically, I was looking for a car stereo at the time, and I accepted his invitation to look at one he had for sale.

He took Denise and me to the trunk of his car, which he opened to reveal a wealth of stereo equipment. The fellow explained to me that he worked at a store on Route 46, and his manager wanted to clear out these models to make way for new stock. I asked him if I could bring the stereo back to the store if I had any problems with it.

"Well, uh, not exactly," he hesitated. "Actually, these models come from the warehouse, and my boss doesn't want people coming to the warehouse. But I'm sure you'll have no problem with it. This here is an expensive unit, and I can give it to you for only $140."

I looked at the unit. It was one of the cheapest, tinniest stereos I have ever seen. Most stores would probably sell it for about $39.95.

Denise leaned over to me and whispered in my ear, "I don't think you should buy this thing."

I leaned back and whispered, "I don't need a psychic to tell me that!"

But I really enjoyed this fellow. He was a perfect flim-flam man. He rapped on and on about the high quality of his product, and he had an answer for every question I asked him. I was not really interested in the stereo, but I was very impressed with his pitch. I love anyone who is masterful at what they do. I prefer a really good bad guy over a mediocre good guy. If someone is really good at being bad, I honor them as a pure character. (Darth Vader is one of my favorite characters. He's so deliciously evil! This stereo salesman must have graduated from the same school.)

"Well, I don't think I'm going to buy the stereo," I told him, "but I

---

[4] T, p. 57

really love your rap. I must tell you that I think you're a great salesman. I bet you'll do well at whatever you put your mind to.''

I shook his hand and Denise and I walked on down Speedwell Avenue. When we rounded the first corner, both of us broke up into hysterics.

"Wasn't he great?" I asked Denise.

"He was phenomenal!" she agreed. "If I ever go into business I'll hire him as my sales rep!"

Both of us truly appreciated this fellow, and we held no grievance toward him. He was playing his part as a great con-man, and it was up to us as to how we wanted to play with him. We chose simply to enjoy him.

Divine Protection

One night a friend of mine was awakened by the sound of a burglar crawling through his apartment window. My friend got up, turned on the light, and spoke to the startled intruder.

"You don't have to break in here like that," he told the man. "I will help you if I can, without your needing to rob me. What is happening in your life that is making you feel you need to steal?"

The burglar sat down and told the man about his life. The conversation ended with my friend giving the man some money and walking him out the front door.

My friend Betty is another person who practices the presence of God. Once she loaned her car to a hitchhiker. The young man that she picked up hitchhiking asked her if she knew the way to a certain town farther than where she was going. "I'm going to patch things up with my wife," he told her. "I've decided to try to make it work this time." Betty offered him her car, and gratefully he accepted. He dropped Betty off at her home, and he went on with the car (a nice one, at that!).

Hours went by, and the man did not return. "I wondered if it was the right thing to do," Betty later confessed to me. "Then, late that evening he showed up at the door with his wife and a little child. Tearfully they thanked me and told me they were taking a new step in their relationship. He returned the keys and blessed me."

Betty also rarely locks her car. Sometimes she leaves the keys on the seat. Yet her car has never been stolen or tampered with. "I just put the car in God's hands," Betty explains. Betty's powerfully faithful outlook and practice reminded me of a statement made to me by one of the boys I used to work with in a youth counseling center. This fellow had stolen a number of things. "Locks are for honest people," he told me. "If someone really wants to steal something, a lock is not going to stop them."

I am thinking, too, of Peace Pilgrim, the saintly minister who travelled thousands of miles on foot to act as an emissary of peace. This noble woman accepted rides and lodging only when they were offered. On several occasions men picked her up in cars, and took her to places where they had less than lofty intentions. "But no harm ever came to me," Peace tells. "I would begin talking to them about who I was, or I would but look into their eyes for a moment, and they realized what I stand for. My divinity and my purpose were my protection."

Belief Creates Experience

You may, of course, be able to cite examples of cases in which you trusted and you felt hurt as a result. All of us have had the experience of feeling that our faith has not been justified. But we find examples of what we want to be true. If you are afraid and you feel you need protection you will find proof that this is so. And if you want to believe that you are protected by virtue of your thoughts and your divinity, you shall find abundant examples to support that belief. And you will create more and more experiences to demonstrate that what you believe is correct. You can create an entire world and have many people live in it with you if your mind is sufficiently dedicated to an idea!

Belief does not stem from examples. Examples arise from belief. Therefore choose well what you would believe.

All Experiences Lead to Awakening

Even if you do seem to get "taken," there is a way to look at such an experience that will bring awakening and healing.

A fellow named Bob telephoned Hilda from California, and he complained that he had been swindled by an unscrupulous auto mechanic. "I paid $400 for this job, and then when I went around the corner I found out I could have gotten it done elsewhere for $75! What do you think I should do?" he anxiously asked.

"Let me ask you this, Bob," Hilda replied. "You take a lot of consciousness trainings and workshops, don't you?''

"Yes, that's right."

"Well, then, imagine that someone offered you a training in discernment, in which you would be taught how to make wise choices about dealing in the business world, choices which would save you money in the long run. Let's say this course was being given over two weekends at a cost of $325. And imagine that you would be absolutely guaranteed to increase your sensitivity to feeling the vibrations of people and making correct decisions in your financial affairs. Would you take the course?"

"You bet!" Bob answered quickly.

"Then you should be grateful to this auto mechanic. You got the course in one afternoon."

The Answer to Fear

At the Human Unity Conference in Hawaii in 1985 Bishop Antonius Markos of Africa gave an address on world peace. He related an experience he had in his motel room.

"There was a bold sign in my room that said, "Please lock your suitcase." So I began to. But something in me felt out of line as I was doing so. I felt that I was attempting to protect myself out of fear. It dawned on me that me locking my suitcase was not much different than the governments of the world arming themselves with nuclear weapons. They claim that the reason they have nuclear weapons is to protect themselves. From who? From other countries who have nuclear weapons! And why do those countries have those armaments? To protect themselves from the countries who are protecting themselves from them! And so it goes on.

"The problem is not nuclear weapons, but fear. It is the consciousness of fear that leads us to believe that we need to protect ourselves. Perhaps if one country would stop protecting itself, it would be an example to the world, and we could start a chain reaction of love. And perhaps if each of us would begin disarmament in our own heart, the nations of the world would follow suit."

Where Freedom Lies

If your world is to change — and it is — there is but one place that trust can begin, and that is in your own mind. If you wait for life to demonstrate to you that it is trustworthy, you shall have long cobwebs upon your cobwebs before you realize that life gives you only the gifts that you bring to it. The only way to prove trust is to practice it. A simple principle, is it not? Yet your practice requires persistent exercise, for you have succeeded in convincing yourself that you need protection from something "out there." There is nothing out there. But you have proved that there is by the amount of effort you have invested in keeping it away from you! A man who builds a fortress to protect himself from demons believes that his walls are affording him safety. But he certainly cannot be considered free. His freedom lies only in removing his walls, for only then can he recognize that he was free without them.

The same mind that hypnotized you into believing that your fears were worth heeding, can teach you that your love is even more worth heeding. That mind is none other than your own, and now is the only moment you can change its direction. That change is not accomplished by force or struggle, but by opening. You will gain far more by releasing your need for defense than by attempting to acquire safety. You cannot acquire what you already have. But you can recognize and acknowledge it. You can fling your dark dreams to the wind, and step forward through the open door that leads to the light. Then, and only then, can you say that you are home free.

There is a plot, and indeed the world is out to get us. But it is not a plot to hurt us at all; it is a plan of the greatest love in all the universe. The game is simple: you keep playing until you realize that there is only love. Then you keep playing until everyone else finds love within their own heart. When everyone knows that there is nothing to fear, the nightmare is over and the celebration begins.

The Final Embarrassment

"My attack thoughts are attacking my invulnerability."
- A Course in Miracles[1]

All of us have had our embarrassing moments. When I was six years old the landlord of our apartment complex called me into our kitchen where he was visiting with some of the ladies in the neighborhood. He beckoned me to come close to him, so he could whisper something in my ear. When I did, he snatched the drawstring of my pajama pants, and dropped them to the floor. I ran out of the room screaming, terribly embarrassed.

When I was in junior high school one of the "coolest" things to do was to go to a high school dance. One Friday night I was invited by some friends to go to the local high school dance, and I was ecstatic. There was a live rock 'n' roll band who wore matching sequined jackets, rhythmically bopped and weaved from side to side, and played loud electric guitar music. As far as I was concerned, I was in Heaven to be in such an "in" place. I sort of wandered around with my friends (I was too shy to dance) and acted cool.

Can you imagine how nerdy I felt when a voice came over the loud-speaker announcing, "Alan Cohen...Please go to the door. Your mother is waiting for you."

The pits!

It seemed like all the kids laughed as I slinked out the door. If there is one thing a fourteen-year-old boy at a high school dance does not want, it is for his mother to come and fetch him from a high school dance in front of his friends.

Years later I found myself sitting on the stage at Hilda's class one Thursday evening. I looked out at the three hundred faces in the audience, and I was excited about performing for them.

"Hilda is ready for us to play now," I heard a whisper over my shoulder. I picked up my guitar and walked to center stage with Toni, the singer I was to accompany.

---

[1] W, p. 40

The first verse went impeccably, and the crowd was pleased. It was a great feeling to have them enjoy the music! Toni was energized, too.

Then, about halfway through the second verse, Toni did something quite alarming. In between her lines she reached over, grabbed my guitar at the frets, and held the strings down so I could not continue playing. Then she told me in a loud voice that everyone could hear, "You're playing the wrong chords!"

Well, I was never so embarrassed in all my life! How dare she do that in front of all those people! I just wanted to shrivel up in my seat and slither off the stage like a little snake. What nerve! I sat there and fumed for a while.

After a few minutes a thought occurred to me. The thought was that I actually might have been playing the wrong chords. (I hadn't considered that before.) Reflecting upon it further, I realized Toni was right. That made me feel even worse. I sat there and felt dumb.

A few minutes later another notion came into my awareness, a thought that came from a different voice than the one that was embarrassed. This voice asked me a question.

"*Think, Alan,*" it gently counselled, "*What is it in you that is embarrassed?*"

Hmmm.

"*What is it in you that cares what these people think about you? What part of you is beating yourself because you made a mistake? Who is it that is upset?*"

Those were quite some questions. As I thought about it I realized that the only part of me that could be embarrassed was my ego. The ego is concerned only with appearances, and the ego really comes to life when appearances come into play. The ego consistently chooses form over content. And we always lose when we see with our eyes instead of our heart.

At the same time I realized that there was more to me than my ego. There was a part of me that could never be hurt; that while the ego was ranting and raving and doing its little dance, there was a place in me — the real me — that could never be touched by any embarrassment. My real self rests safe and secure in the sanctuary of peace within my heart, and nothing that seems to happen can take peace from me as long as I remember who I am.

Can you imagine how freeing it is to find out that you are not something that you were afraid you were? It is like being let out of prison, or being pardoned from execution. And then realizing that it was only you who put yourself there in the first place!

I got so high on this awareness that I just wanted to hug Toni and tell her, "Thank you." The Spirit within me was soaring! While I felt smaller in the public eye, I actually felt freer and greater within myself. It was one of those "Aha!" realizations, like a light breaking through the clouds.

Fifteen minutes later the ego came back to remind me that I had done something foolish not long ago. While I had quelled the ego's initial barrage, there were some reserves hiding in the hills. I looked out over the audience and saw them rapt in Hilda's lecture. The voice of wisdom spoke within me again: *"Alan,"* it laughingly explained, *"No one cares about your mistake as much as you do. Nobody else is thinking about it anymore except you. Everyone else forgot about it the moment it was over. And once you forget about it, it is done. You don't need to keep beating yourself. You are free to get off the cross right now. You put yourself there, and now you can take yourself off. You are free to be happy now."*

I looked out over the audience. I gazed across the sea of smiling faces, and I saw nothing but love. Love for me. Love for life. Love for God and good. And love for the blessing of being in that gift of a class. I, too, could enjoy that precious blessing — but I would have to forgive myself as they had forgiven me.

As I looked at their faces I realized that they were not my enemies or my accusors, but my friends. More than anything else they wanted me to win. I realized that they, too, had probably made mistakes like mine, and they could identify with me. "Who has judged you, now?" Jesus asked the adulterous woman. "No one, sire," she answered. "And neither do I judge you," he told her, and he gave her her release.

I don't think I've ever felt embarrassed like that again. That was pretty much the end of embarrassment in my life. Now, whenever feelings of fear of opinion or embarrassment come up, I ask myself, *"What is it in me that is embarrassed?"* The answer always comes, *"the ego."* Then I smile as I remember that my spirit could never be hurt, and I am free.

The Mirror's Gift

Terry Cole-Whittaker has written a best-selling book called, *What You Think of Me is None of My Business*. It is one of those books from which you can learn a great deal just from the title.

Fear of other people's opinions is actually a reflection of your fear of *your own* opinions. Whatever you are concerned that other people think about you, you are concerned about what *you* think about you. The world is our mirror. What we see out there reflects the thoughts that we harbor within our own mind. But we are not ready to take responsibility for these thoughts, and so we attract people to act out what we are thinking. When we can see the persons in our life as mirrors of our own thoughts, we can learn about how we see ourself, and ultimately take complete responsibility for our life and our healing.

The way to heal our fear of other persons' opinions does not lie in attempting to change their opinions. This would be like a slave trying to escape from slavery by pleasing his master more. That would only cause the master to value the slave's bondage even more. The way to be free is to leave your master and become your own master.

The only way to resolve fear of opinion or criticism is to *heal your own mind* about the issues that are sensitive for you. If you were clear and comfortable about the things that others criticize about you, their opinions could not phase you in the least. But when someone hurts you with their thoughts or words about you, *there is a part of your mind that believes they are correct.* If I call you a frog, and you know that you are not a frog, then you will not think anything further of the idea, for it is clearly a misperception on my part. But if you harbor any doubt in your mind that you may indeed be a frog, my statement will irritate you and probably begin to work on you even after I have left your presence. You will be forced to confront your thoughts that you may be a frog. And that is wonderful, for it is the beginning of the healing that must ultimately result in your awareness of who you truly are.

Thus we see what a great service others offer us when they insult us, for they cause us to face our own doubts and judgements about ourself. Those veils must be lifted before you can see the face of Christ, which is your own. You cannot know that you are the Christ if you think you are a frog. Christhood and froghood have nothing in common, and you had better learn quickly who you are, or else you are doomed to swim around in the swamp for a while. You are free to hop out now and become a prince. Do not wait for some lovely maiden to come along and kiss you. Kiss yourself. Then you release yourself from the spell of disbelief in your own reality. Not that many women are interested in frogs these days. You stand a better chance of finding a princess if you acknowledge that you are a prince.

Take Back Your Power

You have been living in a dream. You have been hypnotized into believing that you are small, that you can be affected by the outside world, and that there is something "out there" that you do not already have. Take back your power now. You have sold yourself out, and it is about time you reeled in the strings that you have given other people to control you. Puppethood does not befit a Child of God. You were born to create marvelous productions instead of bouncing around like a floundering extra in someone else's show.

Wake up! You are not who you thought you were! And be thankful, for you are far greater than you have been taught. You have been taught mostly by people who do not know who they are. How, then, do you expect to learn of your magnanimity? You have studied with teachers who needed to learn what they were teaching. You have gone to therapists whose insanity exceeded your own. You have thrown yourself at the feet of gurus who were still living in darkness. No wonder you have not learned! You have had some very poor teachers!

You cannot fault your teachers for not teaching you what you were not willing to learn. If you were ready to be enlightened you would have found your way to a Christ. And you have. But your vigilance has been wanting. You already know the truth; you have just been taking your time about acknowledging and living it. And that is your right.

But it is also your right to choose Heaven now. There is not one further stone that blocks your way, unless you believe that healing comes from somewhere other than your own mind. Fear will take you down a dark and lonely detour, and you will feel prey to the vultures that rustle in the night. You will be frightened by the slightest sound, including the echoes of your own twisted thoughts. Yet at every intersection in the tangled forest you may choose to find your way out by following the way of forgiveness. There are no depths to which forgiveness will not reach its comforting hand and lift you far above the forest, to be trapped in darkness no more.

The doors to the Kingdom are opened to you. The keys are held by no one other than you. You may deny your identity, but you cannot dissolve it.

You may blaspheme your purity, but you will never violate it. The jewel of your heart has not been stolen by evil thieves. In wisdom your Father has held it for you until you were wise enough to appreciate it and not cast it into the sea. That day has come, beloved one. You have travelled long and hard to reach this moment, and it would be foolish to delay your homecoming any longer.

Open your mind to the beauty of your own being, and never again will the fear of opinion snatch your birthright from you. You live in a castle, and you play in the slums. Wherefore, O Child of Light, have you lost your self? Ah, but it is not lost; it has but been overlooked. The integrity of your innocence has been held in trust for you since you turned your back on it long ago. Here it remains, offered to you now at no cost, sacrifice, or bargain for your guilt in return.

There is one truth that will carry you through storms of doubt, fear, and guilt. It is a shining awareness that heals all pain and restores life to an empty heart. It is the memory of Heaven that has been implanted in your soul, and it remains safe and secure from the winds of fear that batter at the ramparts of your mind. It is the truth that you are a spiritual being, made in the reflection of a perfect Creator, and you are not touchable by any event or experience through which you pass.

What can hurt you now, O Child of God?

Discomfort is aroused only to bring the need for correction into awareness.[2]

---

[2] T, p. 32

The POWER of LOVE

There is no difficulty that enough love will not conquer; no disease that enough love will not heal; no door that enough love will not open; no gulf that enough love will not bridge; no wall that enough love will not throw down; no sin that enough love will not redeem.

It makes no difference how deeply seated may be the trouble, how hopeless the outlook, how muddled the tangle, how great the mistake. A sufficient realization of love will dissolve it all. If only you could love you would be the happiest and most powerful being in the world.

- Emmet Fox

The Miracle Worker

You're not a realist unless you believe in miracles.

- Anwar Sadat

"BASEBALL PLAYER HEALS BOY OF CANCER." The headline caught my eye; it was my kind of story. Before my life was dedicated to healing, it was dedicated to baseball, and the combination of the two loomed as a metaphysical jewel to me. I knew I had to read this account. I invested sixty-five cents in the tabloid and nestled into the front seat of my car, eager to learn the details.

The story was even more intriguing than I had expected. The doctors in a Boston hospital had given up on six-year-old Sean Butler, a little boy whom they had diagnosed as having incurable cancer. His condition, they assessed, was beyond anything they could do for him. They discontinued attempts to reverse the condition and gave the boy just a few days to live.

One night little Sean told the nurses that his favorite sport was baseball, and his hero was Dave Stapleton, the first baseman for the Boston Red Sox. If Sean had one last wish, it would be to meet Dave.

Following the clue, the nurses called Dave Stapleton to ask him if he would visit the child before he passed on. Dave kindly agreed, and that afternoon he came to the hospital with his wife and spent some time with Sean. They talked baseball, laughed, played, and Sean was visibly touched. Before he left, Dave promised Sean that he would get a hit for him the first time he was at bat during the baseball game that night. Sean was thrilled, and he promised to watch the game on TV.

Somehow the word about Dave's promise got around Boston. I was told by a woman who lived in Boston at that time that many eyes in that city were glued to their TV sets that evening. They watched with anticipation as Dave stepped to the home plate in Fenway Park. Several pitches went by. Dave didn't flinch. Then, on the next pitch first baseman Dave Stapleton slammed a triple off the famous green left field wall in that ballpark. Sean was ecstatic.

Then something amazing happened. Sean's condition did not degenerate as the doctors had predicted, but instead he began to improve. Day by day he became stronger until within a few days his symptoms disappeared.

"We have no medical explanation for this," the newspaper quoted the doctors as saying. "It can only be described as a miracle." They released Sean from the hospital, healed.

What healed that boy? I see no other explanation than the power of love. Genuine caring healed that child, and that is the only power that can heal any of us. Perhaps Sean was not feeling important or needed or beautiful. Perhaps he had decided on some subconscious level that life was not worthwhile, and that he was not really wanted here. His illness was really a call for help, a request for some kind of confirmation that he should continue. And who did God call to give him the encouragement he was so desperately seeking? A first baseman. A first baseman with a big heart.

I saw the picture of Dave Stapleton in that newspaper. He did not look anything like what you or I might consider a miracle healer. He was wearing a baseball hat with a big "B" on the front, a moustache, and a few unruly hairs making their statement just above his ears. Actually, he looked more like a baseball player than anything else. And he was smiling.

The kind of healing that Dave Stapleton accomplished is available to all of us — if we are willing to believe in ourselves. We must know that Spirit is eager to use us as we are, as we dedicate ourself to the Light. We do not have to change what we do to be a miracle worker. Dave did not quit the Red Sox to attend the Famous Healer's School or learn any particular incantations. In fact, staying in the work he loved and simply being himself was absolutely necessary for him to accomplish the healing that he did. What a lesson in the importance of being ourself!

But that's not the end of the story. I was so impressed with the account that I wanted to acknowledge the characters. So I sent a package of my books and a love letter to both Dave and Sean. It was my way of saying "Thank you for being willing to be your magnificent self!"

Several months passed, and I received no response. I must confess that some doubts crept into my mind. I began to wonder if the account was real. It had appeared as a headline of the *World Weekly Globe*, a kind of gossip gazette most easily obtained between the bubble gum and plastic shavers at the check-out counter at Foodtown. My credence began to shrivel further when I reread the article to find it sandwiched amid other inspiring reports such as *"John Wayne Now Speaking through Ronald Reagan," "Eleven Year Old Boy Sells His Mom to the Arabs,"* and the intriguing scientific dilemma, *"Is Your Pet an Alien from Space?"* I must admit that my mind began to dabble into the possibility that I had been duped. (I did later learn that the story had also appeared in the New York Times.) Feeling a little foolish, I decided to turn the question over to God and see what Spirit's response would be.

Around Valentine's Day, about five months after reading the article, I received a letter from "Mr. and Mrs. David Butler, Melrose, Mass."

"Who could that be?" I wondered.

Curiously I opened it. There, to my delight, was a lovely letter from Sean's parents thanking me for my books and good wishes. But the real gift was a Valentine's card enclosed with the letter. It was a picture of Spiderman in a ready-to-do-battle stance, advising, "Don't be afraid..." When I opened to the inside of the card I found, "...to have a super Valentine's Day!" And there, in a typical six-year-old handwriting it was signed, *"Love, Sean Butler."*

Natural Miracle Workers

Somehow we have learned to believe that a miracle worker has particular attributes. In some of my classes we make a list of what we believe are the characteristics of a miracle worker, including what one would look like and how he or she is supposed to act. You would not believe some of the ideas that we come up with! Some of us believe that an enlightened person would weigh a certain weight, eat a particular food, drive a certain kind of car, have particular books in their library, and discipline their children in a certain way. I assure you that none of these ideas are true. The only attribute of a miracle worker is that he or she works miracles — and that is quite sufficient!

I have known many miracle workers. Most of them do not wear flowing robes, dispense magic potions, or lecture before great audiences. Some of them smoke cigarettes, read Dear Abby, and occasionally get bugged at their husbands. They appear to be quite normal, and indeed they are. But they have offered themselves to help humanity in whatever way God would like them to do so, and thus their gifts have come forth, independent of any form that you or I might expect.

I am learning to be free of concepts about what an enlightened being says or does. A great lesson came at a holistic health conference I attended. There I met a woman on the panel of psychics who was angry, short-tempered, and told off-color jokes. "Surely this woman cannot be spiritual," I judged her. The limitations I had placed on her were dispelled when I later learned that she is a top consultant for police departments and investigative teams, for whom she has supplied extremely valuable information in finding lost children, solving crimes, and undoing mysteries. I was grateful to see the beauty in this woman, which I had covered over with my opinions about who God could work through. Perhaps Spirit sent her to me to help me learn that God is in no way restricted by the limitations we perceive.

The blessing of allowing for Spirit to work through other persons about whom you have had judgements is that, through releasing them from your opinions, you release *yourself* from the burden of judgement, and you become free to receive miracles and be a miracle worker yourself. As long as you believe that God cannot work miracles through others who seem to have faults, Spirit will be unable to accomplish miracles for you or through you. Not because God is weak, but because Spirit must have your assent to help you. You do not need to know the "how" of miracles — that is God's department. But you do need to offer a little willingness to let your good be. When you let others be magnificent in spite of appearances, you clear the way for your own perfection.

Simple Gifts

Most miracle workers are simple people, like you and me, quietly shining their love-light in the midst of their daily activities. One such man is my friend Richard Ringel, a delightful German tailor with a gold tooth. Whenever I go into his shop I feel healed. Richard always lights up when I enter. He puts his work aside, steps out from behind the counter, and embraces me with all of his heart. We affectionately call one another *"Maivin,"* a Yiddish word meaning "expert." Richard and I do not talk philosophy or discuss evolutionary theories. He is not a Bible scholar. He just shines. And I believe that everyone who walks into his shop walks out a little lighter, a little freer, a bit happier. Richard Ringel is a miracle worker.

My mother is another miracle worker. Someone who did not know Jeane as well as I did might describe her as a Jewish mother. One of her greatest joys was to watch me eat, she asked little more of me than to call her when I got home to my house after visiting her, and she used to encourage me to marry a Jewish girl. Yet I had the great joy to discover that she, too, was a miracle worker. She would heal my friends when they called the house looking for me. A typical conversation would go something like this:

"Hello..." (young girl's voice sobbing) " — Is Alan there?"

"No, he went out for the evening...What's the matter, honey?"

"Well, my life seems to be falling apart, and I need to talk to a friend."

"You can talk to me — I'll be your friend."

"But you don't even know me."

"You sound like a nice girl. Besides, TV can get boring, and it's more fun to talk to a real person."

"Have you ever had a man leave you?"

"Plenty — and thank God!"

(Laughter from the other end of the line) "...Well thanks — it's the first time I've laughed in three days."

"That's good — sometimes laughing makes it easier. Besides, no man is worth crying over."

"You think so?"

"Sure, honey. You do sound nice. I'll bet you're pretty, too. You have a lot going for you! What's the use of wasting a moment of happiness over a man — or anything, for that matter. Go out and have a good time! You're young — enjoy yourself!"

"Wow, Mrs. Cohen — You are really something!"

"Nah, what do I know? I just watch TV."

(More laughter) "Well, thanks a lot — I feel much better."

"That's good. Don't worry, everything will be alright."

"I think I know what you mean."

"Do you want me to give Alan a message?"

"Yes — tell him his mom is pretty wonderful."

When I was in college I studied books and books of psychological theories of healing. I saw films, I participated in seminars, and I observed counseling sessions through two-way mirrors. Once I even once dressed up as a phony doctor in a study on the placebo effect. Yet hardly anything I encountered was as real or as effective or as potent as the kind of healing my mom would accomplish with a few hugs, some jokes, and genuine caring.

Love is the Healer

Dr. William "Cherry" Parker is a well-known and deeply respected psychologist who relies on the power of love as the great healer. When I heard him lecture at a northeastern conference, Dr. Parker told a large audience, "At the age of seventy I have been a successful psychologist for most of those years. I have studied and tried every theory of personality and therapy from Freud to Rogers. In all of my experience, I have come to the conclusion that love is indeed the greatest healer."

Dr. Parker went on to relate a story about a young woman who came into his office for counseling. She had been referred to him after failing in therapy with many doctors.

"She came into my office with a portfolio of her psychiatric records that measured about six inches thick," Dr. Parker told us. "She began the interview by warning me, 'I don't see what you're going to do for me, doctor. Just look at these diagnoses. I'm a manic-depressive schizophrenic with multiple personality disorders. And that's just the first few pages! No one has been able to help me; I think I'm a lost cause.'

"May I please see those papers?" the doctor calmly requested.

She handed them across the desk to him. Dr. Parker sat back in his chair reviewing them for a few moments. Then he threw the papers in the wastepaper basket.

"Doctor! — What are you doing?" the young woman anxiously asked.

"These papers don't mean a thing to me," Dr. Parker answered. "I want to know about *you*, not what some theoretician says. *You*, not your diagnoses, are important to me. Please tell me about yourself and what is in your heart and mind."

That was the beginning of a deeply meaningful and healing relationship for both doctor and patient. This was the first doctor that the woman felt cared about her. In the atmosphere of his genuine caring, she blossomed and grew in ways that she never imagined before.

"Six months later, that girl graduated from therapy," Dr. Parker explained. "She became a new person, for she finally found someone who believed in her more than in her diagnoses. She caught that belief and now she is her own person."

Bloom Where You Are Planted

To be a miracle worker you do not have to get a doctoral degree, become a minister, eat a particular food, or be able to meditate for long hours. All you need to do is to begin to see beauty in your life and in those around you. When you open yourself with the golden key of *appreciation* God will fill your heart with treasures unlike any you have ever imagined.

And you will be amazed at how quickly your life opens up. That opening requires no special circumstances. There are no special circumstances. Only willingness. You can effect the greatest changes in your life and in the lives of those around you by working right where you are, blooming where you are planted.

I would also like to once again call your attention to the beautiful movie *Resurrection*, in which Ellen Burstyn portrays a woman who discovers and develops her healing powers. As a result of her healing work in the public arena she becomes entangled in all kinds of conflict and controversy with persons seeking to deny, debunk, and challenge her. Finally her ex-boyfriend becomes crazed and shoots her because his religious upbringing tells him that she is evil.

After recovering from her wound she retreats to manage a small filling station in the desert. There she quietly blesses all who come to the station. The final scene of the film shows a family pulling into the station in their mobile home. Soon it becomes apparent that their little boy is very ill, and the parents explain that the boy has cancer. After chatting with the family and making friends with the boy, the healer gives him a cute little puppy dog "for the price of one big hug." As she embraces the child we see her place her hands on the affected area of his body, and she goes into silent prayer to heal him. And we are certain that his healing is accomplished — all without any pomp or show.

And neither do you need any pomp or show to be a light in this world. You already are a light, but you may not know it. Your job is not to turn on the light, for indeed it is already lit — and it is promised to be illuminated forever. Your only task is to look at the light, and not the darkness. You cannot expect to see yourself clearly if you look into a distorted mirror. Your problem is not that you hold a lack within you, but that you have not looked to a guide that shows you your wholeness. Look now, and you will see.

Miracles come naturally to those who know their worth. Life is not an exercise in addition, but in recognition — the recognition of your goodness as God created you. That goodness has never been diminished, although it has been forgotten. The remedy, then, is not change, but remembering and awakening.

Ask to see, and you will be shown. Ask to know, and you will understand. Ask to be free, and you will see that you were never bound. And ask to touch others with the power of your love, and you will be healed. This is the promise of the One Who loves you because She knows who you are. Join in that knowledge, and all Heaven and earth will lay their gifts at your door.

The Case for Forgiveness

Living without forgiveness is worse than death.
— Mr. Miyagi, *The Karate Kid II*

"The morning the case was due in court, I was at a loss as to how to handle it," confided Michael Rembolt, a young attorney in Spokane, Washington. A dozen of us had gathered to share in a spiritual support group meeting, and we wanted to hear more.

"This divorce proceeding was a long and bitter battle," Michael told us, "and I could see no way that my client and her husband were going to reach an agreement. Feeling that I had come up against a stone wall, I sat in meditation one morning and prayed for guidance.

"*'Only forgive,'* spoke a voice of inner knowing.

"Yes, that made more sense to me than any other way that I had considered," Michael confided. "I began to think about the ways I was judging or limiting the people involved in the case. I realized that I was feeling put off by my client's husband for making such strong demands. So I started to look past the things I did not like about him, seeking the spark of the Divine within him. Within a short time I saw that all of his outer irritability was actually a disguised call for love. The truth was that he loved his wife, and he felt very hurt by the divorce. His large demands were not really an expression of hatred, as I had thought, but actually a plea for love.

"When I saw this it was easy to see the light in him. I was able to bless him and actually pray for his happiness and well-being. I offered him, his participation in this divorce, and his whole life up to the Light.

"That felt so good that I wanted to look further to see who else I needed to forgive. I discovered that I was a little annoyed at my client as well, for she could have been more flexible in her counter-demands. I released her, too, and I felt the same sense of peace and relief that I did when I prayed for her husband.

"Soon this process of forgiveness became uplifting and actually exhilirating! I began to feel free and light, and I realized I had hit on something

247

extremely powerful, a redemptive secret that was hidden only by my own fear of love.

"I decided to forgive and release everyone and everything associated with the case. I thought of the opposing lawyer, whom I had feared because of his reputation as one of the most ruthless and uncompromising attorneys in the city. I blessed him, the judge, the witnesses, and everyone in the courtroom; all the other litigants, attorneys, clerks, and anyone connected with the case in any way.

"Then I realized there was still one person I needed to forgive — me. I became aware that I had been judging myself for being put off by the other people in the scenario and for feeling inadequate about how I was handling the case. It seemed to follow naturally that if I could bless and wish the others well, I certainly deserved the same love myself.

"I knew that I had hit on the perfect approach for facing the situation. Gratefully I arose from my meditation, confident that with the help of the Holy Spirit I could face the case and the day. I didn't know how it would all work out; I just knew that because I had invited God into the situation, the case would somehow be handled in everyone's best interest."

Michael leaned forward on his chair, resting his elbows on his knees. The entire group was rapt with his account.

"When I arrived at the court I could not find my client. Nor the opposing lawyer. Nor the husband. For that matter I could not find anyone in the courtroom — not even the judge! I looked at my watch and checked my calendar; they confirmed I was in the right place at the right time. But where was everyone? Puzzled, I walked into the lobby to telephone the opposing lawyer.

"'Oh, yes, Mr. Rembolt, I'm glad you called,' answered the secretary. 'I've been trying to get in touch with you all morning. I wanted to tell you that our client has decided to settle out of court; he instructed us to give you anything you want. Just draw up the papers, send them over to us, and we'll get them signed.'"

A spontaneous chorus of "Wow's" and "Yay's" went through our audience. But Michael had more to tell.

"'Amazing!' I remarked to myself — 'Forgiveness really works!'

"I went back to the courtroom to tell the judge, but to my surprise neither he nor anyone else had arrived. 'Strange,' I thought, 'nine-thirty, and still no court.' I went back to the pay phone and called the judge's office.

"'Michael,' answered Judge Hillman, 'the most *miraculous* thing has happened!' (Those were his exact words.) 'We had thirty-two cases on the docket this morning, and every one of them has *settled out of court!*"'

Every one of them. The first lesson of *A Course in Miracles* is that there is no order of difficulty in miracles, and here is a most exciting example of the power of one man's prayer to heal his own mind and the lives of everyone he touches. Michael is no different than you or me, nor does he have any spiritual power that is not available to all of us. Michael simply *put into action* the energy that lives in every divine being. This true story is a cogent testimony for the fact that thoughts are things, and we can make our thoughts work *for* us to bring love, harmony, and real peace into any situation, no matter how bleak it may seem.

There is one message of this story, this book, my life, and all lives:

> *Any hardship can be undone, transformed, and healed to reveal a shining star where once there was but a dark night. The most powerful way to accomplish this miraculous transformation is through* **forgiveness.**

The Sin that Had No Effect

One summer afternoon when I was doing a series of workshops in Washington, a thoughtful masseuse offered me a complimentary massage. Thankful for the opportunity to unwind during a busy week, I gratefully accepted. A friend gave me a ride to her studio on the outskirts of the city. Eagerly I stretched out on the table, laid back, closed my eyes, and began to drift.

The next sound I remember was that of the masseuse's voice calling to me, "It's five o'clock, Alan."

"Five o'clock?!" I awoke with a start; at five o'clock I had an appointment on the other side of town, half an hour away. There my friend Alden was waiting in his car to pick me up to give me a ride to another engagement. Upset, I wondered how I could possibly make it in time to meet him.

Frantically I scurried off the table, threw my garb together and bolted out the door (not exactly the best way to complete a massage!). When we reached the appointed meeting place I was quite late. Alden had given up waiting and left.

I felt terrible. Here this thoughtful man had volunteered to give me a ride, and I stood him up because I nodded out on a massage table. Not a very nice thing to do, I thought. I felt guilty, and shuddered at the thought of facing Alden later that evening.

Sure enough, there he was at the lecture; nervously I thought about what I would say to him. When he approached me after the workshop I immediately apologized to him: "Gosh, Alden, I'm so sorry I didn't show up for our appointment this afternoon; I kept you waiting so long. Could you possibly forgive me?"

There was a pregnant moment before Alden spoke. I felt that my soul was in his hands. I waited for some kind of of chastisement or retaliation.

But it never came. Instead of attempting to punish me, Alden's words sailed to me on a gentle smile: "Would you like a ride home tonight?"

Wow! I felt like a condemned man pardoned from prison. I felt that Alden could have justifiably condemned me, yet he treated me as if I had not wronged him at all. I was free and just as lovable as if I had not done the "sin" with which I perceived I had hurt him. My "sin" had no effect — in fact, it contributed to a miracle of love — and we were both free!

Real Forgiveness

The key to real forgiveness is to understand that forgiveness has nothing at all to do with overlooking a sin or crime that has been committed against you. It is to know and demonstrate that no real harm has been done.

You are in danger nowhere in the universe. There is no person or force outside of your own mind that could ever hurt you. Indeed you have never really been hurt, no more than you are wounded in a dream that dissolves the moment you awaken.

There is very strong agreement in the world that we are vulnerable and subject to the attack thoughts and actions of those around us. Because we have been heavily trained in this way of looking at life, it is very real *in our experience*. But *experience is not always the same as reality*. Our experience of vulnerability seems real not because this is God's truth, but because we have created it to be so with our faulty perceptions based on an erroneous original premise. *Our opportunity in life is to reverse our own thinking that we are weak or hurtable in any way, and to serve others by knowing that they are equally whole.* From this awareness we will demonstrate with our actions that all pain springs from faulty thinking, and suffering need not be.

The Message of Healing

One of the greatest teachers of forgiveness was Jesus. The whole of his ministry was dedicated to teach one lesson: all is good, all is God, and *there is no other force in the universe.* Hell is simply the belief in it. And we discover, too, that even that belief was part of our ascension. *Nothing is outside the picture of our good.* Paint a picture of evil with your mind and you will smudge the portrait where a blessing was meant to be seen. You can make a movie of any idea you generate. But you can't leave the theatre until you see all the credits. You wonder why you have to stick around until the end of the film, and then in the last frame you discover that you are the producer!

Jesus saw the whole picture, and that is why he was able to teach that forgiveness, or looking beyond error into the light, is the way to Heaven. He had no sense of attack, and that is why he said, "Forgive them, Father, for they know not what they do." He recognized that the Father had *already* forgiven them, and he was sharing his Father's freedom in knowing that there was no need for punishment. Both he and his Father — our Father, too — knew that all is forgivable because *there was no real loss.*

What those who crucified Jesus needed was not blame or punishment, but love and understanding, for their error was to believe that the Christ could be killed, and that is a problem in perception that calls not for punishment, but awakening. If they knew who they were, they would have known who Jesus was, and that would have been the end of the drama. Then they could have celebrated their freedom in not needing to change the outer world to gain peace. Jesus was not desirous of revenge, but of sharing with them the understanding — the good news — that they were as invulnerable as he was, and is, as we are. Anyone who knows that he is invulnerable has no interest in killing or hurting anyone, because he realizes that that is impossible. Our purpose in life is to practice and celebrate our spiritual invulnerability, and teach it to others by the very joy we exude as we live with dignity in that truth.

The End of Crucifixion

Many people believe that the purpose of Jesus' life was the crucifixion. The symbol of Christianity has become the crucifix, we glorify the blood of the lamb, and many of us live our lives in a state of crucifixion, an unnecessary emulation wrought of a mistaken understanding of the mission of one who came to teach only love. Even if you believe that Jesus' crucifixion is to be imitated, you will have to admit that the many days, months, or years that you have lived in crucifixion far exceed the three hours that he underwent the cross. And if you believe that his crucifixion did indeed atone for the sins of humanity, what an unnecessary repetition it is for any of us to relive it!

Suffering is not necessary. You can learn from suffering, but you can easily learn the same lessons with joy and celebration. Give up your misery. Once you have seen that there is another way, all misery is self-indulgence. And there is another way. I saw a marvelous bumper sticker that proclaimed: *Misery is Optional.* And so it is. Every moment is a choice between life and death, between celebration and crucifixion, between wonder and despair. What do you choose? It does not matter in the least what you have chosen in the past. It matters only what you choose *now.* Choose the peace of God now, and it is yours for eternity.

Personal Resurrection

It is time for you to come out of the tomb. You have lived in darkness and misery for too long, and none of it was necessary. You could have been dancing in the light, and you still can. All you need to do is forgive yourself. When you truly forgive yourself it is easy to forgive all those around you, for you realize that you were but crucifying them for your sins. And *you have no sins*. You have but made errors in consciousness, and those errors are rectified the moment you see them for what they are. You were not bad; you were just learning. The remedy for error is not punishment, but practice. And you have been practicing a great lesson.

If you are reading this, you are ready to give up your value on suffering and punishment. This may seem like a quantum leap for you, and it is. Yet you are ready for it. When you carry a heavy sack on your shoulders for a long time, you must either release it or fall under it. You have fallen long enough, and now you are ready to arise and walk in dignity.

Join me in the light. There is room for all of us here, for the light knows no boundaries or smallness. Together we can show the world that life is good, that there is nothing to fear, and that we are capable of living in a state of love all of the time. You have come a long way to arrive at this point, and it would be rather foolish to turn back now. And there is no turning back — there is only delay.

Come, for all things are now ready. There is nothing you need do further but say, *"Yes, Father, I am willing to love."* With that invitation the Holy Spirit will come streaming into your mind and you will wonder why you ever resisted love. Child, your pain is over. Forgive yourself and join the ranks of those who have gained Heaven, even while on this earth. You are blessed.

*The holiest place on earth is where an ancient hatred has become a present love.**

---

*T, p. 522

The Lover's Gift

Seeing is believing in the things you see;
Loving is believing in the ones you love.

- Unicorn Song[1]

Bill sat back in the couch and faced his therapist. There was something he had to know, and now was the time to ask.

"Tom, I've been with you a long time, and now I want your advice on something that's very important to me."

"Sure, Bill, what's on your mind?"

"I've been with my wife for nineteen years now. When I married her she was like a queen to me — I loved her so much, and everything she did pleased me. But something's happened, Tom. Somehow over the years she's turned into a shrew. I tell you, she's not the same woman I married. She's cranky, she doesn't take care of herself, and she doesn't do half the things for me that she used to do. She's hurt me too much and frankly, I've had it. Can you tell me what to do that would really hurt her?"

Tom sat back. He folded his hands, and thought. A minute went by, but it seemed like an hour.

"Why, yes, Bill," he responded. "I do have an idea you might be able to use. It's up to you whether or not you will try it, but here it is: When you go home tonight, bring Stephanie a bouquet of her favorite flowers. This weekend take her out to her favorite restaurant. Next Tuesday night tell her, 'Sweetheart, if you would like to go out with your friends tonight, I'll be glad to watch the kids.' For one month treat her like that beautiful, wonderful, lovable person you married. Then, after a month of showering gifts and attention on her — leave her. That will really get her!"

Bill sat up in his chair with a look of amazed excitement on his face. "That's great!" he exclaimed. "Tom, you're a genius — I never would have thought of that! That'll really do her in!"

Bill stood up, shook Tom's hand vigorously, and walked briskly out the

---

[1] M. Adam, *The Unicorn Song*

255

door, on his way to the nearest flower shop.

Several months passed before Tom saw Bill again. Then one night they ran into each other at a party.

"Well, Bill, how are you doing? — I'll bet you're having the time of your life going out with lots of women!"

Tom looked astonished. "Me? Go out with women? — Not me! — I would never do that to my wife."

"But I thought you were leaving that shrew."

Tom smiled.

"Leave her? Shrew?...She's the most wonderful wife in the world! Bill, I must thank you for your advice; the most amazing thing happened! I did exactly as you told me — I brought her flowers, watched the kids, took her out — the whole bit, all with the intention of leaving her. But after the first week of being nice to her, something amazing happened to her. One night when I came home she was dressed up so gorgeous, just like she used to dress when we first were together. And she said it was just for me! Then, the night she came home after going out with her friends she told me, 'Thanks a lot for watching the kids, honey — if you want to go out with the guys Thursday night, I'll be happy to stay home.' I tell you she's a new person — and so am I. It's like starting all over — but better! How can I ever thank you enough, Tom — that was the best advice anyone ever gave me!"

We Create Our World

We create our world by the way we look at it and act in it. Every situation into which we enter is a product of our thoughts. And because the persons around us are sensitive receivers of psychic information (whether they realize it or not), they respond to our vision of them and the actions that follow from that vision.

The good is already there. Perfection already is. Wholeness is wholly created. But it needs your help to bring it forth. Positive thinking does not mean trying to create something that is not there. Real positive thinking acknowledges that good already exists—indeed it is *all* that exists. Your vision and affirmation draw it forth into expression.

It is supremely important to remember that every situation, event, and experience in life springs from your vision of it. In relationships, you will create and recreate situations based upon your vision of who the two of you are. The key to success in relationships is to hold to a vision of the perfection of everyone involved. This means consistently seeing the best in yourself as well as the other person. *A Course in Miracles* tells us, "it is impossible to overestimate your brother's value," and "the only response worthy of your brother is appreciation." This is why you must affirm your vision of beauty in everyone you meet.

Seeing Good Creates Miracles

Dr. Nelson Decker wrote a marvelous book[2] on the Native American ways of healing. One of the most important steps to happiness, the Native Americans teach, is to find something in every situation that you can appreciate.

Dr. Decker relates an experience that changed his life. When he was a young chiropractor in Englewood, New Jersey, a very shabbily dressed man came into his office. The man was dirty, unkempt, and he emanated an unpleasant odor. He had no money, but he asked for treatment. Dr. Decker was reluctant to see him, but he did so. While Dr. Decker's initial reaction was an aversion to the man's appearance, he remembered that a lesson of happiness was to find something you can appreciate in every situation. He scanned the man's appearance, and he could find nothing that he appreciated. Then he looked down at the man's shoes, and he noticed that they were neatly tied. This was the one thing about the man that he could honestly say he liked. So he focused on the tidiness of the man's shoelaces as he treated him. Over the course of the treatment he developed a nice rapport with the fellow, and the man went on his way happily.

A few days later the man returned in significantly better condition. He told Dr. Decker that he owed him a great debt of thanks. Several days earlier he felt that he was at the end of his rope. He walked from New York City to the George Washington Bridge with the intention of jumping off the bridge. When he got to the bridge he decided to give himself one more chance. So he kept walking over the bridge, hoping to find some kind of help on the other side. The first place he saw on the other side was Dr. Decker's office, and so he walked in the door.

"I want to thank you for being so kind to me, Doctor," the man shared. "I think that if you had turned me away I might have gone back to the bridge and jumped. But you didn't, and I am encouraged to live because of your kindness."

---

[2] Dr. Nelson Decker, *The Great Mystery in the Sky*, Benu, Inc., P.O. Drawer 4367, E. Lansing, Michigan 48823

The Beauty in the Beast

If you remember the fable of Beauty and the Beast, you may recall that the young maiden was forced to live in the woods with a beast. At first she was repelled by his appearance, but over time she discovered that he was a kind and gentle creature. After spending more time with him she began to truly love him. Finally she saw so much good in him that she chose to be with him of her own free will. When she kissed him he was revealed to be a handsome prince, upon whom a spell had been cast. Within the beast, there was beauty.

The lesson here is *not* that she learned to put up with his beastliness, but that she discovered his beauty. The moment she accepted the good in him, that became reality. And so it is with our lives. We must see beauty *first*, and then we can be certain it will be manifested.

The Desire to See

If you are seeing pain, ugliness, or emptiness, it is because on some level, probably unconsciously, you have chosen to see these images. And there may in fact have been value in your seeing them, for they are the signposts that you are travelling in the wrong direction. If they help you to return to your proper course, they have served you. But if you have had your fill of hurt and you are ready to see differently, you will see differently.

There is a very simple prayer that always leads to healing. If you pray it with sincerity, you are sure to be released from the limitations that you feel in any situation. Say these words, but mean them, and you will be free:

"I would like to see this differently."

If you make this request sincerely, quickly the situation will be shown to you in a different light. That light will include the way out. The inability to see the way out means that you have been looking in the wrong place. You must see differently before you can find your way to the door.

You may be surprised to find that you do not need to make any or many changes in the outer world to step through the door. You may need but to see the situation in a different light. One correct thought of love and acceptance can transform hell into Heaven.

The Healing Power of Vision

I had a friend who had a ten-year-old boy. When I visited their home, I found the boy to be rather selfish and annoying to me. I judged him as being something of a spoiled child.

One day I was sharing my feelings about the child with another friend of the family. "I don't know what to do about Jason," I told her; "every time I visit the family he gets on my nerves."

"Jason? You mean that sweetie Jason? He's one of the most lovable kids I know! Whenever I go to his house we have a great time together! I love to be with him!"

Hmmm. I had never thought about him like that before. Could it be that the friend was seeing something in the boy that I was missing?

The next time I visited the boy's house, I remembered my friend's words. I tried her perspective on for size. I considered the possibility that Jason was actually a sweet kid. And do you know what I discovered? He *was* a sweet kid. That day he was so kind and loving to me! I wondered how I could have ever thought otherwise.

I needed to hear that woman's perpective as a correction to my own. All she did was see him differently, and I began to see him differently, too.

Who was Jason actually? He was the best we saw him as being.

Who are you, actually? If "the only response worthy of your brother is appreciation," the same must be true for you. Perhaps your problem has not been that there was something wrong with you, but that you temporarily forgot who you are.

Are you so sure that you are weak, lacking, or afraid? Where did you get these ideas from? Who told you that there was something wrong with you? And why did they tell you that? Trace these ideas back in your mind as far as you can, and you may find that your notions of impoverishment are learned. Babies do not have a problem with self-image. They do not beat themselves when they fall down while learning to walk. They do not berate themselves as being weak for wanting and needing momma's breast. They do not see people as old, young, black, white, handsome, or ugly. They are ecstatic about the opportunities that life is offering them to play, discover, and grow. Maybe they are on to something!

Look clearly at what you believe you are, and what you believe you are not. The greatest mistake you have ever made is to stop believing in yourself. You stopped believing in yourself when you adopted a self-image that said you were less than lovable. You made a decision that there was something you had to do to earn love, and you have been trying to buy peace ever since. And of course you have failed. But be thankful that that decision is revokable, and you have the power to undo it entirely by making a new decision now.

The Lover's Gift

Why do we feel so happy in the presence of someone who loves us? They see the good in us, and they remind us that we are lovable. In our heart we know that we are lovable, and we want to live in the love that we deserve. This is why a life that does not reflect the love that we know we deserve is so painful. When someone loves us they help awaken us to the beauty within us. They have discovered the treasure in us, and we want to share in it. They act as a mirror for the best in us, and we want to be with them so we can see it, too. Truly it is an act of love to accept love, for in so doing we acknowledge that we are lovable. We *do* love ourself — that is our greatest purpose — and we want to live in the presence of our own wonder.

The greatest service that we can perform for another, then, is to see their beauty. If you see the good in others, you will experience three major benefits: (1) you will experience tremendous success in all of your endeavors, and enjoy the kind of rewarding relationships that you have dreamed of; (2) you will empower and support those you touch to be successful and happy; and (3) you will love yourself and find phenomenal wonder in your own being.

Surely we can only gain from focusing on the good. It is our most important gift to ourself.

The Final Vision

One of the clearest examples of the transformative power of vision comes in *The Return of the Jedi* movie. In this episode Luke Skywalker, who has mastered the Force, realizes that Darth Vader is his father. Actually, his father is Attikin Skywalker, but Attikin has become enamored by the dark side of the Force, and he has put on an intimidating mask, to become known as Darth Vader. But the man behind the mask is not the one who has created havoc. He is actually a being of radiant light. This is the man that Luke recognizes as his father.

Luke goes to the very core of the Empire's headquarters and confronts Darth Vader with the fact that he knows he is his father. But Vader has become so hardened in the ways of darkness that his response is to attempt to influence Luke to join the dark side of the Force with him. He even threatens Luke's life.

But Luke, a true Jedi Knight, is undaunted. "You cannot fool me, father," he tells Vader, "I know who you are. I know that you belong to the light."

Though Vader's mask is expressionless, we can feel the inner transformation taking place as his heart begins to awaken. The layers of armor begin to dissolve around him.

Vader brings Luke to the Emperor — the very monarch of the dark Empire. There, when the Emperor realizes that he cannot persuade Luke to join the dark side, he begins to electrocute him with lightning bolts of anger.

Darth Vader stands by and watches. But his heart has been opened. Finally he can stand it no longer. He makes the decision to honor the light. He picks up the evil Emperor and hurls him into a bottomless chasm.

But Vader is wounded in the process. He is dying. He asks Luke to take off Vader's mask. Finally, after years of fear, pain, and terror, Darth Vader's true face is revealad — it is the original countenance of Luke's father, Attikin Skywalker.

In the final scene of this saga we see Ben (Obi-Wan Kenobe — Luke's first teacher) and Yoda (Luke's elf-like guru) standing together in Spirit, blessing the celebration of the victory of the light over the darkness. And standing with them, in fully glory, is another figure: it is the spirit body of Attikin Skywalker, known in life as Darth Vader. But now he shines brightly, with the same radiant dignity as Ben and Yoda. We see a vision of his true being as a master of light. The nightmare is over.

It was Luke's willingness to see the light in Darth Vader that set the transformation into motion. Luke walked directly into the lair of the Empire to face Darth Vader with the truth of his being. Vision preceded victory. And so it always is.

261

You and I must have the same kind of vision to effect true transformation in our lives. The world is hungry for the vision of perfection. You can break the agreement of limitation by seeing freedom. You can transform ugliness by acknowledging beauty. You can awaken love by seeing it where hatred now seems to rule.

You must have the faith and the courage to act upon your vision. Luke walked into the center of the Empire because that is where he had the most power to transform it. The Empire that you and I must penetrate is not a place, an institution, or a country, and it is not founded on the actions of other people. The Empire that you and I must conquer is the fortress of fear that has been erected in our own mind. We have allowed a dark perception to cast a shadow in the land of light. We have accepted the idea that evil has power. We have believed in a force outside our own divinity.

Yet correction lies within the same mind that led us astray. And that correction begins with vision. Begin now to see yourself in a new light. Begin to affirm, empower, and celebrate the greatness in you. Naturally your enthusiasm will spill over onto those you contact, and you will become a miracle worker. You will be astounded at how far your vision will carry you.

And you will not be alone. You will see for many, for many are in need of your sight. Do not belittle this responsibility, for it is the one you were born to accomplish. And it will be the easiest task you have ever mastered, for One will walk with you Who will see with you. And that One will affirm that all you see is born of goodness. You must believe that you are entrusted with the power to heal, for so you are.

The Letter

If, while you are presenting your offering upon the altar,
You remember that your brother has a grievance against you,
Leave your offering there upon the altar,
And go and make peace with your brother.
Then come back and present your offering.

- Jesus the Christ[1]

One Christmas a group of us gathered at a friend's house to create our own Christmas pageant. We celebrated song, laughter, prayer, and feasting. It was a wonderful day that we created according to the spirit of devotion in our own hearts.

At one point someone read from the Bible. Randomly he chose a passage that contained the verse, "If, while you are presenting your offering upon the altar, you remember that your brother has a grievance against you, leave your offering there upon the altar, and go and make peace with your brother. Then come back and present your offering." In other words, to have a clean slate with God you must have a clean slate with your brothers.

"Do I have a clean slate with my brothers?" I wondered.

I searched my mind for any grievances. I did not find any, but I did not feel totally peaceful. "Father," I asked God, "Is there anyone against whom I am holding a grievance?"

Immediately into my mind flashed the face of a fellow named Ronald. Ronald was a man I met many years ago at a professional conference. At this workshop Ronald attacked me verbally and physically for something I had said that he did not like. The thought of our relationship was a painful emotional memory for me. During the ensuing eleven years, whenever I thought of Ronald or my experience with him, I felt anxious. If I would even hear his name, I would lose my peace. I realized that I had been stuffing, or repressing my feelings about Ronald for a long, long time. And now the entire experience was ready for healing.

---

[1] Matthew 5:23

"If you remember that your brother has any grievance against you, go and make peace with him, and then come to the altar." I have fancied myself to be a pretty good meditator. I have often closed my eyes and dived into peace for long periods of time. Yet if I harbored feelings of resentment toward Ronald - or anyone - could I truly say that I have been peaceful? I realized that before I could come wholeheartedly to God, I would need to do something to heal my relationship with Ronald.

I sat down and wrote Ronald a letter. Upon reading it when I was done, I decided it was too stiff, and I tore it up. I wrote him another letter. This one was too sappy. I tore it up and tried again. The next one, I felt included a tinge of laying guilt on him. Into the wastebasket it went, with the others. I went on with draft after draft. Some were not completely honest; others, too honest. Some were bravado, others fawning. I kept going until I felt that the words on the paper said what I wanted to say.

Finally I held a sheet of paper in my hand and read, in my handwriting:

> *Dear Ronald,*
>
> *I don't know if you remember me. We met at a professional meeting about ten years ago. There we had a bit of a confrontation.*
>
> *I am writing to you now to let you know that I have not felt peaceful about that for all these years. I have come to a point in my life where my relationships are very important to me, and more than anything else I want all of my relationships to reflect love. I would like to bring my feelings about us into the light of peace.*
>
> *I want you to know that if I offended or upset you in any way, I am sorry for that. I respect you as a person and a professional, and it was never my intention to interfere with the work that you are doing.*
>
> *I would now like to count you among my friends. I know that we have not been in touch for a long time, but perhaps we could consider our friendship like a fine wine that took a long time to mellow.*
>
> *Please know that my love and support are with you.*
>
> *Yours truly,*
> *Alan*

That felt right.

I signed, sealed, and stamped the letter, said a prayer over it, and took it to the mailbox.

As I was about to drop it into the slot, my mind began to wriggle with all kinds of hesitations and warnings.

"He's going to think you're a real jerk," one voice in my mind warned me.

Another thought threatened, "What if he comes to see you and he hits you again?"

Yet another voice questioned, "What if he doesn't answer?"

But quickly I saw that those voices were all the ego, disguised as different characters. I have learned not to heed such ravings. I dropped the letter in the box.

When the letter dropped out of sight a feeling came over me that was so beautiful! I was a free man. *Eleven years* of hurt and anger and fear were dumped that day. And I was proud of myself for doing it!

It didn't matter if he thought I was a jerk, or if he got angry, or if he didn't answer. I did what I had to do, and the relationship was healed in *my heart*.

"It is the destiny of all relationships to become holy," *A Course in Miracles* tells us.[2] That was the day for that one.

I went home and sat down to meditate. How sweet it was.

---

[2] M, p. 7

Love Always Answers

A miracle is never lost. It may touch many people you have not even met, and produce undreamed of changes in situations of which you are not even aware.

- A Course in Miracles*

There was a woman who was married to a very cold and emotionally insensitive man. For many years the man did not show his feelings or acknowledge his wife's love for him. Often over the years she thought about leaving him, and at times she almost did. But each time she was about to walk out the door, a voice within her heart told her to stay. And so she did.

Many years passed. Still the man showed little appreciation for this devoted woman. She wondered where it was all leading to.

Then the husband passed away. The wife went to the family safe deposit box to collect their valuables, and there she found a letter that her husband had written to her some time before he passed away. The letter said,

> *Dear Betty,*
>
> *I want you to know how much I love and appreciate you. As you know, I am a man who does not show his feelings very much or very well. But that does not mean I do not feel. It has been very difficult for me to express appreciation, and perhaps that is why I am writing this letter to you instead of speaking what I want to say.*
>
> *Betty, I have been aware of all the kindnesses and thoughtful acts you have done for me over all these years. You have been a wonderfully devoted and giving wife, and I want to acknowledge you for it. Please do not ever feel that what you have done with me and for me has gone unnoticed or unappreciated. I am thankful for all of it. Please know that I love you, I value you, and I am very grateful for our years together.*

---

* T, p. 4

God bless you for being such an angel in my life.
Always,
John

Do you have any idea of the power of your loving acts? Perhaps you do not. Every act of kindness, yea, every *thought* of loving creates a wave in the ocean of the universe, and ripples out to touch, affect, and heal everything everywhere. The value of your love can never be overestimated. Your simple caring deeds are supremely important, and you must never underestimate how you can help someone in gentle ways that may seem to go unnoticed. In reality such acts have healing power of unbelievable magnitude.

Sometimes, when I think of the people in my life who have had the most profound and transformative effect on me, I realize that some of these beautiful souls have no idea how they have contributed to my life. Two of the people whom I think of as my most important guides are individuals that I spent just a few minutes with. I am certain that neither of them is aware of how valuable those few minutes were to me.

One summer, when I was thirteen years old, my Cousin Ethel invited me to spend a few weeks with her and her family at her home in the suburbs of Wilmington, Delaware. As I was raised in the city, the experience of spending a vacation in a country setting was a special gift. I accepted.

One afternoon Ethel took me to the community pool just down the street from her house. There she introduced me to a man named Mr. Simmons. Mr. Simmons was a schoolteacher, I believe. I don't really remember much else about him, except for one very important and, for me, unusual feeling: I felt happy in his presence. During our time together he asked me questions about my life and my interests, and he really listened to what I was saying. He was the first and perhaps the only person in many years, who I felt loved me unconditionally. The significance of our interaction was life-changing for me, and I was with him for no more than about half an hour. But in those thirty minutes I felt loved, cared for, and listened to. I felt like I was a worthwhile person, and that was a very important feeling for me at that time of my life.

Another person who touched me deeply was a man named Bill, a rather jovial fellow whom I met at a Unity retreat in Allentown, Pennsylvania. The gift that Bill gave me was that he hugged me very warmly. At retreats such as that one, many people share hugs. But when Bill hugged me, I felt that he was really giving me all of himself; he was not just wrapping his arms around me and squeezing;—he was really hugging! I felt that his heart was wholly with me, and that he was communicating *all* of his being in that hug. In short, he meant it and I felt it. Bill's hug encouraged me to share myself like that with others in my life, and more and more I have been doing so. Bill ignited within me the desire to give the gift that I had been given. And as we receive what we give, I have gained much.

I never saw Bill again; I do not even know his last name. I am certain that he does not know how much he gave me in one strong and genuine hug. But I have been passing it on, and I know the blessings are returning to Bill thousands and thousands of times over.

How many times I have heard a lecture, read a book, or studied with a teacher from which I gleaned one sentence, one word, one idea, or one feeling, and then taken the idea into meditation and found new and wondrous avenues opened to me! Most of these speakers or authors have no idea how they have touched me. To many I was just a face in an audience. If I was not smiling, perhaps they wondered if they were reaching me at all. Yet all the while inside my soul wheels of fire were churning. Insights and healings were coming. Doors were opening. All of these important changes were invisible to the world the eye sees. Yet they were indeed real and magnificent in the realm of the spirit.

Does it not stand to reason, then, that you and I must be affecting other persons without our knowing it? Could it be that our love is more powerful than we see? Let us know the value of every kind word, caring touch, and encouraging deed. Every act of love goes a long way, and though it may not be acknowledged openly, the heart knows. "What is essential," the Little Prince learned, "is invisible to the eye."

When Negativity is a Blessing

Sometimes we may seem to be affecting a person negatively, while actually they are undergoing an important positive transformation. Once I received a letter from a woman who complained vehemently about the content of one of my seminars. She objected to my emphasis on meditation, the sharing of my personal experiences, and my references to *A Course in Miracles*. This was rather surprising to me, as I have found these methods to be among the most powerful and well-received of the material I present. Yet she was disturbed enough about these ideas to write an emotionally-charged letter protesting them.

I took the letter into meditation, and the answer I received was a very important one. My guidance told me that actually the seminar touched a sensitive chord within her. I perceived that she had a lot of repressed anger and resistance to spiritual awakening, and the mention of these ideas set off deep issues within her, issues that were ready to be resolved.

My reasoning further told me that her response was actually a very positive one, for her experience was forcing her to bring these issues into the light and look at them. Looking at the things that press our sensitive buttons is healthy, for they are hidden fears seeking healing. Her response also got me to look at how I was presenting my materials; I had to ask myself if I could find a way to offer these ideas in a form that would reach more people.

Thinking about our interaction even more, I wondered if perhaps she had actually gotten more than some persons in the seminar who listened politely and took notes without filtering the material through their thoughts and feelings.

I also remembered that some of the people and groups that have been the most important in my life are those to whom I initially had an emotionally adverse reaction. Later I became deeply involved with these persons and organizations, and I ultimately learned and gained much through my participation with them. Sometimes when we meet a person or group that has come into our life to offer us an important healing, the ego steps in, and in its effort to resist healing it makes the situation out to be the exact reverse of what it is. But that is only temporary. Sooner or later we must accept our next step to the light. Our destiny is happiness.

I wrote this lady a letter telling her that I was sorry she found the material so unacceptable, and I offered to get together with her for lunch to chat some more if she liked. She did not take me up on the invitation, but she did send me back a lovely letter of thanks for my personal response to her.

The Perfect Timing of Love

Spirit never leaves us comfortless. Sometimes when things seem to be going all wrong, an angel of comfort will come to make our way easier and give us the strength to carry us over the bumps and move us up to the high country. Angels do not always appear with wings, halos, or wands. Sometimes they come in letters, animals, or sunsets.

A musician friend of mine told me that an angel once came to him when he most needed it. Peter was experiencing what seemed to be the end of his rope. His girlfriend had left him, and when he went to work that night at the club at which he had a standing engagement, the manager told him that his band had been discontinued at the club.

Peter felt that he had nothing. On his way home he became so overwhelmed with his difficulties that he stopped on the sidewalk, laid down his guitar, fell to his knees, and began to weep. "Where can I turn, now?" he wondered.

At that moment a little puppy dog crawled under Peter's arms and began to lick the tears off his cheeks. Peter had never seen this cute little fellow before, and you can imagine his joy at having this friend come to him at this time of his greatest need. He felt that someone cared about him, and he decided to carry on. He brought the dog home with him, and had it sit on the porch while he went inside to get him some food.

When Peter got in the door, his girlfriend was there waiting for him. She told him that she did not really want to leave him. She also told him that he had received a phone message about some wonderful new musical opportunities for him. His whole direction had been reversed in those few minutes.

When Peter went outside for the puppy dog, it had vanished. Peter reasoned that the little guy was an angel.

And I must share for myself that sometimes I wonder if I am doing anything worthwhile in this world. I wonder if my writing or workshops are the most powerful things I could be doing. Sometimes I wonder if maybe I should make candles for a living, or something like that.

Then, it seems to never fail, just as I start to doubt, someone calls, writes, or visits me and tells me quite specifically (without my asking), "When is your next book coming out? You must keep writing! What you are saying and doing is touching many more people than you realize."

I feel sort of ignorant for a minute. Then I sit down at my typewriter.

What's in the Minutes

I recently saw a wonderful film called *Vision Quest*. It is the captivating story of a high school wrestler who devotes nearly all of his time — and life — to training for a big match in which he intends to win the state championship from an undefeated and a seemingly invulnerable champion.

The young man, Louden, becomes obsessed with winning this match, and his friends accuse him of insanity in his passion to prove himself. He agrees that he may indeed be crazy, and he carries on with his training program of unbelievable intensity. He occupies nearly every moment exercising, jogging, dieting, visualizing, studying his opponent, and demanding top performance of himself at every turn.

The night before the match Louden's girlfriend leaves him, and he is crestfallen. He is so downhearted that he changes his mind about competing, and he goes instead to visit his friend Elmo. Elmo is an older man that Louden works with, who has become like a big brother to him. To Louden's surprise he finds Elmo dressed up nicely, fixing his tie as he is ready to go out. Elmo tells Louden that he has taken off from work this evening to go see Louden win his match.

Feeling rotten and trying to find a way to tell Elmo that he has copped out of the match, Louden asks, "Why would you want to take off work and lose money to see me wrestle? — It's just a lousy six minute match."

Elmo stops tying his necktie and asks Louden, "Have you ever heard of Pele?"

"Yeah, I think he's a soccer player, right?"

"I was sitting here alone one night," Elmo tells Louden, "and I discovered this soccer game on the Mexican channel. In that game I saw Pele flip his entire body into the air in a somersault, and then kick the ball into the goal while he was upside down — and backward. The ball was in the net before the goalee had a chance to think about it.

"You know, Louden," the older man says, "I'm sort of a tough guy — you know me. But when I saw that, I began to cry."

Elmo begins to weep even as he speaks to Louden.

"I began to cry because I knew that there were millions of us little people watching him, and most of us have not had our lives amount to anything. But when Pele made that goal like he did, for one shining moment he lifted me and everyone else into a higher place. It was as if he was saying, 'Look what a person can do if he puts his mind to it.' In that one glorious moment he was showing everyone that there is nothing that is impossible to someone who sets his mind and heart on something. In that moment he saved me and the millions who were watching him. We were small, and he made us great.

"No, Louden..." Elmo tells him, "It does not matter that the match is only six minutes long — It's what happens in those six minutes that is important."

Louden is touched. He got it. He dashes down to the high school and gets into the match just before he is about to default for being absent. And he wins.

The Sure Investment

Loving is an investment that always pays off. But do not dictate the how and the when of the payoff. You do not know. You cannot know. You may never know. But there is one truth of which you may be assured: God's payment plan is the best insurance in the world — you are guaranteed to always have what you need when you need it.

Always keep putting your love out there. This does not mean you need to be a doormat, a martyr, or a fool. All it means is that you keep on loving, and you trust that your love is working, even when you do not see the results on *your terms*. Your terms are based on an extremely limited picture. There is One who sees a bigger picture. Entrust your vision to Him, and you cannot lose.

Do not be attached to seeing the results of your giving. An act of love may go unacknowledged, but this does not mean that the effect has not occurred. All it means is that you did not see the effect. You must know that what you are doing is very much appreciated on some level, and it is improving the world significantly.

The real reward of giving is in the act of loving. The results in the outer world are the icing on the cake. The feeling of joy in truly giving love far exceeds the need to see a response. If you need a response, you have confused giving with getting, and that is a poor bargain to strike. Your love is real, it is felt, and it is working. Never doubt this. When you doubt, you begin to devise silly games to find proofs that you are loved, and those proofs are never satisfactory, even when they come. The real proof lies within your heart, where you feel peace when you give love.

Your faith is your greatest asset in this world of shadows and illusions. It will not fail you when all else is falling away. Your faith will tell you that nothing is taken away that you need, and nothing is given you that you cannot use. The gifts that you are given are based not upon your achievement, but upon your identity. Your identity is the heir to the Kingdom of God, and surely such a noble child would not be cast to the winds of fate. You make your own fate by believing that you deserve love, and you prove your destiny by accepting only good. Thus you go far beyond the meager property of time and space. You find the answer to your love in giving it.

My Beloved Son

Behold, this is My Beloved Son, in whom I am well pleased.
- Matthew 3:17

The crisp winter evening nipped at my ears as I approached the door of the laundromat. It would be good to get inside and feel the warmth. I emptied my laundry into the first available machine and, realizing I had half an hour to fill, I decided to stroll down the mall to Bradlees to return some Christmas gifts.

Heading toward the department store, my tummy told me it was dinnertime. Suddenly I felt a deep craving for eggplant parmesan. Instantly I conceived a whole menu of thought-forms about that savory dish, and in my mind I was quickly transported to an astral pasta palace.

As the divine plan would have it, there just happened to be an Italian restaurant right between the laundromat and Bradlees (It is not a random universe!) and I set my tastebuds on course toward Tony's.

As I approached the restaurant my mind began to generate all kinds of reasons why I shouldn't have an eggplant parmesan sandwich.

"You know," said the mind, "the bread will probably be made of white flour, and you should eat only whole wheat."

"Hmmm," I began to ponder, "maybe that's true."

Given an opening, the mind continued: "And don't you remember that radio program that said, 'Watch out for tomatoes — they are nightshades'?"

"Maybe this is a test of temptation!" I speculated.

In hot pursuit, the mind waged its final assault: "Just think: the cheese will not be organic!"

I stopped with my hand on the knob of the restaurant door. There I found myself at the crossroads of indecision, stymied at the intersection of the gulley of guilt and the freeway to freedom. It was an old familiar position of attempting to decide what to do to be good, how to please God, how to avoid the punishment that comes of being bad.

Then an inner guidance came, a voice nudging me in a direction I had

275

not before considered.

"Alan, imagine you had a child, a little boy about five years old."

O.K., I could do that.

"Now imagine that you loved this child with the depth and breadth of your being, to the point that this child's happiness was more important to you than anything else in the world."

That was quite a feeling.

"Now, Alan, if you were out shopping with this son of yours one winter evening around dinnertime and your beautiful little boy, holding your hand, looked up into your eyes and asked, 'Daddy, I'm hungry...Could you please buy me an eggplant sandwich?' what would you do?"

The answer was easy, and so obvious. I would take the deepest delight in taking that child to the nearest Italian restaurant, sitting down with him at a table with a red and white checkered cloth, and ordering him the biggest eggplant parmesan sandwich on the menu — with ice cream for dessert! And I would sit with him and be thrilled by his enjoying it.

"Why, then, would you expect that I would want any less for you? For you are My Beloved Son, in whom I am well pleased."

Upon hearing those words a feeling came over me that was totally fulfilling and complete, unlike anything I have known in this world. It was the simplest and yet most profound feeling of being loved by God. For so long I felt that I was unworthy and punishable. But in just a few moments of feeling what I would do for a child that I loved, I became the child that God loved.

Then I received a garland of words I had read and heard many times before, but as I heard them that day I heard them anew. I understood the meaning of these words, for I heard them from the mouth of the One Who spoke them:

> *If a man's son asked him for a loaf of bread,*
> *would he give him a stone?*

I realized, as if for the first time, that God wants only for us to be happy, and He would never hurt us. I knew that God is a God of only love, the source of everything that is good. The idea of God punishing us or giving us something we didn't ask for is inside out (and it has been the cause of our doing some very crazy things!). I knew that my relationship with God is not one in which He is a demanding authority figure requiring me to prove my worth, but a loving Father taking delight in seeing me happy. I further reasoned that one of the purposes of our having children is to feel how much joy God derives from giving us what makes us happy. We can use the best of our relationships on earth to see what our relationships in Spirit are really like.

As Thyself

Once I was visiting some friends who had a little child. As her mom and I were conversing in the kitchen, the little girl tugged at her mom's dress and asked her for some orange juice. Mommy gave her the juice in a glass with a straw, and within a few seconds the child had imbibed the entire glass. She concluded her drink with a symphony of delightful slurping sounds indicating that the straw was vacuuming the bottom of a nearly empty glass.

"She sure did a quick job on that one!" mom commented. We both smiled, as we enjoyed the child's joy in drinking the juice and her playfulness.

Then it occurred to me that if I had drunk the juice that quickly, I probably would have considered myself a glutton. Sometimes when I have been very thirsty I have drunk something quickly, and I have judged myself for it. But I had no judgement for this child in my heart — I loved watching her enjoy it.

I wondered, then, why could I not extend the same freedom to myself? Jesus' most often quoted teaching is "Love thy neighbor as thyself," and we usually interpret this to mean that we should be as kind to our neighbor as we would like them to be to us. And this is surely true.

But perhaps there is another meaning to this great teaching. Perhaps we are being reminded to extend the same forgiveness to ourself that we offer our neighbors. We are much harder on ourself than we are on others. How often do we forgive a neighbor for something for which we would judge ourself harshly? If so, we are loving our neighbor *more* than ourself, and we need to love ourself just as much.

Years ago when I was in college I would sometimes go to x-rated movies. I felt rather guilty about this, as I judged myself for it. One evening when my roommate was out I decided to go to the local art cinema. I slinked into the theatre, feeling strange about being there. I took a seat and waited for my eyes to adjust to the darkness. After a few minutes I looked down the row, and who did I see sitting there, but my roommate!

Now here is a great lesson that I learned: Upon seeing him my initial reaction was, "I must not let him see me — he will think I'm weird." It was fine with me that he was there; I did not judge him for it — lots of college guys go to x-rated films, and he was just out enjoying himself one evening. I certainly did not love him any the less. Perhaps I even loved him more, knowing that he was like me. But I felt that I was bad for being there. Even when confronted with the truth that I and my brother are one, my ego found a way to fabricate a separation between myself and my brother. I let him know I was there, and we had a good laugh together. "All sin ends in laughter."

That night I learned to love my neighbor as myself, or should I say, to love myself as much as my neighbor.

Forgiveness Clears the Way

We need to forgive ourself before we can make progress with any challenge. At a workshop a woman approached me and told me that she was having a very hard time quitting smoking pot. "I've been smoking every day for ten years, and I have tried everything to help me stop. I've been hypnotized, I've asked my friends to hide my joints, — I even went to Pot Smokers Anonymous — yet I haven't been able to stop. I just don't know what to do!"

"Who says you have to stop?" I asked her.

She was startled. "But it's a terrible habit!"

"Here's my suggestion," I offered. "Don't judge yourself or make an issue of smoking. Just love yourself. If you smoke, you smoke; if you don't smoke, you don't. Learn that smoking pot has nothing to do with your worthiness or lovability. But do this: Go for the light. Do the things that really bring you peace. Meditate, pray, sing, come to my workshops or others — do whatever brings real joy to your heart. Don't curse the darkness; light a light. Then you will see exactly what pot smoking is all about."

Several months later the woman came to me, ecstatic. "It's amazing!" she raved. "I haven't smoked pot in months — for the first time in ten years!"

"Tell me more!" I encouraged her.

"Well, I did just as you said. I decided not to let smoking or not smoking be a big deal. I decided to love myself no matter what. I did more of the things that bring me real peace.

"Then one night I went to a party and before long a joint came my way. I took one toke, and it was nothing — I tell you, *nothing!* It wasn't good, it wasn't bad — it just wasn't interesting. I passed it by, for the first time in all those years. The same situation came up once or twice since then, and my experience was the same. I think I am done with pot."

I am happy to report to you that I have seen this woman often since her report and she has not smoked in years. In fact, she is an entirely new person — all because she was willing to forgive herself and love herself just as she was.

When we hate ourself, we energize the thing we hate. Hatred is a powerfully creative emotion, for it feeds the object of our wrath and causes it to loom even larger in our mind. Ironically, we tie ourself to that which we resent. Thoughts are targets, and emotions (e-*motions*) are the fuel that moves us toward those targets. To hate anything we do, therefore, is to cause us to do it more. The only antidote to a bad habit is to love yourself for what you are, and then to cultivate the habit we do want. Love and hate both move us toward their objects. We must choose what we really want.

Good and Truth

One of the ways that we violate ourselves is by trying to prove that we are good. To try to prove that you are good is to affirm that you are not already good. So in a sense you are trying to fill in a hole that does not exist. No wonder your life has been bumpy!

The Indian saint Neem Karoli Baba said, *"Truth does not come from good; good comes from truth."* When you tell the truth, much good comes, but if you try to attain truth by doing what you believe is good, you may not gain truth, but confusion. It is very difficult to know exactly what good should come of any particular situation. To attempt to manipulate circumstances so *your* idea of good can come about, is to let the ego play God — and that, as you know, can and does backfire. "You cannot be your own guide to miracles, for it was you who made them necessary."[1]

I first learned about the pitfalls of being a do-gooder several years ago when I was invited to visit the home of Maurice B. Cooke, the author of the *Hilarion Series*,[2] a powerful collection of spiritual teachings. I had respected

---

[1] T, p. 277
[2] M.B. Cooke, *The Hilarion Series*, Marcus Books

and admired Mr. Cooke's work for a long time, and I considered it a great honor and opportunity to be with him and his family.

The first evening of our visit we shared a lovely dinner, and after some intriguing conversation the dishes from the main course were collected. Now, what would any self-respecting do-gooder do at that moment? The dishes, of course! I arose and went straight for the sink. "They'll really appreciate this," I subconsciously thought; "I'll do all the dishes, and they'll see what a good person I am! Then they'll like me and invite me back." So, while everyone else was sitting at the dinner table enjoying apple pie, Dudley Do-Right was in the kitchen washing away. (I whistled occasionally to let them know that I was on the job.)

The final piece was the wok in which the Chinese vegetables had been stir-fried. "What an oily wok!" I remarked to myself. "This needs a real scrubbing...I'll clean it up, and then I will have done really good!" Out came the Brillo, and away I scrubbed.

Soon Maurice's wife Christine came into the kitchen to see what had happened to me. With great pride I held up the shiny scrubbed wok, and like a little boy showing his mom the finger-painting he made in kindergarten, I proclaimed, "Look, Christine, how clean the wok is!"

Christine's jaw dropped about six inches. (With a remarkable amount of self control) she exclaimed, "It took me three years to season that wok!"

What I didn't know was that you're not supposed to scrub a wok until it shines. Woks, I learned (quickly) are better when they are seasoned. But I was busy doing good — which is not always so good!

Christine was a good sport and we had a good laugh. It was a priceless lesson to me. If I had listened to my inner voice, I probably would have stayed in the dining room and enjoyed dessert with my friends. Then perhaps several of us would have gone into the kitchen together and played through the cleanup in song and laughter. And saved the wok. That was the last time I did good.

Stand Up and Be Counted

One of my most important lessons of this life has been that is it more important to be myself than to prove myself. I have gotten into all kinds of trouble in relationships, business, and communications because I wanted to be nice at the expense of telling the truth. I was afraid that I would be rejected or somehow lose if I said something that another person would not like to hear. Yet time and time again I have found that people value the truth more than sugar-coating. Loving honesty is much more productive in the long run.

The only thing more frustrating than being a nice guy is to be with a bunch of nice guys trying to make a decision. It doesn't happen!

Several years ago I was spending a day in New York City with some friends. As evening approached we were deciding whether to go to a movie in the city or return home.

The driver of the car turned to the rest of us and asked, "Well, folks, what would you like to do tonight?"

"Anything's fine with me!" Charley answered.

"I'm flexible!" we heard from Susan.

"I will go with the flow!" responded Artie.

When the poll got around to me, I answered, "Whatever you like!"

"Now wait a minute!" the driver retorted. "No one is saying anything that will help us decide! We really need to have some opinions here. This is just one of those situations where everyone is going to have to be honest about what they want. Let's go around again, and everyone please take a stand."

As it turned out, none of us really wanted to go to the movie, and so we went home. But we could have said that the first time.

Love Proves Itself

Love requires no defense and bears no need to prove itself. It knows that it is lovable, and all that comes from love must be lovable, too. You, who *are* love, need no method to demonstrate your worth, for your value speaks for itself before you even say a word or begin a deed. You accomplish far more by allowing your true goodness to shine than by attempting to neurotically demonstrate that you are valuable. Any attempt that you make to convince another that you are good will interrupt the One who stands with you to speak on your behalf, and you will demonstrate to the contrary. There is nothing you can do to make yourself more worthy, but you can, and *must*, awaken to your own greatness.

God needs no proof of who you are. Why should you? The fact that you do not remember your Origin is not a statement about your Source, but about your memory. One day you will learn that you have always been whole, despite your lapses in recollection. Thank God that your perfection is not dependent upon your recall.

Imagine for a moment that everything you do, that you have done, and that you will do is good. Imagine that you could not possibly do any bad if you tried. Can you get a taste of the feeling of forgiveness and release? That is how God sees you now. God has not been fooled in the least by your facade of unworthiness. The only difference between God and your self-image is that God always remembers how much you are loved, while you have sometimes forgotten.

You are lovable not because of what you do; you are lovable because of what you *are*. And that can never change. Your true nature as a loving being is *invulnerable and inviolable*. Spirit knows this about you now, and this is how you will learn to see yourself. When you see yourself as God sees you, you will have become God. And that is very possible indeed. In fact, you will not be finished with your wondrous journey of consciousness until you have claimed the vision of yourself as healed.

My Beloved Son

At an intensive healing retreat my roommate Lou sat in the center of a circle of supportive friends, describing the most important transformational events of his life. After painfully describing many years of challenge, hardship, and feelings of unworthiness, his face lit up as he described his experience of being at his first son's birth. Immediately he burst into tears, calling the child's name, "Andrew! My God, Andrew! How beautiful you are! How blessed I feel that you have come to be with me as my son! I have never felt so much love in all my life!"

The group of listeners began to weep with him, for the depth of his appreciation struck a chord deep within all of us. Here was a man who was totally grateful for the gift of his child.

After hearing Lou's entire story the facilitator began to offer her insights and counsel him. She encouraged him to know above all else his worthiness and beauty in the eyes of God. At the end of her sharing with Lou she stopped, thought for a moment, and told him: "And if there is one thing I would like you to remember the next time you do not love yourself, it is this: The way you felt when Andrew was born is the way God felt when you were born, multiplied ten thousandfold, and lasting unto eternity."

Story of a Soul

Nothing you can do can change Eternal Love.
- A Course in Miracles[1]

There are some experiences in life that come to us as gifts of grace. Sometimes we receive blessings that clearly do not bear a relationship to anything we have done. They are bestowed upon us to remind us that we are lovable not for what we do, but for what we are.

A blessing such as this was given to me during a planetary healing pilgrimage that I undertook to the European continent. Thirty of us gathered to find and explore the ancient mystical healing sites of the continent. It was during this journey that I had one of the most treasured and transforming experiences of my life, and I would like to share it with you now.

One of the shrines we visited was the Church of St. Theresa of Lisieux, who was affectionately known as "The Little Flower." St. Theresa was a little-known nun who lived in the late nineteenth century. Her devotion as a child was so compelling that she obtained the Pope's permission to enter a Carmelite convent at the age of thirteen. For seven years she served in the order, seeking to emulate the innocence that she found exemplified by the Child Jesus.

During her stay in the convent Theresa often underwent criticism and blame from the elder sisters. Once Theresa loaned her last favored possession, a water pitcher, to a sister in the convent. When it was returned with a crack in it, Theresa thanked God for removing the last barrier to peace from her heart. Such was the gentle willingness of Theresa to find Heaven above all else.

Around the age of twenty Theresa became ill. When it became apparent that she would not be living in this world much longer, her elder sister asked her to write the story of her life and her devotion to the way of simple loving. Theresa did so, more out of obedience than desire, and left the *Story of a*

---

[1] M, p.84

Soul [2] as a tender, shining legacy of her short but meaningful life. Theresa promised that she would "spend my Heaven doing good on earth," and "let fall a shower of roses to all who need love."

When the book was published after Theresa's passing, it became a sensation, selling out almost as fast as it could be printed. Theresa's readers discovered an immense spiritual power in her uncomplicated words and childlike devotion. The unassuming strength of her conviction won the hearts and souls of readers throughout the world. Soon Theresa began to appear in visions and accomplish miracles for many persons in need of help. The healings were often accompanied by the sweet fragrance of roses. Sometimes a rose would be found at the site of a miracle.

I was told the story of a woman who prayed to St. Theresa for help for her mother, who was undergoing a surgical operation. After the daughter waited for a long time in the anteroom of the surgical suite, a doctor emerged from the operating room, exhibiting a sweaty brow and a half-smile.

"It looks like your mother is going to be alright," he comforted her, "...but I don't know how I could have done it without the guidance of that nun."

"What nun?" inquired the daughter.

"The nun who came into the operating room and gave me directions during the surgery — Didn't you see her?"

"No, I didn't," answered the young woman "...and I was sitting here the whole time."

At that moment the two of them looked down, and found a rose at their feet.

It was with great anticipation and devotion that the thirty of us bussed toward Lisieux on that rainy September morning. How light we became as we sang songs and told miracle stories woven about our love for The Little Flower! The bus seemed to lift a few inches off the highway as we rode through the French countryside. What a reason to "arise at dawn," as Kahlil Gibran wrote, "and give thanks for another day of loving!"

Can you imagine our delight to learn upon arriving in Lisieux that this, the one day that we would be there, was St. Theresa's feast day! We joined thousands of pilgrims scaling the sloping hill to the pastel basilica high atop the picturesque little town. Gratefully we gazed upon the patchwork countryside of Brittany, a soft mirror of the gentleness that Theresa lived to extol.

---

[2] *Story of a Soul: the Autobiography of St. Theresa of Lisieux*, ICS Publications, Institute of Carmelite Studies, Washington DC 1972

As I entered the church I saw a thousand candles burning a thousand prayers into the high archways of the basilica. The contoured ceilings were elaborately yet tastefully decorated with painted roses, portraits of St. Theresa, and quotes from her brief but eternal lifetime.

My gaze was drawn to the high altar, hundreds of feet away yet nearer than my breath. There I beheld a score of white-robed, hooded priests chanting hymns to God and celebrating the virtues of their dear patroness.

Love filled the air; it was a moment of pure adoration. The service that followed was a touching communion of souls. We held hands with the elderly ladies who had come many miles to attend this mass. They appeared to be peasants, but I saw that they were queens. We hugged them warmly as the celebration concluded. The fact that we spoke no French did not matter; we were united in love, and that language transcended all apparent differences. It was a moment orchestrated by angels.

Exiting from the mass I noticed a sign pointing "To the Crypt." The word "crypt" has never had a great appeal to me, as I have always associated it with maudlin tales of sardonica *a la* Edgar Allen Poe. Yet today I felt guided to step inside this place to see what was there.

What I found was a blessing of the highest Light. The feeling in this sanctuary was sweet, nourishing, and deeply healing. Slowly, reverently I made my way beneath the painted arches to the golden altar at the front of the sanctuary. I sat down for a minute to listen to the music and feel the peace. What happened to me then I shall never forget.

As I settled into my seat a feeling of the deepest serenity enfolded me. It was as if I was being bathed in a pool of tenderness. Glued to my seat, I felt myself washed over and healed in a golden light. I looked at the gold of the altar and I realized that it was but symbolic of the wealth of the healing energy emanating from the crypt. There was no death in that crypt, only eternal life in the most magnificent testimony of its own reality. There I knew with all my heart that Spirit is the only reality; that love and service are the real essence of life; and that this physical plane is not even like unto dust covering a lamp. Everything physical, everything of this world seemed as nothing compared to the peace flowing over and through me.

There I felt a *living presence* — not just an idea or a belief — it was the essence of a living being, created and creating of love itself. If I could give it a voice, it was saying, *"My Child, God is real; Love is real; all the teachings of the Christ and the saints are true. Nothing you do in this physical world can touch the power of the presence of God, Who is Love and Love alone."*

Then I understood the meaning of the *Course in Miracles* teaching, *"Nothing you can do can change Eternal Love."*

I wanted to sit there forever; there was nothing more I wanted, nothing I needed, nowhere to go, nothing to do, not a thing to say but, "Thank you, I love you." I felt comforted in a universal womb, safe and sure of my protection, nourished to my depths. I felt that I could have stayed there for eternity. Perhaps I did. It was a taste of Heaven, one that remains imprinted in my heart like the soft warmth of the first spring rain. It was a true gift from God.

Realizing at some point that it was time to go, I arose a changed man. A saint had taken my hand and shown me the lawns of Heaven. I was told very directly that God is with me and all of us all the time, and there is nothing to fear in all the universe, for all there is, is the love of God.

As I made my way out of the church I saw a lifesize statue of The Little Flower standing by the door. Posted beside it was a sign promising that "Those who sign the book at St. Theresa's feet are assured of her protection." I signed the book, including my name and those dear to me.

As I laid down the pen, my eye was drawn to a collection of plaques from persons who had received answers to their prayers in the name of The Little Flower. Most of them said simply, "Thank you, St. Theresa," gently meaningful testimonies that I know she appreciated and offered to her Lord.

I thought that I, too, should like to offer The Little Flower a plaque of thanks for blessing me so richly. I would like to designate this testimony as my plaque of appreciation to my Little Flower. I want to say publicly, St. Theresa, that I believe in you; to me you are more real than this physical world, and if, as a result of reading this, others are inspired to seek and find help through your intercession, I will celebrate with you the shower of roses that you have sent to a world pining to know the joy of true love. You have taught me that the path of the pure of heart is the straightest road to God, and that the simplicity of a child is the way to find the peace you discovered. Thank you, St. Theresa, for spending your Heaven doing good on earth. I should like to join you in your noble cause.

Saint Theresa

The HEALING of the PLANET EARTH

LIVING from
the HEART

Now, Voyager

We are on the verge of the new age, a whole new world.
Human consciousness, our mutual awareness,
is going to make a quantum leap.
Everything will change...
All this is going to happen just as soon as you're ready.
                                        - Paul Williams, *Das Energi*[1]

One night I had a most symbolic dream. In the dream I was in an airplane flying from New Jersey to Hawaii. En route I experienced incredible delays. First, the plane landed in Kansas City where I had to make a connection. But the airplane landed in an old, rundown baseball field, as if I had gone into a time warp — it was back in the 1950's! Then the plane had to go to another airport in the city to make the connection. But instead of flying to the airport, the plane drove on the highway with the automobiles — and it was rush hour. It seemed like it was taking forever to get there!

When I asked the steward when my next flight was scheduled to leave, he answered, "That flight is scheduled to depart in one year, sir." *One year!* Then I noticed that I was the only one on the plane. And it was not the airline I had originally scheduled. Finally, when the flight was airborne, the stewardess announced, "We are scheduled to arrive in New Jersey in two hours." After all that, I was back where I started!

Finally I got disgusted with this dream, and I decided to wake up. And do you know where I woke up? In Hawaii, where I had gone to sleep the night before.

It can be very frustrating trying to get where you already are. If you are already home, you can be sure that any attempt to get there will cause delays, and ultimately will not work. You need but realize you are already home.

I had another experience which also had to do with airplanes and

---

[1] Paul Williams, *Das Energi*, Warner Books, 1978, p. 50

airports, but this time it was in a waking dream.

Last spring I went to North Carolina to participate in a healing conference. It was a long weekend of travelling and workshops, and when Sunday came I looked forward to returning home, stretching out on my couch, and relaxing. My plane touched down to the Newark runway at 9 o'clock on Sunday night, and I was glad to be home. My friend Anne would be waiting for me at the gate, and it would be good to see her.

When I reached the lobby, Anne was not there. I waited five, ten, fifteen minutes, and still there was no sign of her. Where was she?

I phoned the house, and to my surprise Anne answered.

"Where are you?" I asked. (Actually, it was a rhetorical question. I already knew the answer, but it was not the one I wanted to hear.)

"I'm home," she brightly replied. "Where are you?"

"I'm at Newark Airport."

"Noooo!"

"That's what this sign here says."

"But you're not coming in until tomorrow night."

I looked at my ticket. "The ticket says I'm here tonight."

"The message from your office says Monday night."

"I think the pilot didn't get that message."

"O.K...Hang in there — I'll be right there." Right there meant at least forty-five minutes. I felt annoyed. "Why is this happening, God? What am I going to do in Newark Airport for almost an hour?"

The Voice came loud and clear: *"Why not practice being happy?"*

"Yeah, that's easy for You to say," I retorted. "You get to hang out on some celestial cloud, listening to harp music and watching sunsets — You don't have to sit in Newark Airport on a Sunday night."

"What makes you think Newark Airport is outside of Heaven?"

"Now, really, God, You're stretching it on that one."

"Am I?"

"Of course You are. If You're so great, why didn't You have Anne here on time?"

"Listen, Son," the Big Air Traffic Controller went on, *"It's really up to you. You can be bugged, or you can have the greatest hour of your life. You can choose to be upset or you can be in love. That's the power I gave you. Don't you remember all those books you wrote telling people that happiness is available at any moment?"*

(Why is it that God always has to hit you with the truth when you're upset?)

"Sure, I remember."

"Well, here's your chance to practice. Imagine that you are in Heaven now."

"You sure do have a great imagination."

"I know — that's how I created the entire universe! Not a bad production, wouldn't you agree?"

I had to agree. I had my assignment.

So I decided to play a game while I waited. I decided to imagine that I was in Heaven, and everything I saw happening before me was actually happening in Heaven. I saw that the porters were smiling as they were ticketing luggage. "Wow," I exclaimed to myself, "...they are ticketing suitcases in Heaven — what a great job!"

Then I saw families greeting their children at the baggage carousel. "What a wonderful scene," I remarked to myself; " — families reuniting in Heaven!" My heart felt warm.

Then I noticed several people standing at the rent-a-car desks, making arrangements to pick up transportation. "How beautiful!" I considered. "These folks have arrived in Heaven and they are going to tour or find their new homes!"

As I continued to play the game, I found myself in a state of deep tranquility. The flight attendant had said, "Welcome to New Jersey," but I was beginning to see that that was but a part of a bigger picture.

Sitting there in what seemed to be Newark Airport, I went into an exquisitely beautiful meditation — with my eyes open. Why would I need to close my eyes to find Heaven, if I were seeing it all around me?

My reveries were interrupted by Anne's hand on my shoulder. "Hi!" she smiled.

Had it been forty-five minutes?

"Ready to go?" she asked, car keys jingling in her hand.

"Sit down," I invited her. "This is a wonderful place!"

"What are you talking about?"

"This is Heaven!" I told her.

"Noooo!"

Anne sat down, and I explained to her what had happened. She loved the idea; she was happy to be in Heaven, too.

Then came the icing on the cake. A rather harried fellow came up to us and asked us if we would mind watching his bags for a few minutes while he went to make a phone call. Already in Heaven, we had no place to go; so we were happy to tell him "sure." A short while later he returned and thanked us profusely for our help.

Then it occurred to me that we had just brought Heaven to earth. Because we were in a heavenly state of consciousness, we served our brother and made his life easier. (George Eliot said, "What do we live for if not to make life less difficult for one another?") If we were in a state of fear or impatience, we might have said no or acquiesced begrudgingly. But we were at peace, and in that consciousness it was our joy to bring him peace.

I saw that we had actually *created* Heaven in Newark Airport, and we saw it manifest in a very material, practical, and grounded way. So I learned that Heaven begins with our thoughts.

This is It

At a workshop I attended, the leader taught a strong lesson about the power of the now. "This is it," he stated, "and it doesn't get much 'itter' than this!"

There is just as much love, God, peace, and healing in the room in which you are now reading, as there is or ever will be anywhere in the universe. There is a great ocean of love, which includes every kind of fulfillment you have ever dreamed of, inviting you to swim in it. But you have to step into it. And it is even easier than that — you don't even need to know how to step into it; you just have to let go of the ways that you have devised to dam it away from you. *"The course does not aim at teaching the meaning of love, for that is beyond what can be taught. It does aim, however, at removing the blocks to the awareness of love's presence, which is your natural inheritance."*[2]

One of the ways we deny love's presence is by placing it in the future or the past. We see Heaven as being in the future, like a carrot on a stick which we will get a bite of if we are good between now and then. But *there is no "then."* All there will be in the future is here now. We deserve good not by earning it, but by accepting it.

The concept of future peace actually works against peace, for if there is no peace now, there is no peace. Jesus was not a pie-in-the-sky teacher, although many who claim to teach in his name use the carrot of Heaven as a tool of fear. Jesus taught, "The Kingdom of Heaven is at hand," and "It is within you." He was a teacher of love in the present moment. Indeed this moment is the only one in which we will find true love.

---

[2] T, Introduction

In a way similar to misplacing our trust in the illusion of a future Heaven, we hurt ourselves by believing in a Heaven that existed in the past. "If only I could go back to the good ole' days," we think, or "if I could just recapture that moment." But what we need to realize is that the joy of those moments came from being in those moments, and if we would be willing to be in the present moment, we would find the same wonder waiting for us to enjoy it.

Even in new age teaching, we may tend to glamorize our "former" innocence or the heavenly realm from which we came to earth. This, too, is a trap, for the way we lose that innocence is to wander into thoughts about it being in the past. The same innocence and light are available to us here, now, in a body, on the earth. "On earth as it is in Heaven," prayed Jesus. He wouldn't have declared it if it weren't possible and true. We have *not* lost our innocence, except in our thoughts, and our thoughts alone. Paradise has not been removed from us. But we have removed ourselves from It by believing it was there or then, and not here and now.

One afternoon when I was in Olympia, Washington, I was riding in a car with Unity minister John Wingfield and his lovely five-year-old daughter, Leanna. Somehow our conversation got around to where we came from.

"I know where I came from, Daddy!" Leanna offered.

"Where's that, sweetheart?" Daddy inquired.

"Heaven!"

John and I looked at one another and we smiled. It was, of course, a perfectly cute answer.

Then John turned to Leanna and added something quite profound to her response:

"That's right, Leanna...And you are still in Heaven!"

That got me. John's words put it all in perspective. His statement was the missing link, the truth that bridged the supposed gap between the Heaven that we came from and the Heaven that we are taught we will go to (if we are good). We *are* good, and we are good *now*. This knowledge is the key that unlocks the door to the Heaven that we deserve, now and always.

The Invitation

Life is not a delicatessen where you have to take a number and wait until your turn is called. It is an always alive and fully exciting gift of total love.

Many times Jesus likened the Kingdom of Heaven to a great banquet to which everyone is invited. The table is set, and all are free to partake. But if you believe there is something you have to do first, you will delay your homecoming and you will be hungry. Not because the food is kept from you, but because you had something you believed was more important.

That something may be a job or a marriage or a new car, or any of the glittering things of this world. Or it may be a thought that you need to suffer first or do something to earn Heaven. Suffering has no place in the Kingdom, and the idea of earning God's love is as preposterous as an infant earning his mother's adoration or proving himself worthy to be sheltered by his father. A child receives love because she is lovable. That lovableness has nothing to do with what she does, but it has everything to do with what she *is*. *Is* is a present tense verb. Because you are always in a state of *is*ness, you are always in the Kingdom. Any concepts that you harbor about what you have to do first to deserve Heaven are roadblocks which you have erected between yourself and your happiness. They push Heaven away from you by exactly the distance of the width of your fear of It.

The Door to the Light

Even a little consideration of the possibility that you are already healed will begin to undo the tight ball of knotted fears which has bound you, and set into motion the dynamics of mind that will open the door to the Light. Real healing in your life is possible only now, and it is up to you to accept it or delay it. Please accept it all now. You have no karma to pay off, no more tests to face, and no further lessons to learn. All of those ideas are products of past, future, and separation thinking. If all there is, is now, from when could you have incurred a karmic debt? If you are one with God and there is no power outside your own Self, who could test you? And if your mind is one with the Mind of God, Whose knowledge of the whole of the cosmos is imbued in your soul, what lesson would further be required of you?

These concepts of salvation in time may have served you to bring you to the point at which you now stand, but beyond this moment they will act only as an encumberment. *Be free now!* This moment is the only one in which liberation can be found. *Future salvation is no salvation.* You have allowed thoughts of past and future Paradise to edge you out of eternity. This need not be. The same eternity that was available to you before you chose to step out of it is available to you now, as it always has been, and always will be. That step was taken in thought only, and not in reality. You are free to think with

God or against Her, but you are not free to be outside Her love. Peace is here for you to choose, but the only moment in which you are free to choose it is the present one.

Who would wander into past guilt or future fear if he knew that he could have all the peace he has ever dreamed of, now? Who would make a plan for her liberation if she knew that plans were the ego's tools to avoid freedom now? Who would preach the way to escape from a future hell unless he were in hell already? And how clearly do you think one in hell can see the way out?

But one who walks with God at this moment can show you the way to healing. You are not a body, but an idea, and ideas are alive only as you think them. Think another, and the original idea is gone. Return to the original one, and what you interposed between its inception and your return was but a dream. No matter how long you have dreamed of loss, only a moment's awakening is required for you to realize that all is quite intact.

Celebration, not Anticipation

To attempt to act to create a new age in the future is to fall into the subtle trap of denying that it is already with us. To manufacture a future Heaven is to judge the present One, and the present One is all there is. In so judging you will see separation, find people who are wrong, and feel that you are a victim — none of which are true.

The Millenium that you rightfully seek lives within you even as you read these words. But it needs your assent to be made real on earth. God has done His part to create it, and now your part is but to accept it.

Do not delay your healing by doubting, questioning, or waiting. You are never farther than one thought away from peace, and if you choose to think a peaceful thought, the Kingdom of Heaven is at hand. Every great sage has taught this truth, and if you are willing to accept it, you may count yourselves among those who see God.

> *Do you not say, "There are yet four months, then comes the harvest"? I tell you, lift up your eyes, and see how the fields are already white for harvest!*
>
> - Jesus the Christ[3]

---

[3] John 4:35

The Day After the Prayer

Someday, after mastering the wind, the waves, and the tides,
We shall harness for God the power of love,
And then, for the second time in history,
Man will have discovered fire.

- Teilhard de Chardin

God, what can I do to heal the earth?'' I asked as I sat in the quiet of my room late that Sunday evening. Thirty of us had gathered to watch the television docudrama "The Day After," and though I had expected the movie to be grimly depressing, I found myself more inspired than despairing. Deeply I yearned to be guided to know the way I could contribute to eliminating any possibility of the horrific scenes I beheld on the television screen.

There was one scene in particular that stood out in my memory. It was a scene in which a young woman was about to give birth to her child in a musty, dimly lit hospital. This was after the bomb had dropped, and she and her doctor were discussing the possibility of her child growing up healthy. The possibilities were slim.

"This did not have to happen," she said. "We knew about nuclear power for forty years. We knew its dangers and what it would do to the earth. But nobody cared. If someone cared enough, this would not have happened."

I thought about it, and I cared. I cared enough to want to do something about it. Perhaps if there were more people like me, we could make a difference.

Then came to me a thought, the kind of inspired awareness that is bestowed as a graceful gift, delivered by angels of the kindest intention. I remembered a project which a friend had told me about, in which American and Russian families were exchanging photographs and keeping one another's pictures in their living rooms as constant reminders of our abiding sameness. To me this was a guiding vision that there is nothing to fear of one another, that we are all children of One God.

A voice of inner guidance blended with the memory. *"This project is symbolic of the way that the healing of the planet will be born, through overcoming fear with genuine love. The people of the world can create peace simply by finding peace within each one's own heart. As that happens — and it is happening, now — the governments of the world must follow suit. The politics of the world are nothing more or less than the reflection of the consciousness of the people. Make peace with the Russian **people**. Pray for Soviet families. Let there be a healing within **your** heart and mind, and the strength of your love will be the cornerstone upon which the temple of peace on earth will rest."*

Of course, it made so much sense. I began to see the wisdom of this way. As the outer world is but a mirror of my own mind, if I want to make a change in the world I see, I must first transform, or re-create, my pattern of thinking. If I seek to build a bridge of peace between nations, I must first find unity within my own self. This is the law of mind, love, and life, a principle I have seen demonstrated thousands of times in my own experience. And because the world I see is a reflection of my own self, what heals my own life must also heal the planet.

With the firmest confidence in the power of my intention, I began to radiate love and genuine caring to the people of Russia. As I did so I realized so clearly that they are just like me, appreciating life, enjoying their children, and yearning for peace and good will on our garden planet. Mentally I enfolded the Soviet people in my arms and told them that they need not be afraid of me. I let them know that I cared for them, that I would never do anything to hurt them. In a flash I saw the insanity of fear and the futility of casting anyone out of my heart. It was a vision of how easily love can transform our world.

As the power of the prayer increased, my relationship with the Soviet people became a reality. The thought occurred to me that I would love to visit the Soviet Union, to get to know the Russian people, to celebrate the truth that we are not really different after all. I imagined meeting Russian families, embracing them as my own, and sharing my books with them as an expression of our real unity. As I visualized these scenes I felt a warm glow in my heart, as if God was confirming to me that my desire was aligned with Divine Intention. I felt not so much that I was praying to God, but that God was praying through me.

Divine Appointment

The next morning I found myself in the USAir waiting room at Toronto Airport, en route to Newark, hardly able to think of anything but the destruction my eyes had beheld the night before. I watched the smiles of the families greeting one another at the gates. Light was dancing in the eyes of the children with their noses pressed against the viewport windows. I noticed the gaily-colored wall murals with scenes of international celebration, a striking contrast to the charred grey rubble of the razed, radioactive Kansas City depicted in the movie.

I wanted to see what effect the movie had had on the people of the world. Half-anxiously, half-eagerly I peered over some shoulders to catch a glimpse of the morning headlines. I hoped to read, *"'The Day After' Births New Efforts Toward World Peace."* Instead I found, *"Nuke Film Stirs Debate."*

"Debate?" I exclaimed to myself, "The last thing we need more of is debate — Didn't that film wake everyone up, as it did me? Didn't it make any difference?"

At that moment my reflections were interrupted by the sound of a mother reading a children's story to her little daughter, sitting just a few inches to my right. I couldn't make out the words she was reading, so I scanned the book. It looked like *"Babar,"* but I couldn't understand the characters of the writing on the page.

"Excuse me," I carefully interrupted them, "Could you please tell me what language that is you're reading?"

The mother lifted her head, and with the kindest smile she answered, "Russian."

My heart soared like a sailing star. The previous evening I had prayed with the deepest fervor to meet and make peace with Russian families, and now, *less than twelve hours after the prayer*, I found myself seated next to a lovely Russian family.

Silently I said a prayer of gratefulness. The night before I had seen the grim vision of our holy planet reduced to a mound of burning cinders because the American and Russian people forgot our mutual divinity, and this morning I found myself with another chance. It was as if I had awakened from a grievous nightmare, and here I was given the ability to personally stop the horror from becoming a reality.

"How to make contact, now?" I deliberated. I wanted to approach them in a way that would be comfortable for both of us. (There is a bumper sticker that advises, *"Expect a Miracle Today,"* and what a marvelous counsel that proved to be on that special day!) I reached into the pouch of my parka and there found a multicolored strip of heart stickers, the kind that children love to collect.

"That's it!" I silently celebrated. I tore off a section, held it firmly between my hands, and silently prayed, *"God, I'm going to give this little girl these hearts, and I ask you, Father, to imbue these hearts with Your Heart. Let this act of sharing symbolize the healing of the planet. With these hearts I offer all the love and understanding that will renew the truth of the real brotherhood and sisterhood of the American and Soviet peoples. Let this gift heal the earth of all separation, fear, and warfare forever. Let Your Light be shared now. The fate of the whole world and all humanity rests in my hands, and I ask You to use this act for your healing purposes. Let your blessing ripple out like waves on the ocean of eternal love. Thank you, Father, for I know You have heard and answered."*

With full confidence that what I had just done may have been one of the most important acts of my life, I turned to the little girl and asked her, "Would you like some hearts?" Though she had not been paying much attention to me, her eyes instantly lit up. Her mom, humbly grateful, asked her if she could say "thank you" in English. Shyly she did her best. As I gave her the strip I peeled off one heart, the color of the sun, and gently pressed it onto the page she was reading.

The girl's father, having watched our meeting, walked over to thank me, and we began to converse.

"What kind of work do you do?" he asked.

"I write books...some for children."

"Oh, really?" mom perked up, "On what subjects?"

"On themes like making friends."

An idea lighted in my mind. "Say, I have a book called *Have You Hugged A Monster Today?* If you'd give me your address, I'd love to send one to your beautiful daughter."

"Isn't that kind of you!..." the father began to respond, and just then we were shuffled onto the plane. As I took my seat about ten rows behind the family, I wondered if he was just being polite, or if I would have the joy to complete my offer. I sat and beamed prayers of thankfulness nearly the whole flight, tears welling up in my eyes at the thought of the immediacy with which last night's prayer was answered. Earnestly I hoped that more good would come of our meeting.

A few minutes before the plane was about to land, the burly man with a kind face rose from his seat and walked toward me with a slip of paper in his hand.

"Here is our address...You must come and visit us for dinner sometime!"

My joy at his invitation was exceeded only by the amazement that welled up within me as I read what was written on the paper. The girl's name was "Shlomit," which means "Peace." She was born in Jerusalem, which in Hebrew means "The City of Peace." The icing on the cake, the real cosmic giggle, however, was their address: Einstein Drive, Princeton. That is where Albert Einstein developed the formula for atomic energy. The symbology of the meeting is awesome: Peace is growing up on the street that Einstein paved.

A Formula for Planetary Healing

As this lesson was received for all of us, I would like to share with you some of the very important principles I gained from this miraculous experience:

WE CAN USE OUR THOUGHTS TO CREATE PEACE ON EARTH.

Thoughts are things, and every thought is a prayer. Our thoughts are very powerful, and we attract to ourselves that which we think upon. The Law of Mind is perfectly consistent, and it can be focused upon any chosen goal. The formula for healing ourselves, one another, and our planet is:

$$C + B = A$$

CONCEIVE + BELIEVE = ACHIEVE

I *conceived* of the idea of making peace with Russian families. (Mental conception, like physical conception, requires two partners. In this case God impregnated my mind with an idea, and I accepted it; thus was consummated the marriage of God and man.) Then I *believed* that such a marvelous healing could take place. A feeling of joyous completion vibrated through me. Finally, the idea was *achieved* as it was realized on the physical plane.

This incident is a dramatic example of how the Law of Mind works, a ubiquitous principle that governs all of our thoughts and their subsequent manifestations. The divine promise of the Law of Mind is that *we can change our life by changing our thoughts.* If we seek to change our planetary life, we must begin by

visualizing, feeling, and *accepting*

the reality of a peaceful, healed world. All actions that stem from these thoughts work instantaneously and dynamically to create peace.

Peace is an Idea
Whose Time Has Come

Since my vision, I have seen many indications that others have been inspired by the same lofty idea, and they are acting on it. Within a week after my prayer I saw a newspaper headline proclaiming, *"New York Town Launches First Strike for Peace."* The city of Saratoga Springs, New York has been matched by the Ground Zero Pairing Project[1] with a city in the Soviet Union, Kashin, U.S.S.R. (It is interesting to me that the USA and USSR both start with *US.*) The sister cities were chosen for similarities in climate, geography, population, industry, and in this case a special interest: both cities are known and celebrated for their natural spring water. The people of Saratoga Springs sent the Russian townspeople a three-pound love package, called a "Community Portrait," containing a scrapbook of items that are personally meaningful to the Saratogans, and it was arranged that the Kashin people do the same.

In Seattle, Washington, three thousand miles from where the idea came to me, I was given a flyer entitled "Send Your Heart to Russia," announcing the *Earthstewards Network* [2], a group without any particular religious, secular, or political affiliation, bound together only by their desire to make contact and share understanding with the Soviet people. The group organizes personal good-will tours of the Soviet Union (exactly my idea!).

---

[1] Ground Zero Pairing Project, Community Portrait Exchange, PO Box 19049, Portland, Oregon 97219

[2] Earthstewards Network, 6330 Eagle Harbor Drive N.E., Bainbridge Island, WA 98110

Besides inviting people to make a personal statement by visiting Russia, some of the Earthstewards were collecting small hand-made gifts from regular American people like you and me, to be personally delivered to Russian people like you and me, along with hugs and arrangements for pen-pal relationships. The trip includes a meeting with the Peace Committee of Moscow, visits to the sister cities, and sharing circle dances with the Russian people in the parks of Crimea, Georgia, and Muldavia. What a wonderful way to make contact!

Since that time I have learned of many other citizen diplomacy groups, each offering a unique and creative method of making human contact. "Play for Peace"[3] joins American and Russian people for frisbee throws and other light-hearted activities. One sculptor has proposed a Soviet-American "clay stomp," in which Russian and American persons of all ages come together, stomp a huge vat of modeling clay into mouldability, and then create ceramic ornaments to share and display in the spirit of mutual support. Other groups include volleyball tournaments, musical collaboration, and clowning. The possibilities for healing through creativity are endless! And many of them are being explored. Last year there were seventy-three citizen diplomacy groups scheduled to visit the Soviet Union from the *Seattle area alone*. Surely we are awakening to our own power to build bridges of love, no matter what the distance that seems to separate the shores. Love knows no distance or limitation.

The Way Out

As I was meditating after watching "The Day After," all I could see in my mind's eye were the two nuclear bombs bursting over Kansas City. Though in the movie they were red, in my field of vision I saw two dark masses, expanding into a nightmare of death and destruction. Then I remembered that a friend with whom I had watched the film had suggested the affirmation, *"The love of God is now pouring through the whole earth."* I began to repeat this affirmation, asking my Heavenly Father to show me the truth of these words. Then I saw a great beam of golden light coming down from far up in the heavens. This light was like a wonderful shaft of healing power pouring through the clouds. This wondrous ray shined down right where the bombs had burst, and the golden light began to dissipate the darkness. Like a horror film vanquished by a bright dome light switched on

---

[3] Play for Peace, PO Box 8910, La Jolla, CA 92038

in a theatre, this bright beam completely outshined the black mass of the bombs, until there was only golden light where the bombs had been.

With this healing vision came these words:

The power of God is far greater than nuclear power.

This message of encouragement was followed with this explanation:

> *Atomic power is not even an eyelash compared to the arsenal of love that is God. The Power of the Divine, given cooperation, can free you from the seeming nuclear dilemma in a thousand ways that you haven't even begun to think of.*

In other words, *God has a way out*, and indeed God is the *only* way out. God always has a way out, and just because we haven't discovered it yet, doesn't mean that it isn't there — it just means that we haven't approached it from the right angle yet. God's power begins where thoughts of limitation leave off. A miracle is simply something that God does as easily and naturally as anything else, except that we didn't think He could. The miracle, then, is not a reflection of God's ability to transcend law, but a statement of our willingness to accept the Law of Love as the only law.

In my lifetime I have seen many miracles, wondrous healings that have left me with the firmest conviction that God can indeed do anything. I have seen the lifetime crippled arise and walk at the touch of a healing hand; I have friends who have had seemingly inoperable cancers disappear in a matter of minutes; and I know of Padre Pio, the twentieth-century saint who prayed for a man with no corneas in his eyes, and the man had his sight restored. These are not supernatural occurrences, but natural expressions of God's Healing Love shining through the door of the opened mind. *A Course in Miracles* teaches that "Miracles are natural. When they do not occur, something has gone wrong."[4] Our problem is not that miracles are not available to us, but that we do not live in the expectation of miracles. The key to transforming our lives is to gladly *let go of our attempts to change other people, and use that energy to expand our expectation of what God can do for us.*

As the ancient orientals taught, every crisis equals danger plus opportunity. Where there is apparent danger, you can be sure there is a lesson, really a precious gift, waiting to be learned. When we accept the gift, our life

---

[4] T, p. 1

is infinitely enriched. Indeed the whole nuclear dilemma is actually our first planetary lesson, a cause for rejoicing, for through solving it we shall be firmly established in the great awareness that we live, breathe, and love as one family on this one planet — under one God.

Love's Way of Transformation

Nuclear power seems fearful — as does anything — only when we forget that God is in charge of the universe. *A Course in Miracles* reminds us, "The presence of fear is a sure sign that you are trusting in your own strength." The belief that we are lost, helpless, and unloved children is the source of all of our problems, and the nuclear situation is a magnification of our self-image as being outside of God. Who that believes God is present would need an atomic bomb? And who that believes God is not present could possibly secure his safety with ten thousand atomic bombs?

Whenever we act on a false idea, only more confusion can result. And so our world has become a nuclear porcupine, the natural result of unnatural thinking. We are like a family of children feeling deserted by a father who would gladly embrace us if we would only drop our defenses long enough to let a hug in. The only way out of the confusion is the memory that there is indeed a Divine Order to the universe, no matter how confused it may *seem* to be. The truth is that if we are willing to love, we shall surely discover we *are* loved.

The Heart is the Real Peacemaker

President Eisenhower said that

> *"One day the people of the world will want peace so much that the governments are going to have to get out of their way and let them have it."*

This is exactly what is happening on our planet now, and you and I have the great privilege to participate in this miraculous transformation and watch it unfold before our eyes. We are the channels through which a new age is being delivered upon the earth. The new age will not happen *to* us, but *through* us. There is no use in waiting for a savior. The savior is within each of us, patiently awaiting our expression.

We have now come to the moment in planetary evolution at which we must allow destiny to be delivered through us.

We are all expressions of the Mother Principle, and we can now all participate in the birth of a safe and healed world — a holy child that belongs to all of us.

Peace Needs Your Belief

It is possible that the only wall remaining between us and the complete healing of the planet is the *belief* that war is an inevitable part of life on earth. If this is so, then you and I can make a major contribution to the healing of our earth by simply understanding and knowing that war is *not* a necessary part of anyone's life, and certainly not of our collective lives. In fact, peace is what life on earth was intended to be about, and indeed *will* be about, as soon as we cease to believe that war is necessary. The course of human evolution involves shifts — sometimes radically rapid shifts — in what we *believe* to be so, and consequently what *is* so on the planet.

Until about a hundred years ago slavery was an accepted common practice in life on earth. Yet now slavery has almost entirely disappeared, and it is certainly unthinkable to us. The idea of slavery seems so outlandish that we can hardly conceive of it at all. Yet only a hundred years ago millions of human beings were indentured as slaves.

Although the idea of complete — *complete* — peace on earth may seem impossible, we need to look at planetary healing from the point of view of *the possible*. The first principle of miracles is that *there is no order of difficulty in miracles.* There is no reason to believe that healing the world of nuclear arms is any harder or needs to take any longer than the shift of one thought in your mind or mine, which are one. If we can see one possibility in a million for peace, it will surely come, for the mind works in terms of *possibilities*, and *it is only a matter of time until that which we can see to be possible becomes real.*

Peace Begins with Me

The most powerful way to bring about peace on the planet is to create peace in our personal relationships. Because the world is a manifestation of many small relationships, *we can create global peace by initiating interpersonal peace.* The fate of the world literally rests on our daily interactions with our husbands, wives, children, parents, roommates, friends, and co-workers. The politics of the world are simply a magnified reflection of the way we handle our daily personal politics. How can we expect the earth to be healed of separation if we are operating our individual lives under the illusion of personal separateness? And how can all the pain of the world but be healed, as we exchange our idea of being alone for the truth of being all one? Spake Paul, ''When I was a child, I talked like a child, I thought like a child, I reasoned like a child. When I became a man I put childish ways behind me.'' [5]

There is one truth upon which we can found all of our precious work toward the healing of the planet earth:

> *Peace in the physical world can be built only upon the cornerstone of peace in each of our hearts, and as we heal our sense of interpersonal separation, peace on earth is sure to follow.*

Metaphysicians tell us that all of the bullets, bombs, and nuclear warheads in the arsenals of the nations are the manifestations of the collective fear and anger thoughts of the people of the world over all of history. And now, we are told, we are facing the results of our thoughts. This may at first seem intimidating, but actually it is a cause for celebration, for if we created weapons with our thoughts of hatred, *we can dismantle them with our thoughts of love.* As we begin to think, feel, speak, and live in harmony with our treasured goal of peace, so must peace surely come.

This is Grace, which far supercedes karma. Grace means that no matter how big of a mess we seem to have made, it can all be erased, eradicated, and undone by correcting the way we *think*. No error, personal or global, is so great that a transformation of thinking cannot accomplish its complete

---

[5] Corinthians 13:11

correction. When our intention changes, so do our results.

> *The most significant contribution you and I can make toward*
> *world peace is to be peaceful ourselves, to give peacefulness to*
> *those whose lives we touch daily, and to forgive ourselves for*
> *our errors, to the point at which we love ourselves no matter*
> *what we have ever done.*

When we find no sin in ourselves we will find no sin in the world, and thus, after our long, thirsty trek through the desert of human separation, we find ourself at the holy gate of New Jerusalem, key in hand.

> *If the people lived their lives*
> *As if it were a song!*
> *For singing out the light*
> *Provides the music for the stars*
> *To be dancing circles in the night.*

> — Russian folk song

If we can build great bridges
Across the mighty waves, between the distant ridges
Is it a task too great
To build a bridge across the depths of hate?

For now more than ever
What the world needs more of
Is to reach for each other
With bridges of love [1]

If we can reach so far
To send men up to the moon and rockets to the stars
Why are we still so far apart?
Why can't we find the way from soul to soul,
From heart to heart?

For now more than ever
What the world needs more of
Is to reach for each other
With bridges of love

Bridges of steel reach from shore to shore
Bridges of love reach so much more
They link our common hopes, our common ground
Joining one and all, the whole world round

We all can build bridges of love each day
With our eyes, our smiles, our touch
With our will to find a way
There is no distance we cannot span
The vision is in our hearts
The power is in our hands

For now more than ever
What the world needs more of
Is to reach for each other
With bridges of love [1]

---

[1] Steven Longfellow Fiske and Jai Michael Josephs, "Bridges of Love," Fiske Music, 1983

Bridges of Love

In a gentle way, you can shake the world.
                                    - Mahatma Gandhi

It was no surprise to me, then, that several months after my encounter with Shlomit and her family, I received a telephone call from a friend in Washington who was also committed to building bridges of love between nations. "Would you like to come to Russia with us in May, Alan?" she asked.

Think you not the goal itself will gladly arrange the means for its accomplishment?[2]

When I asked about the details, I was thrilled to learn that some of the people I most admire would be joining us: visionary woman of integrity Barbara Marx Hubbard, the great Swami Satchidananda, who has touched and inspired millions through his way of living yoga, and Patricia Sun, one of my favorite healers and teachers of love. I was also impressed to know that some well-known people from the entertainment industry would be with us, such as Dennis Weaver, Mike Farrell, and Shelly Fabares. The entire group was to be comprised of eighty spiritually-oriented teachers, business leaders, physicians, and artistically talented people, all dedicated to making a personal contribution to world healing. I took a deep breath in, and as I breathed out I realized I was about to undertake a great adventure.

Laughter and Sorrow

We arrived in Helsinki, Finland, where we spent three days undergoing an intense orientation to prepare us for our entry into the Soviet Union. Amidst the backdrop of a beautiful resort on the shores of the Baltic Sea, we got to know one another and learned much about Soviet history, the Russian people, and their culture.

---

[2] T, p. 340

Many of us brought gifts for the Soviet people, which we distributed among our group for each of us to give to individuals that we met in our travels. The first evening we came into our meeting room to find a glittering display of one hundred quartz crystals laid out on a table in a mandala geometric pattern. We filed up to the table and each of us chose a crystal that called to us vibrationally.

The next morning Patch Adams gave a lecture on the healing power of humor. Stunning the audience with his outrageous clown outfit, Patch revealed a table with one hundred rubber noses of all shapes and sizes, laid out in a mandala pattern. Each of us was invited to file up to the table and choose a nose, program it with our vibration, and give it to a Russian! (And we did. We "nosed" policemen, teachers, diplomats, children, shopkeepers, and anyone to whom we felt guided to give one. Without exception the noses were received joyfully, in the spirit of fun and sharing with which they were given. Long live nasal diplomacy!)

When the time came for our orientation about Soviet history, I learned some facts about Russia that stimulated a very deep process of transforming my attitude and understanding of Russia and her people.

The Russian people have had a horribly painful history. The country has been invaded and plundered over the centuries. From the Turks, to Napoleon, to Hitler, ambitious moguls have sought to overrun Russia, against which the Russians have taken up resistance. It is no wonder they are an isolated and defensive people.

Until 1917, the Russians were essentially a kingdom of peons. At the beginning of the twentieth century two percent of the population controlled eighty percent of the nation's wealth, and there were gross injustices in the dichotomous standards of living. We visited the Czar's Summer Palace in Pushkin, a staggeringly beautiful and glamorous estate with a thousand rooms embodying unbelievable wealth. One room had walls covered with pure gold; the next, malachite; and the next, ebony. Phenomenal treasures! We were told that eight of the royalty lived here, and they were staffed by three thousand servants! Artisans and craftsmen were paid next to nothing for their work. So in 1917 the people got fed up, they overthrew the Czar, and established a country where the ideal, at least, was for everyone to have an equal share of ownership and control of the country. Now that ideal has certainly not been realized, but an understanding of this history gives us a perspective on where the Russian people have come from in the brief space of seventy years.

Another very astounding fact was that the Soviet Union lost twenty million of her people in World War II. Ten million were killed through the war with the Nazis, and another ten million were lost to Russia's own Stalin. This is a rarely publicized fact. In all of the wars the United States has been involved in, from the American Revolution through Vietnam, this country has lost one million of our citizens. So you may begin to appreciate the kind of challenges the Russian have had to face. As so many families were touched by the war, there is still a strong memory of it. I would say that the Russian people have an extremely high value on peace — perhaps even more than our generation in America — for they have seen war, and they do not want to see it again. Be assured that all of their armaments and bravado arise from their feelings of insecurity; that they need to protect themselves from what they consider to be outside aggressors.

These facts gave me a great deal of insight into the life and genetic psyche of the Russian people. The purpose of our journey was to learn how to make contact with the hearts of the Russians, and knowing more about their history certainly helped me to do so. Here would be an important point to remember Longfellow's statement, "If we could look into the secret history of our enemies, we would find sorrow and suffering sufficient to disarm all hostilities."

Vicki's Tears

In Leningrad we were taken to the War Memorial, where nearly five hundred thousand Leningrad citizens — half of the city's population lost in World War II — are buried in mass graves the size of six football fields. At the head of the park stands a huge statue of Mother Russia, looming with the solemn dignity of a people who feel. The Mother holds a great granite wreath lain across her open arms, a symbol of respect and life. Somber music stirs in the background as Russian citizens lay rare, expensive flowers at the feet of the mass graves, not knowing exactly where the ones dear to them lie. There is the feeling that all are dear to them.

Our tour guide, Vicki, guides us to the head of the memorial, under the arms of Mother Russia, where she recounts to us the story of the war. An entire generation was lost from the body of the nation. The Russian people remember.

Vicki, I am told, is a KGB agent, a party member, an avowed atheist. And Vicki, in the midst of her canned discourse, stops and breaks into tears, a striking contrast to her otherwise controlled presentation.

"Please forgive me for digressing," she mutters through the mascara running down her round cheeks.

"I want you to know how grateful I am that you have come here...Our countries must unite...We cannot go on like this...For the sake of our children...there is no other way."

We weep with her. There is a moment of spontaneous silence, deeper and firmer than the granite from which Mother Russia herself is hewn.

Behind Vicki we hear a munchkin-like *babushka* explaining that four men from her family are buried here. We think, we feel, we begin to see.

Vicki returns to her lecture, slightly disarrayed, yet still professional. She points out the age of some buildings, the style of the architecture, the method of construction. To walk past us now one would not know, except perhaps for a few undried mascara lines just below the eyes, that just moments before this one all the borders on the planet were erased, fifty thousand nuclear warheads disarmed, hearts opened as they never had before, and the people of America and the Soviet Union united as one on a healed planet.

But I would know. I would know that behind the most threatening facade, underneath the most terrifying mask, is but a frightened child, calling desperately for the love he feels he has lost. I would know that a huge aggressive bear acts ornery only because he has felt wounded; that there is no real distance between hearts; that the pain of the planet's past is shared by all of us; and the healing of that pain lies within our very hearts, now. I would know.

Gorgi's Gift

While standing in a bookstore in Leningrad one afternoon, I felt a hand on my shoulder as I heard a voice ask, "Do you want to sell your pants?" (There is a big black market for blue jeans in the Soviet Union.) When I turned my head I saw that it was a fellow from our group, playing a little trick on me.

But with him was a Russian man, Gorgi, a handsome young fellow with deep-set dark eyes and a sort of early-Beatle-ish crop of raven-black hair sweeping across his forehead. Gorgi spoke almost impeccable English. We chatted amiably for a while, and then he invited us back to his apartment. It felt right, and we decided to go.

He guided us up the back stairway of a shabby apartment building and cautioned us to please not speak English in the halls. We understood.

Stepping into his apartment, we were appalled. One wall of Gorgi's living room was completely covered with picture post cards of the United States. This panorama was composed of most of the great sights of this country, from the Statue of Liberty to the Golden Gate Bridge. The adjacent wall displayed a collage of peace posters and buttons, similar to ones you might find in a young person's room in this country: pictures of doves, olive leaves, flags with peace symbols, and buttons with bombs crossed out by x's. The only difference was that the lettering was in Russian. Another wall contained a stereo cassette player. He put on a Michael Jackson tape.

Gorgi invited us to sit down at his little kitchenette table, and he put up water for tea. Then he went to his refrigerator and took out a luscious chocolate cake that looked as if it had been decorated by Michelangelo.

"What are you going to do with that cake, Gorgi?" we asked.

"Serve it to you!" he answered. " — It may be another fortnight before I meet some more American friends."

We enjoyed the cake and conversation immensely. None of us were as interested in discussing politics as we were enthusiastic about getting to know one another.

After some very vibrant conversation, we realized we needed to get back to our hotel. We thanked Gorgi for his warmth and hospitality. On our way out, Gorgi called, "Oh, wait a minute — I have something for you!" He went to his cabinet and took out a beautiful shawl, woven of cotton and printed with red roses. Humbly Gorgi handed it to me, and I did not know what to say. As I was admiring the shawl he dashed to the kitchen and brought me a jar of caviar. I did not even know what it was. Later I learned it was worth about eighteen dollars — a lot for a Russian tailor.

I thought for a moment, and I gave him my Sony Walkman — He was visibly touched. (I knew I would not come home with that Walkman.) I threw in some tapes.

"One more moment, please," Gorgi requested as we were about to step out the door. "Would you like some of these?"

He opened a cardboard tube and took out a thick pile of large printed posters. As he unfurled one for us to see, I could hardly believe the picture — it was an illustration of a little naked child, holding the earth close to his/her heart. At the top of the poster there were two words in Russian.

"What does that mean, Gorgi?" I asked.

"Embrace peace," he answered.

I was almost at the point of tears. He is not different than us. We love the same things. We want peace. We have been afraid of our brothers. We have been afraid of our self. We have been ignorant. That will change.

"Gorgi, is there anything we can do for you?" we wanted to know. "Can we send you anything or help you in any way?"

Gorgi smiled politely and shook his head, pushing his hands away from him as if to stop the idea.

"Thank you, no," he answered. "They read the mail, and packages do not always get through. It would not be a good idea."

We were disappointed.

"But there is something I would like."

"Please tell us."

"You can send me a picture post card every now and then!"

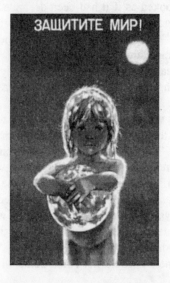

Gorgi's message: "Protect Peace"

Heart to Heart

On the evening of Ascension Thursday Swami Satchidananda was invited to address the Baptist Church in Moscow. (If you have any doubt that we have entered the new age, that invitation should dispell any question!)

It was raining in Moscow as the eighty of us dashed from our busses into the stone church, which was marked only by a small sign. We were ushered with great hospitality up to a lounge adjoining the balcony of the church, where we huddled together and enjoyed the flavored mineral water and tasty cookies put out by our hosts. There we presented the minister of the church with many hand-made dolls for his congregation, which we delivered as love gifts from a church in Washington. Each of the dolls contained a photo of the family that made it, a copy of the Silent Unity Prayer, and a love letter from the maker, stuffed into the doll's clothing. The minister and the elders of the church were delighted to receive these special gifts, and their faces lit up as they accepted them.

We filed into the balcony, but it seemed as if we were going into another world. In contrast to the gray concrete starkness of the streets of the city, here was warmth and wood and people gathered to sing to God. Most of the people in the sanctuary were *babushkas*, elderly women who had nothing to lose in the society by coming to church and celebrating their spiritual nature. They greeted us with their humble smiles, and made us feel welcome. It felt as if we had arrived home to grandma's house.

Our group stood and sang the One World Anthem, a song of international peace. It is sung to the tune of "My Country 'Tis of Thee," the melody of which is used as the national anthem of four countries on the globe. But instead of glorifying one nation over another, the One World Anthem glorifies the unity of all people everywhere.

Then we sang the anthem in Russian. Hardly any of us knew the Russian language, but we had rehearsed the song phonetically, and here was our chance to see if anyone would understand us. To our amazement, they did! Their faces lit up as we sang, and we were happy to see them elbowing their neighbors to listen carefully to what we were singing. There is something very touching about singing to someone in their own language.

Then Swami rose to offer his address. There are not many swamis in Russia, and to have a yogi give a spiritual address in Russia is quite a phenomenon. The congregants were leaning over the edge of the balcony to see and hear the man in the flowing robes.

And what an address he delivered! His words were simple, universal, and sincere. Swami spoke about the strength of our spiritual unity with the Soviet people. He said that Spirit is the Father of all of us, and the Earth is our Mother. That makes us all Children of the same Parents, brothers and sisters of one family. He even made a few jokes that the people enjoyed, even in translation. It was a perfect speech for the event.

After Swami's discourse it was time for us to leave. Everyone in the church had been emotionally moved, and we could feel the electricity in the air. The church choir rose, and to the accompaniment of the stirring tones of a pipe organ, they sang a Russian hymn that resonated deep within us. It sounded like "God Be With You 'Til We Meet Again," and it had the haunting flavor of the old Russia in which the soul of the people flourished like deeply-rooted flowers waving in the wind. It was a key to the real spiritual nature of the people.

As we began to file out of the church all of the *babushkas* rose to their feet, took white hankies out of their pockets, and began to wave them high in the air. They called, *"Mir, mir,"* ("Peace, peace") over and over again, in a chorus that shook the very bastions of the edifice.

I think there was not one dry eye in the house. Nearly every person in the church was moved to tears. We hugged and kissed and held the hands of many of the *babushkas* on our way out, and gave them our personal blessings as we received theirs. It was a holy moment.

When we arrived back at our bus, there was hardly a word spoken or heard. I sat in silence, wanting to bathe in the feelings of that magnificent experience. An awesome feeling of confirmation rolled through me; it was as if God was saying, *"This is surely the way to peace — from heart to heart."*

Vessels

The Russian people have a very high value on the exchanging of gifts. They do not take giving or receiving gifts lightly, and you can be sure that if a Russian gives you a gift or receives one from you, it means a lot to them.

One couple in our group took one of the homemade dolls on the subway, and gave it to a little girl they met there. The little girl's parents could hardly believe this was happening, and they were deeply moved. After accepting the doll they put their hands over their hearts, and bowed their heads toward the couple who gave their daughter the gift. The Soviet family's gratefulness was the best gift they could have given to the American couple.

Jim Barlow, a beautiful businessman with a huge heart, went to visit some Soviet dissidents, or peaceniks. There is a small group of peace activists in the Soviet Union who stage various forms of demonstrations and make statements for disarmament, ecology, and peace initiatives. Many of them dress in late-sixties garb, and one of their greatest heroes is John Lennon (an interesting variation on "Lenin"). To come out as a peacenik in Russia is quite a step, for although the government has become much more lenient than it used to be, those in power do not have as much patience for dissidence as do western governments, and those who rock the boat too much lose privileges. The man whom Jim visited had been demoted from a computer programmmer to an elevator operator. But, as Jim described him, "the light shined in his eyes very brightly indeed."

Upon the conclusion of Jim's visit with this couple, the wife went into the bedroom and brought Jim a gift. "Do you love God?" she asked Jim.

"Yes, very much." he answered.

"Then we would like you to have this." Jim saw that it was a silver-plated Bible in the Russian language. "It is over a hundred years old," the woman explained. "We have treasured it, and now we would like you to have it as a symbol of our appreciation for your visit and your love."

A woman from our group, Dulcie, is a make-up artist for movies in Hollywood. Her dream was to visit a Russian movie set and learn about their make-up techniques. As this was a rather unusual occupation, the organizers of the trip were not able to arrange such a contact before the journey. But Dulcie was determined.

While we were in Moscow Dulcie learned that *Peter the Great* was being filmed there, and it was in the last few days of shooting. This, Dulcie reasoned, would be a marvelous opportunity to make contact. She found her way to the studio, but now the question was, "How to get in?" She had heard that one of the make-up artist's name was Tania, but that was all she had to go on. She had brought with her an American pictorial book on popular make-up techniques that she could show to someone who would be interested.

Dulcie began to nonchalantly walk through the security gate when she was stopped by a guard. He asked her in Russian, "Where are you going?" Dulcie knew no Russian, but she held up the make-up book and pointed to the cover, on which was a picture of one of the Ape-Men from *Planet of the Apes*. The guard looked at the photo, laughed, and began jumping up and down, scratching his sides, imitating an ape. Then he waved her into the studio.

Once inside, Dulcie still had no idea how to make contact. "Looking for a Tania on a movie set in Russia would be like walking into Universal

City and asking for Susan," she explained. After making several inquiries she did not find Tania, but she was directed to a very kind and hospitable make-up artist who spent hours sharing and discussing make-up techniques and movie production with Dulcie. "That, in itself, was quite a gift," Dulcie told our group. "To give an uninvited visitor even a few minutes during the last three days of a shoot in Hollywood would be unheard of. But this lady gave me her full attention and the gift of her time, which was very valuable indeed!"

And what about our friend Patch? Patch was a little disappointed, because although he is a doctor, he went on this pilgrimage as a clown, and he wanted to meet a Russian clown. On our last evening in Moscow we attended the Moscow circus, at which we saw an excellent clown. After the circus Patch went backstage to meet the man. Patch came out glowing. "Look what he gave me!" Patch announced, pointing to his feet. We looked down and there we saw some funny-looking clown's shoes, about two feet long. "He has been wearing these shoes in his act for twenty years!" Patch told us. "They were his first clowning shoes — and he told me he wants me to take them home as a gift from him!"

It is said that the only function of the things of this world is to communicate love. A gift of a material object is a vessel through which love and caring and encouragement are communicated. Through sharing gifts with the Russian people we discovered the highest purpose of the things of this world.

Star Peace

It was arranged for us to visit the Canadian-American Institute where, we were told in advance, the Russians observe and analyze our political, economic, and social trends. "I've never before been to a place where they study me," I joked as we walked through the large doors of the old yet stately building.

Several of the Soviet political analysts who staff the institute entered and sat at the head of a horseshoe of meeting tables. These men were more casually dressed than we expected, but they were neat and dapper.

They began our meeting with a brief description of their purpose, their work, and some of their methods. It was clear that they were not into propagandizing or giving any speeches. They were, however, very open and receptive to answering questions, which is what we preferred, as well.

(As our hosts concluded their introduction, someone in our group told me that these people had the ear of Premier Gorbachev. I later saw one of the advisors on television during the news reports of the summit meetings.)

Several of our group asked more probing questions about their methods. I wondered how much these men actually knew about us and our country. Did they just read propaganda literature? Had they ever visited our country? What were their sources? As I wondered, they answered all of our questions cordially. They seemed to be glad we were there. I sensed that these people were truly interested in communicating.

Some of the people in our group began to challenge the Russians on political issues such as the Soviet invasion of Afghanistan and the "Star Wars" militarization of outer space. I cringed a little bit, as political debate seemed so out of context with the goal of our visit. The people in our group who were asking the questions got a little hot under the collar, but the Russians handled the challenges in a cool, dignified, and respectful way. Our people looked a little foolish by contrast.

Then someone in our group asked them what they felt were the reasons that Ronald Reagan had won the American presidency.

"What kind of question is that?" I wondered to myself. "Why would you come to Russia and ask something like that?"

The answer took all of us by surprise. The gentleman who responded was a genius. A soft-skinned twenty-seven-year-old fellow with a boyish face, he gave an astute, unbiased, and enlightening discourse on the dynamics of the election. His explanation was so fascinating, in fact, that all of us were on the edge of our seats as we listened. In just a few short minutes he explained the economic conditions in the United States at the time, the influence of the fundamentalist Christians, an analysis of the strengths and deficits of Jimmy Carter's campaign, and several other insights which exemplified a deep working knowledge of how the American people think, act, and react. This fellow had lived in Washington for a number of years, and he put our newscasters to shame. His analysis was so well-integrated, interesting, and nonjudgemental that our entire group broke into a wave of spontaneous applause when he had completed his observations.

A little while later, as we concluded our session with this group, one of their members called out, "I would like to say just one more thing before you leave."

This gentleman had been stting quietly and doodling while he was listening to the discussion.

"Here is what I would like to share about my feelings and reaction to your group and today's meeting..." he stated.

He held up the paper on which he had been doodling. On it was drawn a gold star next to a red star.

"The symbol for both of our countries is a five-pointed star," he explained. "Meeting your group and feeling what you stand for, confirms to me that we are indeed more alike than we are different."

We looked at the picture. Above the stars he had written in bold letters, *"Star Peace — not Star Wars."*

Helen's Response

Helen was our tour guide, and to me she appeared to be tough. From the moment she greeted us at the train station in Leningrad, my feeling was that this woman was not to be messed with. She marched us from the train to our bus like a bunch of cub scouts on their first camp-out (maybe Patch Adams in his clown outfit told her something).

As she conducted the first day's tour Helen was rather authoritative, and it was clear that while she was very efficient she also seemed mechanical. I respected Helen, but I kept my distance.

One afternoon I was the first to return to the tour bus after a walking tour. There I found Helen alone, sitting and reading a book. I noticed a lovely softness in her face, a lightness I had not seen before. Helen was relaxed and her eyes were gentle, and it made me happy to see her in a peaceful way. She showed me the book; it was an American book about Samantha Smith's visit to Russia. Samantha was a twelve-year-old American girl who made international headlines when she wrote to then-Premier Breznhev telling him that she knew very little about the Soviet Union, and that she would like to get to know the Russian people herself. Both nations were shocked when the Premier replied and invited Samantha and her family to come to Russia as guests of the Soviet government. The book was the pictorial account of Samantha's journey in which she, in her own way, opened the door to citizen diplomacy. I looked at the page to which the book was opened, and there was Helen's picture — she had been Samantha's tour guide.

(Since that time, Samantha has become something of a heroine to the Russian people. After she and her father were killed in a private airplane crash in Maine, the Russian government issued a Samantha Smith commemorative stamp, and they named several streets after her.)

Still, I felt a little leery about Helen. Could I trust her? I had brought a bunch of my pamphlets, *"If We Only Have Love"* (printed in this book as *The Day After the Prayer*). I had had them translated into Russian, and I gave them to persons whom I felt would be receptive. I had given one to Vicki, our other tour guide, but I was still reluctant to give one to Helen. I had been told that she was KGB, and as some of my like materials had been seized at the border, I wondered if it would be wise to give it to her. I played it safe and said nothing.

Then one afternoon Helen approached me and told me quite sincerely, "Alan, Vicki told me you gave her a pamphlet which she liked very much. Why did you not give me one? I would love to read it and show it to my children." I felt a little embarrassed, but more grateful than anything else. I was glad that Helen reached out to me. *A Course in Miracles* tells us that if one person in a relationship remains sane, it will help both to be sane. I was glad that Helen was sane.

Helen softened and unfolded as the tour progressed. The real miracle, however, came at our closing luncheon, at which each person in our group stood and shared what they had gained from our journey. When the microphone came to Helen, she rose and began to speak with tears streaming down her cheeks. "I have grown to feel that I am one with you...And I want to tell you that I love you very, very, very, very much." All of us were deeply moved. Helen received a long standing ovation.

We Will Always Be with You

One evening we were invited to something of a new age party in Moscow. Our group piled into several little cars and taxied to a rather large apartment of a Belgian journalist living on the outskirts of Moscow.

And what a party it was! For me it was a momentous evening, for I had the opportunity to be with some of the people I most admire. In one room Swami Satchidananda was leading chanting. In the living room, Patricia Sun was offering her healing sounds. In the next room Barbara Marx Hubbard was discussing a satellite space bridge with several Russian geniuses.

Elsewhere in the house a talented Russian icon painter was describing how he tunes his mind to serve as a channel to paint beautiful holy pictures, into which he imbeds crystals for healing. A little later a tiny Greek fellow showed up at the door, offering a concert on this nifty little cello-like musical

325

instrument he carried with him. We accepted, and he found himself a place on the couch, where he droned on for the remainder of the evening. Like I say, it was quite an evening.

At this party was a young man with a shining face. He was an accomplished artist, and his specialty was etching. He showed us some of his work, and we were astounded. He had taken birch bark, rolled it into a flat canvas-like medium, and into pieces of the bark he had etched exquisite scenes of the Russian countryside, concentrating mainly on churches. All of us were taken aback by the beauty and the craftsmanship in these renderings.

This young man was especially touched by the presence of Swami Satchidananda. He had never seen a yogi before, and to this young man, Swami represented God (to us, too!). The young man watched Swami from afar for most of the evening, and when we left to get a cab back to the hotel, the man followed us to the parking lot of the apartment building. The man approached Swami and gave him one of his portraits. Then he took Swami's hands and kissed them, and almost tearfully asked him, "You're leaving now?" It was a very moving scene to behold.

Swami took the young man's hands, pressed them to his own heart, looked the fellow in the eyes, and answered, "No — we will never leave you — our hearts will always be with you."

How the Forest Answers

When we arrived back in Finland to get our plane to the states, our tour guide joyfully told us, "I heard your tour was very successful." We all assented. "Yes," she went on, "there is an old Finnish saying: *'The forest answers you the way you call into it.'*"

And indeed that is how the forest answered us. We went with a clear purpose: to build bridges of love between the American and Russian peoples, and to make a personal statement that we are ready to have peace in our world. And because our statement was honest and simple and undisguised, it was heard and reflected back to us in the spirit in which we gave it.

We learned the power of unconditional love and communication from the heart. We saw the importance of valuing peace above all other goals. We found that the way to real communication is to focus on how we are alike, instead of analyzing our differences. We learned that the Russian people want peace as much as we do, and that they are one with us in so many ways We discovered that the real menace is not nuclear weapons, but fear. If we as a people knew more about the Russian people, we would not be afraid of them, and we would feel no need to be pointing nuclear weapons at them. We would want to be with them more and seek to learn from them as they have learned from us.

A long time ago someone said, "We have met the enemy, and he is us." This is so, and now I would add, "and we have loved him, and in discovering his beauty, we have unveiled the doorway to peace."

> *For now more than ever*
> *What the world needs more of*
> *Is to reach for each other*
> *With bridges of love*

Power, Peace, and Pedestals

There remains but one lesson for the Children of God to master to enter into the Age of God: the reclaiming of personal power to be used in the service of Love, free of guilt, and dedicated to the celebration of light in human experience.

This is not a power *over*, but a power *for*. We cannot afford to misuse our power, and neither can we afford to deny it. Both errors, actually forms of fear, can be rectified only by knowing ourselves. There is but one reason that a being of light would lose the power to be happy, and that is that such a one does not remember who he or she is. Yet in the regaining of that precious awareness is the entire world restored to the soul to whom it rightfully belongs.

Let us now discover the process by which that error can be undone.

Shadows

Many times and in many ways we have spoken of the shadow that stands between you and your own light. Now we must focus on it so clearly and with such keen determination that you will be able to see clearly, without any question, how you have divested yourself of joy by the denial of your power.

The Dark Shadow

When we become appalled at the evil we *believe* is in us, one of the ways that we attempt to get rid of it is to project what we do not like about ourself onto the outside world. By seeing the unwanted trait in someone else instead of ourself, we believe we have relieved ourself of the "sin." Once the feared trait is "out there," we identify with the opposite "good" quality, and then engage in obvious or hidden attack against the negative trait that we have projected outward. Sometimes, for example, we may find newspaper stories about persons who are well-known for their personal combat against some kind of evil, who are discovered to be engaging in the very evil they are fighting. This is because we only fight ourself, and if someone has a personal vendetta against any cause, you can be sure that within themself they are harboring some kind of guilt or fear over the same issue, or a variation of it. If they had made peace with that issue in their own heart, they would feel only compassion for persons still struggling with that situation, and they would treat the problem not as an attack, but as the call for help that it is.

It is impossible to project a shadow and not engage in a war against it. Inherent in our view of the outer shadow is the self-hatred that caused us to project it originally. Hence we see the most important dynamic that *all attack is a statement of self-hatred*, and thus a *desperate plea for healing*. But because the entire dynamics of shadow-making are veiled from conscious awareness by the ego (like the greater part of an iceberg under the surface of awareness), no one in a state of war is aware that it is himself that he is attacking.

While all of us have engaged in shadow war in our personal life, perhaps the clearest and most dramatic example of shadow-making is Adolph Hitler and Nazi Germany. During the time of that regime an entire culture projected a shadow of unprecedented proportions and then attempted to get rid of it by annihilating the persons onto whom they had projected it. The Nazis took every trait and weakness that they hated in themselves, projected those characteristics onto the Jewish people, and then attempted to purge themselves by getting rid of the Jews.

Seen on such a massive scale, the insanity of such a plan and its utter hopelessness is obvious. What we need to see, little though we may be willing to admit it, is that *we engage in the same type of "windmill-warfare" each day*. Every time we feel angry or judgemental of someone, we are fighting our own shadow. We may not rally a nation around us to support our insanity, but we certainly blame and attack others for the faults that we are not willing to look at within ourself. (And then we solicit agreement to support our attack on ourself.)

The answer to the dark shadow is obviously not in attempting to attack or destroy the screen onto which we have projected our fear. Imagine a motion picture theatre in which a beautiful movie is marred by a huge, ten-foot fly crawling all over the the screen. Then imagine the audience becoming so fearful and irate that they throw objects at the big black bug and ultimately tear the screen apart in an effort to get rid of the intruder. How mistaken they would find themselves to be as they discover that the problem was not a ten-foot fly on the screen, but a quarter-inch fly on the lens of the projector! The answer was not at all to attack what they were seeing, but to examine and purify its source.

The mind is the source of all that we see in the "external" world. No matter how many years or lifetimes we may spend trying to purge the outer world of problems, the only path to real healing is to return our attention to the great projector of our mind and polish the mirror that reflects the Light that illuminates all that we see.

Our analogy becomes even more striking when we remember that it was a beautiful movie that was intended to be projected onto the viewing screen. To attack or destroy a brother or sister is to remove the one field on which we could behold the beatific image of Itself that Spirit projected into the world. We *need* one another to see the God in this world.

The understanding that the person "out there" is *not* the cause of our problem is a major first step toward the healing of any relationship. Acting upon this understanding offers a gift to your brother and the world that cannot be measured in any way except in the depths of the heart.

Correction versus Attack

The question may occur to you, "Does this mean that I am not to correct anyone? People certainly do make mistakes that I do not do." This is quite true.

There is one sure way to know if you are fighting with your shadow, or offering useful help: *Do you have an emotional charge when offering the correction?* If you feel in any way upset or less than peaceful when pointing out a problem to someone, you can be sure that it is yourself that you are attempting to correct. At such a time, your most productive step would be to stop for a moment, perhaps take a deep breath, and ask yourself, "Will the way I am about to speak to my brother or sister bring about healing, or more separation?" or "What do I really want to create in my life?" But a brief moment's consideration of this question will reveal the way that you can be most helpful to your friend and yourself.

The Healing of the Dark Shadow

The healing of the dark shadow involves a process which, if followed with sincerity, is certain to create most rewarding transformations in your relationships and your entire life. Life is made of relationships, and your sense of peacefulness in all that you do is directly related to how you see your sisters and brothers.

The first step to healing is releasing the person "out there" from the responsibility for your pain. It is a major premise of miracles that *no one and no thing can cause you pain except your own thoughts.* Every time you ascribe your suffering to a source outside your mind you not only perpetuate your hurt, but you divest yourself of the power that God gave to you to create a loving and rewarding life. You do not stand a chance to be truly healed until you own everything that happens to you as your own creation.

The second step to undoing the shadow is to acknowledge that you believe you do the same thing for which you find the other party guilty. You may not see yourself as doing it in exactly the same form, or you may not find yourself doing it now, or you may have done it in thought but not action. This attribute may not even be true about you, but you may believe it is true or harbor fears that it may be true. Your sense of guilt may disguise itself in any one of a thousand forms. But of one thing you may be sure: if you see it in another, you see it in yourself. You would not have needed to cast it onto another if you had not first found it too overwhelming to accept in yourself.

The third step is a joyful and liberating one: Forgive yourself. You may rejoice in the knowledge that you were wrong about being guilty. You have not sinned. You may have made an error, but that is not the same as a sin. Sins require punishment, but errors require only correction. Your judgements about yourself were too heavy. God has found no sin in you, and now it is for you to align your vision of yourself with God's, which is always merciful. You must transform your attitude about this so-called sin; you must cease to see it is evil, and begin to see it as a call for healing, which you deserve. Such a perspective will bring great peace to your heart, for now you can use your experience as a springboard to greater love. Thus, with just a slight change of mind, you have transformed your "sin" into a blessing, and you see yourself as God sees you, which is totally lovable.

Then you can turn the whole situation over to God. It is not your job to heal yourself. Your job is but to see yourself clearly. Looking at yourself in this light, constructive change must flow naturally. Problems are not a call for condemnation, but vision. When you see yourself as innocent you defuse the need for punishment which you have called upon yourself by your sense of guilt. And you are innocent. You deserve only good. You are here to reflect only peace. This awareness will take you all the way Home.

If you follow this healing process whenever you feel angry, victimized, afraid, hurt, or rejected, you will quickly reclaim the power that you have given to fear. You always had the power, but you gave it away because you believed that someone else could be the source of your experience. In so believing, you reversed the sequence of cause and effect in your life. *You* are the cause, and your experience is the effect. To see the world as the cause is to make yourself helpless; to know that your mind is the cause is to make yourself helpful. The time has come for you to reclaim power over your life.

The White Shadow

Many teachers, psychologists, and consciousness trainers have intelligently and productively identified the dynamics of the dark shadow. But there is one aspect of shadow-making that has rarely been illuminated: the white shadow.

The dark shadow is projected when we are unwilling to accept our faults. The white shadow is projected when we are unwilling to accept our beauty. If we are afraid of being beautiful we hurt ourself as much as we do when we are afraid of being ugly. We cannot afford to be afraid, and the most direct way to disarm the fear in our life is to undo the fear of ourself.

In some of my workshops I ask the participants to take a sheet of paper and list their positive traits in one column, and their negative traits in another. Then I ask each person to stand up and share their list with the members of the class.

You would not believe the length of the negative lists, and the brevity of the positives! Most people have little difficulty describing what is wrong with them, but when it comes to reading the list of their wonderful attributes, they inject a symphony of "uh"s, "sort-of"s, and screwed-up faces. Most of us are embarrassed to be beautiful, and that is a great problem indeed! The white shadow is projected when we are afraid to own our goodness. Feeling unworthy to accept holiness as a part of our real being, we throw it off of ourselves, create someone out there to be wonderful in the ways that we are not, and then we worship them. This is a terrible disservice to ourselves, and in the long run it hurts the other person as well, because sooner or later their humanness becomes obvious, and when we realize that they are not who we thought they were, we may tend to blame them for defrauding us or leading us to believe that they are something they are not. The problem is not that they misrepresented themselves, but that we made them out to be something they never could be. We gave our power away and blamed them for stealing it. All because we didn't love ourself in the first place.

White shadow-making has destructive ramifications to an astonishing degree. It has been a part of nearly every marriage and relationship, as many of us are attracted to the persons that we believe are the things that we are not. When we enter into any relationship with the premise that we are empty and the other person will fill us in, we are sure to fail. We can win only when we proceed from wholeness. A relationship in which two halves seek to become whole will be extremely disappointing, for you bring to the relationship only what you believe you are. To see both of you as incomplete is a very debilitating gift to offer to a marriage or relationship.

This does not mean that such a marriage or relationship is doomed; in fact, the reversal or transmutation of the white shadow releases healing energy that can build a real and nourishing relationship. When the two halves realize they are *already whole*, the relationship ceases to be a litany to emptiness and becomes a celebration of perfection. Two persons agreeing on their mutual innocence makes them quite invulnerable and opens the door to a cornucopia of miracles which only continue to surpass themselves. The energy generated in such a relationship is an example of the power of joining. So, you see, the thought that we are empty must ultimately lead to the discovery that we are whole. And therefore our adventure into shadowland is actually a steppingstone to the joy of self-realization.

Real Teachers

Another example of white shadow-making that is especially ripe for understanding in our time and culture occurs in cults and guru-worship. Cult members are especially prone to divest themselves of the responsibility for their wisdom, strength, and independence, and place their own magnificence in the lap of the leader. Here it is easy to see that just as we cannot afford to ascribe our pain to a source outside ourself, neither can we place our salvation in the hands of another person.

If the leader in such a situation does not have a high degree of integrity they will play on the followers' sense of lack and unworthiness, and use the power that their followers have given them for spiritual tyranny. We do not have to go into the details or offer many examples of teachers who have led disciples into darkness or students who have hurt themselves by offering their power to someone who was not worthy of it.

If, on the other hand, the leader is a true teacher, they will take advantage of the disciples' attention to teach them that the power they would like to give away rightfully belongs within themselves. It is said that a real teacher is one who makes himself or herself progressively unnecessary. A good guru teaches the disciples to go beyond his or her form. Hilda used to tell us that the best compliment we could give her would be for us to graduate from her teachings and become our own teacher. One of the lessons in *A Course in Miracles* tells the students to "forget this course."[1] And Jesus said, "Even greater things than I, shall you do."

The word "guru" means "from darkness to light." If a guru guides his or her disciples to the light, they are fulfilling their function in a powerful way. If they keep the disciples in darkness, they may not be called a guru. Beware of teachers or groups that threaten you with evil things that will happen to you if you leave the organization. Some students of certain cults are told that if they leave they will go to hell, lose their spirituality, or be cursed in one form or another. I was told by one ex-cult member that he was told that if he left the organization he would be reincarnated as a cockroach. Well, maybe that would be an improvement over his current situation. There is no curse worse than fear, and if you allow fear to motivate you on the spiritual path, you are already cursed. But that can all be undone instantly as you choose love as your guide instead of fear.

The desire of a disciple to stay with his or her teacher should be born of love for the teachings, a feeling of increasing strength, and the manifestation of real healing in the student's life. The student should have little patience for healing that is promised just around the corner, after death, or after obtaining a high rank in the organization. It may be said that the presentation of a threat at the suggestion of leaving the organization is a clear sign to leave the organization. The purpose of any guru, church, therapy, or conscious-ness organization is to teach that God is everywhere. If Spirit is purported to be only in this group, it is a poor spirit indeed, and one that is not worthy of

---

[1] W, p. 350

learning more about. If you are told that you are too weak to leave, you must respond with the knowledge that you are too strong to stay.

The Right to Power

The bottom line, of course, is that no teacher, therapist, cult-leader, or guru can hurt you or hold power over you unless you first give him or her that power. The tendency to project blame can and must be transmuted to appreciation for a valuable lesson in personal responsibility. The moment you are ready and willing to reclaim the power you gave away, you are free. If you know how to think with God, you will bless the leader for having played an important role in the lessons that ultimately lead to your liberation.

Thus we see the wisdom in the *Course in Miracles* teaching that "all things, events, encounters and circumstances are helpful."[2]

From Pedestals to Power

We can no longer afford to hold idols before the face of God. To be afraid of our power is to be afraid of God, and in turning our back on our source of Light we create shadows. In so doing we severely limit who we are and what we can do, and such a way of walking this world is very much out of context with the purpose of our life.

But the awareness of our misunderstanding is the perfect prelude to understanding. We must learn that God is a God of only love, and knows nothing of the punishment that we fear. The awareness of God's unfailing knowledge of our innocence is enough to dethrone our idols and place us on equal footing with our Self, where we belong.

Placing one who is equal with us on a pedestal is not to raise him or her up, but to lower ourself. All of us are equal Children of Perfect Spirit, and to deny our perfection in any way is to suffer. Pain would not be possible if we knew without a doubt that only good dwells within us, regardless of what we may seem to see to the contrary. In Spirit's eyes there is no contrary, and it is for us to see ourselves through those uplifted eyes. To love ourself in the same light in which Spirit holds us is to live free of judgement, purified of fear, and confident in the knowledge that we may walk in poise and dignity.

[2] M, p. 9

From Power to Peace

Power and peace are one and the same. Any dichotomy that we hold between the two is a function of a split mind, born of the fear of our own being. When we trust our feelings, our intuitions, our love, we honor the power that we have been given to find our way Home and know ourself. There is no greater gift in all the universe than discovering our own beauty, and we do have the power to do it. But we must accept it. When you are asked to surrender, you are not asked to surrender to death, but to life. You are not asked to become weak or subservient, but to accept your own strength. You are not summoned to give up your joy, but your lack of confidence in your ability to be grand. You already are grand. And so you are asked only to know yourself.

You cannot know yourself as long as you see others as shining brighter than you or lesser than you. You must love yourself so much that you are unwilling to deny your own wonder by seeing it in another instead of you, or in yourself to the exclusion of another. You must enfold everyone you meet in that same dignity, or else your dignity is lost. It is not only possible to hold all in the highest esteem — it is imperative. There is room at the top for everyone, and none of us are Home until all of us are Home. And all of us *are* Home.

You must appreciate yourself with such integrity that your heart beats a blessing to you and the world every time it pumps. Each breath you take is an affirmation of God's need for you. Do not fear, deny, or misappropriate your greatness — it is what you came to know and live.

Peace *is* power, and all of it has been given to you. It is now for you to take what you have been given and use it. The world rejoices at your peace.

> There is a hush in Heaven, a happy expectancy, a little pause of gladness in acknowledgement of the journey's end...No illusions stand between you now. Look not upon the little wall of shadows. The sun has risen over it...No more can you be kept by shadows from the light in which illusions end. Every miracle is but the end of an illusion. Such was the journey; such its ending.[3]

---

[3] T, p. 381

What One Can Do

The pure, unadulterated love of one person can nullify the hatred of millions.

- Mahatma Gandhi

Your personal power is as unlimited as you would have it be. You are under no restriction of age, gender, education, or experience. The only thing that can bind you is your mind, and that is something over which you have total control. You are a free soul, and if you do not allow fear to stand between you and your vision, you will walk with dignity upon the earth and bring healing to the world.

The world cannot defeat you. Only you can defeat yourself. There have been many persons who have caught a glimpse of their personal power, and moved with that vision. One morning they woke up and realized that they were not small. They understood that those who told them that they couldn't make it were seeing but their own illusions of limitation. And then they went out and did something about it.

The difference between an ordinary person and a saint is that the ordinary person dismisses his dreams as fantasies, and a saint takes a step to making them realities. Never underestimate the power of your vision. Your dreams are your fuel, given to you to lift you out of the mire of small thinking and power your way to the stars. Your vision of who you can be and what you were born to do is a gift from a loving God, to help you find your way home. You are not meant to live in the mud — your home is in the heavens. Your dreams will carry you past obstacles that would otherwise defeat you. You were not born to be defeated. You were born to triumph.

At times your vision may be your only window to God. If you do not look through it, all you will see is limitation and despair. But lift up your eyes and you will see a golden destiny that is sure to bring healing to your heart and to all that you touch. This is God's promise of success, and you have every right to claim it.

You have sometimes, perhaps often considered how much you need

God. Now you must consider how much God needs you. There are certain questions that you must ask, for you are now ready to receive the answer: Does God want you to succeed? Does God want you to be happy? Does God want you to make a special contribution to the healing of this planet?

If you believe that Spirit wants anything less than total joy for your life, you have allowed guilt to cast its shadow upon the light that burns within you and yearns to be expressed as you. The shadow cannot take away the light, but it can hide it from your awareness. This is tragic, not because you could lose who you are, but because time in life is given you to celebrate your beauty, and every moment that you do not see yourself is literally a waste of time.

Make time your friend by finding a cause for joy in every moment. If you look, you will find. Spiritual enlightenment is not a matter of finding the right answer in one place, but discovering God in *all* places. The journey is complete when you see God everywhere. And because God *is* everywhere, such a vision will be profusely rewarded.

In Your Own Way

There are no standards in the outer world to which you must adhere. If you attempt to live your life to fulfill external pressures, you will prolong the illusion of death, you will not create anything new, and you will be miserable. But there is a standard to which you must be true, and that is to do what is personally meaningful to you. Whether or not it is meaningful to anyone else does not matter. But that it is meaningful to you matters a great deal. Your destiny lies at the end of that path, as well as in every step of the way. If you follow that path, you will be at peace and your acts of integrity will change the world. To be at peace with yourself is to make the greatest contribution to life.

Stepping into Your Own Shoes

One who succeeded gloriously in living her truth was a remarkable woman known as Peace Pilgrim.[1] After years of contemplation about what is required to bring personal and planetary healing, Peace Pilgrim renounced her past, possessions, and name, and walked for over twenty-five thousand

---

[1] Peace Pilgrim Center, 43480 Cedar Avenue, Hemet, California 92344

miles in the name of peace. Owning only the clothes she wore, including a tunic that said *PEACE PILGRIM* on the front and *25,000 MILES ON FOOT FOR PEACE* on the back, this courageous lady crossed America for nearly three decades, sharing with anyone who had ears to hear the simple principles for which she walked and lived:

Overcome evil with good,
falsehood with truth,
and hatred with good.

Peace Pilgrim placed herself entirely in the hands of the Lord; she would not eat unless offered food, she did not seek shelter unless invited, and she solicited no money for her work. In spite of her renunciation Peace Pilgrim became something of a celebrity. She was sought after as a speaker and teacher, and she was invited to speak on radio and television and in schools nearly everywhere she went. She sought no personal glory, and yet her influence was so profound that many articles and books have been written about her life.

I saw a video and several photographs of Peace Pilgrim, and the clarity of the light in her eyes was a teaching of tranquility. Here was one person who made a stand for what she believed in, and many hearts were opened as a result of the purity of her love.

We do not all need to renounce our homes and literally walk for peace as Peace Pilgrim did, but we do need to live for it. Peace Pilgrim was guided to serve in her own way, and if you are willing to listen to the Voice of Truth within your own heart, you will be given clear, unfailing direction toward the discovery and fulfillment of your destiny.

We do not need to be statesmen or diplomats or revered celebrities; we do not need to demonstrate the riches of royalty or the sacrifice of martyrs; neither need we be lauded, applauded, or acclaimed. All we need to be is real. There is but one requirement to feel the peace of God in every activity of life: We need to live our lives according to the integrity that we know, and love ourself and our life just as it is.

The Power of Giving

One man who has touched my life is "Highrise Joe," a blind man who attended one of my workshops near Minneapolis. What a contribution he made to our class! Joe was a positive, inspiring, and dynamically alive giver in our group. During one session someone in our group asked Joe how he has come to shine so brightly, and he told us this story:

"One day I became so frustrated that I was about to pack it all in. I felt that I had had it, and I didn't think I wanted to live any longer. Then the telephone rang; it was a caller who had the wrong number. He was in desperate need. It was a teenager who was contemplating suicide. My heart opened as I talked to the boy, and after a long conversation he changed his mind. I decided at that time that if there is one person out there who needs me, it is worth it for me to be here. I can make a useful contribution to the world, and that gives me great joy."

Joe's life has changed quite a bit as a result of that experience. He has since become a one-man hotline for teenage crisis intervention, and now he receives calls from all over the country, from teenagers who need help. Joe has developed remarkable relationships with many of these young people, which have continued over the years.

Another experience that has shaped Joe's life occurred when he tripped over some packages of groceries that were left in the hallway of his apartment house. As he picked himself up he was feeling clumsy and upset. At that moment he heard the sobbing of a woman. He followed the sounds into an apartment near the groceries, and there he found a neighbor in deep despair. Upon returning home from shopping she had received a telephone call that her husband had been taken to the hospital, and suddenly he had passed away. The woman was sitting at her kitchen table weeping, in something of a stupor.

Joe sat with this woman and comforted her. He gave her loving support and helped her make some necessary telephone calls. Joe spent four hours being fully with her, and when she was in a better frame of mind and in a position to act more effectively he left her in greater peace.

How God uses us when we are willing to be of service! Joe's tripping over those bundles was not an accident at all, and he was not clumsy. He was in his right and perfect place, and he was actually an angel in that situation. How appropriately he is called "Highrise Joe"!

You, too, are in your right and perfect place. When you seem to be tripping up or clumsy, you need but shift your focus slightly, and you will find that God is right where you are. Never forget this. It can make the difference between despair and great triumph.

Be a Lighthouse

Another person who has changed the world in his own way is Willie, a shining soul in a nursing home in New Jersey. Willie is diagnosed as a paraplegic, but he is not a disabled person. After speaking with Willie for just a few minutes the first day I met him, I saw that he is a bright light in that hospital. There his positivity and his love have worked wonders. He is like a beacon in the halls. Many patients approach Willie for moral support and counseling, and I have seen doctors and nurses come to him to renew and energize themselves. Sitting in the hall with Willie, it is difficult to have a continuous conversation, for so many people, from the custodians to the hospital director, stop to talk with this man. He has a smile, a joke, and an encouraging word for everyone who passes him.

When I had originally gone to the hospital to conduct a weekly yoga class, I felt put off by the pain and limitation that I saw. But Willie showed me that happiness goes far beyond circumstances; it is really a state of mind.

Not Afflicted

Willie is not the only one to make a stand for joy in the hospital. During one of our classes I instructed the group to "Raise your arm like this..." One fellow, Earl, called out, "I can't see what you're doing — I'm blind."

A woman down the row responded abruptly, "Well, we all have our afflictions."

"I'm not afflicted," answered Earl, " — I'm just blind."

Perhaps we can learn from this man's willingness not to see himself as a victim. I learned so much from the hospital patients, and I honor them as my teachers. I had thought that I was going there to teach them something, and I did. But along the way I learned a great deal from them.

To Feel Full Inside

There is a young woman in a Unity church who has won the hearts of the entire congregation. In the world of appearances Wendy is a paraplegic. Some may see her as a limited victim of a disease. But that is not how she sees herself! And therefore that is not who she is. Wendy is a vibrant, energetic, loving being, and she is an inspiration to all who meet her. I have never met Wendy in person, but someone gave me her card, by which I feel I know her totally. Her wallet-sized card shows a sun, a rainbow, and a pot of gold at the rainbow's end, colored with beautiful water-colors painted by Wendy, with a brush that she directs by holding it in her mouth.

The card says,

> My belief is that life is like a rainbow.
> At the beginning you struggle uphill,
> But at the end, if you make it,
> You find the "Pot of Gold."
> I found the gold in all of you here.

I found it in true friendship and love.
To me you shine just like gold.
I found out what God's plan and gift to me is:
The ability to help other people.
I feel full inside! Love is **everything.**

Wendy

How Wishes Come True

As I was sitting and writing this on the patio of my back yard, the wind blew a piece of newspaper into the yard. My friend Anne, who had been assisting, picked up the paper, read it, and handed it to me. The title of the article was, "Wishes Can Come True." It was a story about the Make-a-Wish Foundation[2], which has been created to grant wishes of children suffering with life-threatening illnesses.

The organization was founded when a seven-year-old Phoenix boy who was dying said his dream was to become a policeman. The State Department of Public Safety became aware of his vision and made him an honorary policeman for a day. On his day they gave him a custom-made helmet, a badge, and a glorious helicopter ride. The boy passed on a few days later, but before he did, he had an adventure he had always dreamed of.

Other examples of the work of the Make-a-Wish Foundation have included arranging a leave of absence and paying the salary of a working woman whose fifteen-year-old daughter's last wish was for her mom to be able to spend more time with her; sending a group of forty children with cancer to Disney World; and providing children with cassette players, VCR's, and computers to make their time in bed more comfortable and stimulating.

The heart of the Foundation, the article reports, is the volunteer staff, a cross-section of persons with all kinds of occupations and interests, who are described as being generous, compassionate, and "giving two hundred percent." "When something reaches way down inside you and grabs at your heart," Jane Martens (a high school teacher and founder of one chapter) describes, "you just know you have to help in some way."

---

[2] Make-A-Wish Foundation, 4601 North 16th St., Suite 205, Phoenix, Arizona 85016

The Best Teacher

Perhaps the miracle change agent closest to me is a beautiful and sensitive man named Lou. At an early age Lou found in himself a degree of sensitivity which the persons around him did not understand or appreciate. As a result he entered a long struggle with his identity, and he went through a very challenging and difficult adolescence and early adulthood. Eventually Lou entered a monastary in hopes of escaping from the harshness of the world. But there he found monks flagellating themselves and being surprisingly unkind to their fellows.

As Lou grew he learned not to look outside himself for solace. He discovered that to be happy he would have to find worth in his own self, just as he was. He made a decision that gentleness and sensitivity are gifts and not deficits, and that suffering and separation are not necessary. Lou worked his way through all kinds of questions, fears, and doubts, and ultimately Lou's sensitivity made him a healer in his own right.

As a teacher, Lou established a new program in his high school. The course, called "Humanities," is an elective for seniors in which the students are offered a full semester to explore themselves and discover who they are and what they would like to do with their life. Lou employs methods such as inviting each student to sit with him in two director's chairs in front of the class, where he interviews them about their ideas, their feelings, and their aspirations. His goal is for the students to learn to see themselves as whole persons, and to love and accept themselves in the process. And it works. The kind of rapport that Lou develops with his students is one that every teacher has dreamed of, for he inspires them to open their minds and hearts to a greater vision of themselves and the possibilities for their life. They appreciate his gift in the deepest possible way. During the three years that I shared a home with Lou, he received many phone calls and loving letters from students and former students who wanted to stay in touch with him. "Please tell Mr. Chalupa that Gary Carlson called...I am in the Air Force now, and I just wanted Mr. Chalupa to know that I am doing great." One day Lou took the day off from work to go canoeing with a former student who had just lost his father unexpectedly. Another time I saw a copy of a teacher's evaluation form lying on our kitchen table. It was an evaluation made by the school vice-principle who sits in on classes unannounced, and grades each teacher on various kinds of performance. Curious as to what the school administration thought of Lou, I picked it up and read, "Mr. Chalupa did not seem to be scientifically organized, and I didn't really understand what he was talking about; but it should be noted that once again the students have voted Mr. Chalupa the best teacher in the school, and therefore I recommend him to continue." Largely as a result of Lou's quality of inspired teaching, two other full-time teachers have been hired to teach the same course, and last semester so many seniors signed up for the class that even though six hundred of them were able to take it, many were turned away.

Lou's latest triumph was gaining the approval of the Board of Education to allow senior citizens to join the high school students in his classes. In an unprecedented project, the senior citizens come to class every day and participate with the younger students in dialogues, sharing, and study. Lou reports that the results are phenomenal; the wisdom of the seniors' experience is melded with the vitality of the teenagers. During a Halloween costume contest, the teens voted one of the golden agers as having the best costume as a sailor. (Another student came to school dressed as Mr. Chalupa.) The Board is so impressed with the quality of what is happening in this project that they are planning to expand it to the entire high school. What one man can do.

The Power of Willingness

As we can see through the example of all of these courageous people, it is not your position in society that allows you to become an effective change agent, but your willingness to shine where you are. The number of people that you seem to affect is not as important as the quality of the effect that you have on those you do touch. Some of us have chosen to touch large numbers of people, and some have chosen to work intensively with a few. Both are equally important, and both serve the entire universe profoundly. Never be fooled into believing that you are judged on the number of people you help. God is impressed by a loving heart more than pure volume. More is good, but it is not always better. A mother who gives one child unconditional love is making an enormous contribution to the universe. A friend of mine, a young mother who used to be very active in social, political, and spiritual organizations, wrote me a letter describing her life with two infants. "Most of my time is occupied with feeding, cleaning, and diapers," she wrote, "but it's the strangest feeling; I feel like I am accomplishing less in the world than I ever have, but I feel more rewarded and content within my self than ever before." And no one could ask for more.

The Most Effective Healer

There is but one further awareness that all who would serve the world must accept: It is not up to you alone to do it all. Remember that the real healer is Spirit, and that Spirit will work through you if you are willing to listen with a quiet mind and a receptive heart.

The first step in changing the world is to change the way you see the world. You must acknowledge God's presence in the world before that presence can be made manifest. If you proceed with a picture of victimization, injustice, fear, or anger, your work will largely be ineffective. Wrath is a vicious temptress, and if you fight under her bloodied flag, your losses will most surely outweigh your gains.

Love will afford you your most powerful position, and draw to you all manner of strength and support. The energies that you make available to yourself when you are at peace will enfold you with a mantle of comfort and protection that cannot be violated by any sense of fear or loss. When your goal is to be truly helpful, you are literally invulnerable. Being truly helpful means that you seek only the solution in which everyone wins. If anyone loses, everyone loses. The only real victory is one which brings peace to everyone involved. To understand this kind of victory you must see with your heart, and not your eyes.

This shift absolutely requires that you know who you are and Who is your Source. If you believe that you are your own source, you are doomed to failure and you will wither behind the walls of your self-imposed loneliness. But to know that there is a higher power that is acting though you, and in fact needs you to accomplish its great goal, is to find your full strength. You don't have to go it alone, do it alone, or be it alone. The knowledge that God is with you is the strength that will carry you over the hurdles at which lonely warriors falter. Everything you need to succeed is already within you, and it has been but awaiting your assent to pour forth in creative healing.

The Healing Vision

Like you, the world already has what it needs to be perfect. Some have feared the healing of our world because they have equated healing with ending. But this could not be so. All healing is a beginning. The resurrection of our life will come not through destruction, but through transformation. The caterpillar does not die; it becomes something entirely new and more wonderful. To hold our world in the willingness to have it continue to live, and to acknowledge that such a world already lives within our hearts, is the greatest gift that you and I can offer to our planet.

Thus we arrive at the ultimate awareness of the spiritual warrior, a joyful renunciation which only the stoutest of heart can embrace: the world is already saved. The healing of the Planet Earth has already been accomplished by God, and you are free of this awesome burden. Spirit does, however, vitally need one contribution from you, something that only you can choose to offer: *your vision.*

You will not see a perfect world until you see a perfect world. This is the first and final element of healing, the part that you came here to play. You may delay it, but you cannot change it. Nor would you want to. Who but an insane person would focus on chaos when he or she could create healing through a vision of perfection? You are not insane, but you have been asleep. The world does not need your manipulation, but it is desperate for your awakening. With your arising to the truth within you, you will carry all who have slumbered to their healing, as well. You are not separate from the world. Heal your mind, and you will transform your world. Thus you have the key to the healing of the Planet Earth.

Offer, then, this gift with me. We need each other to share in this vision. Joined, our minds are an unstoppable force. Jesus said that "the gates of hell shall not prevail against the Son of God," and we join him in his identity as a peaceful warrior. He came as a harbinger of what we have come to accomplish. And we shall not fail. We cannot fail because we act in the name of the One Who sent us. And I assure you that we are sent in the name of Love.

> *What one man can do is change the world*
> *And make it new again*
>   - John Denver

One day, you will sit on a plateau and the wind will blow through your hair, and you'll have a simple cloak on. And you will sit there and you will contemplate your life and you will realize the magnificent creature that you really are. And you will have not done one thing that would have ever harmed you or hurt you or would have disrespected you in any way, because, above all, it was your respect that you upheld and no one else's. That is when you can sleep and slumber at night and rejoice during the day and love what you are. Then you are a happy entity and, indeed, a happy God.

- Ramtha

A personal note from Alan Cohen:
If you have been touched and inspired by the vision and principles
of this book, I invite you to join me personally in Hawaii for a
life-transforming week dedicated to rediscovering who you are and
celebrating your magnificence.

THE MASTERY TRAINING

An Intimate Adventure in Spiritual Destiny in Hawaii

THE MASTERY TRAINING is a
highly focused retreat for those
who are ready to take the next
step in their spiritual growth.
Limited to twelve participants,
this unique program offers
maximal personal attention
and support to move beyond
limits and manifest your
chosen goals. This five-star

training is for those seeking deeper self-appreciation, greater intimacy
and unprecedented empowerment in creativity, relationships, prosperity and physical well-being.

PROGRAM INCLUDES:

- Full training process in a group of twelve
- Lodging at an elegant retreat center
- Gourmet meals
- All transportation on the island
- Pre- and post-training consultations with
  Alan Cohen
- A nurturing massage
- Guided adventures to Hawaiian sites of
  power and beauty—hidden waterfalls,
  ancient temple sites, pristine beaches,
  sailing/snorkeling, and more
- Music and colorful entertainment

Your Future Isn't What It Used to Be.

For next training dates, tuition, & further information, write to:
The Mastery Foundation, 430 Kukuna Rd., Haiku, HI 96708
or Call: (808) 572-0001 Fax: (808) 572-1023 E-mail: acpubs@aloha.net

About the Author

Alan Cohen is the author of ten popular inspirational books, including the classics, *The Dragon Doesn't Live Here Anymore* and *I Had It All the Time*. *The Celestine Prophecy* author James Redfield calls Alan "the most eloquent spokesman of the heart." Alan's column "From the Heart" appears in many New Thought newspapers and magazines internationally, and he is a contributing writer for the bestselling *Chicken Soup for the Soul* series.

Mr. Cohen resides in Maui, Hawaii, where he conducts seminars on spiritual awakening and visionary living. *The Mastery Training* is a highly focused small group intensive for individuals seeking to bring greater authenticity, love, and integrity to their chosen goals. *Celebrating Paradise* invites participants to reclaim their inner riches in a spirit of greater joy and aliveness. Alan also keynotes and presents workshops at many conferences and expos throughout the United States and abroad.

For a free catalog of Alan Cohen's books and audiocassettes, more information on his Hawaii seminars, and a listing of his upcoming seminars in your area, call (800) 462-3013, or write to Alan in c/o the Publicity Director at Hay House, Inc., P.O. Box 5100, Carlsbad, CA 92018-5100.

To write to Alan Cohen directly or receive more detailed information about his programs, write to The Mastery Foundation, 430 Kukuna Road, Haiku, Hawaii 96708, or call (808) 572-0001.

We hope you enjoyed this Hay House book.
If you would like to receive a free catalog featuring
additional Hay House books and products,
or if you would like information about the
Hay Foundation, please write or call:

Hay House, Inc.
P.O. Box 5100
Carlsbad, CA 92018-5100

(800) 654-5126